Baldock
Thaxted
Harwich
HERTFORDSHIRE
LUTON
Bishop's Stortford
ESS
Hertford
St. Albans
Chelmsford
Epping
Watford
Brentwood
SOUTHEND
Shoebury Ness
LONDON
R Thames
Tilbury
Sheerness
1
North Foreland
Richmond
Gravesend
Margate
Kingston
Rochester
Chatham
Herne Bay
Broadstairs
Croydon
R Medway
R Stour
Ramsgate
R Mole
Faversham
2
Maidstone
CANTERBURY
Sandwich
Goodwin Sands
Deal
KENT
3
Guildford
Reigate
Redhill
Tonbridge
South Foreland
SURREY
Ashford
4
Tunbridge Wells
DOVER
Crawley
Cranbrook
Folkestone
Sandgate
Hythe
STRAITS OF DOVER
Dymchurch
Cuckfield
5
New Romney
Petworth
Uckfield
Rye
R Adur
SUSSEX
Battle
Dungeness
R Arun
Winchelsea
6
Arundel
Lewes
Hailsham
7
Hastings
St. Leonards
BRIGHTON
8
Bexhill-on-Sea
Pevensey
Hove
Shoreham
Worthing
Newhaven
Seaford
9
EASTBOURNE
BOULOGNE
Littlehampton
Bognor Regis
11
10
Beachy Head
H CHANNEL
DIEPPE

THE COMPANION GUIDE TO

The Coast of South-East England

Uniform with this volume

The Coast of South-West England
The Coast of North-East England

In preparation

The Coast of East Anglia and the Thames Estuary

THE COMPANION GUIDE TO

The Coast of

South-East England

John Seymour

COLLINS
ST JAMES'S PLACE, LONDON

William Collins Sons & Co Ltd
London · Glasgow · Sydney · Auckland
Toronto · Johannesburg

First published 1975

ISBN 0 00 219630 1

Made and Printed in Great Britain by
William Collins Sons & Co Ltd Glasgow

Contents

Illustrations

CHAPTER I

North Foreland to Ramsgate

WE start, somewhat arbitrarily, at the **North Foreland**, which, terrestrially, is a piece of no-man's-land dividing Margate from Broadstairs, but nautically is more important for it is the southern limit of the Thames Estuary, which is still one of the greatest shipping channels of the world. Here is a lighthouse, built as long ago as 1683, made higher in 1793, and made lower again in the late nineteenth century.

This North Foreland owes its existence to an upfold in the same chalk stratum as that which forms the North Downs. This outcrop is separated from the North Downs by a syncline which is overlaid by the Tertiary sands and clays which form Pegwell Bay, and the chalk outcrop forms the **Isle of Thanet**: an island now no longer, for the Wantsum Channel that used to separate it from the mainland has silted up.

Thanet cannot be called an attractive piece of countryside – unless you happen to own land there, when it is attractive financially. Cobbett, writing in September, 1823, describes it thus:

> In this beautiful island every inch of land is appropriated by the rich. No hedges, no ditches, no commons, no grassy lanes: a country divided into great farms; a few trees surround the great farmhouse. All the rest is bare of trees; and the wretched labourer has not a stick of wood, and has no place for a pig or cow to graze, or even to lie down upon.

Cobbett wrote of the intense fertility of this land, which was then devoted exclusively to the growing of great crops of wheat:

> Barns, I should think, two hundred feet long; ricks of enormous size and most numerous; crops of wheat, five quarters to an acre, on the average; and a public-house without either bacon or corn!

Since Cobbett's day corn has largely given way to enormous fields of market-garden crops on Thanet, and the other great change is that Margate and Ramsgate have spread far over the countryside and a sort of messy suburbanism is never far away. The land is still extremely productive, often producing three crops in a year: spring greens, second-early potatoes, and then broccoli. Land, for purely agricultural use, can cost a thousand pounds an

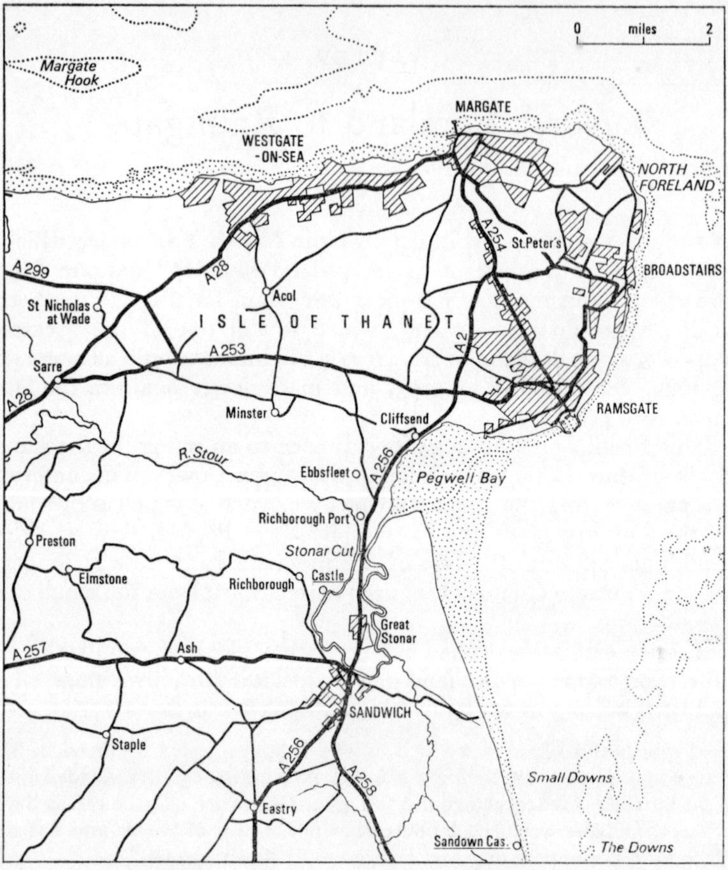

acre. Thanet is unusual in that it never went through an enclosure period after its Open Field stage. It merely got cut up among a few huge farmers, and owned by huge farmers it still is.

But on to **Broadstairs**. The ancient village was built about a mile inland, at St Peter's, in order to be concealed from Danish pirates. In St Peter's Church is buried a gentleman named Richard Troy, who lifted a weight of 2,240 pounds, and broke, with his bare hands, a rope which had just lifted thirty-five hundredweight, and he had a sister who could do nearly as well. This lady failed, we are told, to find a husband: whether *in spite* of her great strength or *because* of it we are left to imagine.

In Tudor times a little pier was built to form a harbour, or a half-harbour, in which boats could be beached on the sand. It is hard to believe, when you look at this now, sheltering as it does a few beached motor boats and one or two boats that take trippers out, that Broadstairs once owned and built ocean-going ships, sent fishing boats to Iceland, owned coasting schooners, and had a large population engaged in *foying*, or taking passengers and supplies out to passing ships. These foy boats also engaged in rendering assistance to vessels in distress. This latter activity was a considerable industry off this coast. In sailing ship days thousands of ships converged on London, and thousands sailed away from it. It was then by far the busiest port in the world. And all the ships from south, or bound south, had to round the North Foreland. This meant that the narrow channel off Broadstairs was more crowded than any other shipping channel in the world. So the local men kept fine luggers, which were rowed or sailed to sea every time there was a bad gale. If a ship were in distress (and in nearly every gale some were) then a pilot could be put aboard her to get her in to some safe harbour. If a ship had gone on the sands a big lugger could sometimes carry an anchor from her out into deep water for her to heave herself off to. As an example of many hundreds, when the schooner *Mizpah* was stranded in a fog in the eighteen eighties a tug from Ramsgate rescued her crew, which had taken to their boat, and it was left to a lugger from Broadstairs to put a crew aboard the schooner, get her off the sands, and sail her into Ramsgate Harbour, for which they got £350 salvage: a fortune to poor fishermen in those days.

A lifeboat was eventually stationed at Broadstairs, but even then there was plenty of work for the luggers, for a lugger could sail to windward much faster than a lifeboat and the lugger could often get there first. Nowadays, of course, with powered ships and radar and far far fewer ships anyway (ships were smaller in the old days and therefore there were more of them) this salvage industry has gone.

The railway came in 1863 and the fate of Broadstairs was sealed. It immediately began to develop into a commuter's residential area and a small seaside resort which it still is. Charles Dickens stayed here, and in 1973 the Dickens House Museum was opened, with relics of the author, and every year, in June, there is a Dickens festival.

Ramsgate, almost continuous with Broadstairs along the steep chalk cliffs, is a bigger place and one with a fine harbour: a royal harbour in fact, for so it was designated after George IV had sailed from Ramsgate to Hanover and back again in 1821. There is an obelisk down by the harbour to commemorate this momentous occasion with a suitably obsequious inscription on it.

Like Broadstairs, the first Ramsgate was inland a mile or two, and there are Saxon elements visible in St Lawrence Church. The town as we see it is principally the result of the sea-bathing craze, which started in the mid-eighteenth century. By 1764 we hear of sea bathers at Ramsgate, by 1780 there were a dozen bathing machines, Nelson Crescent was built about 1798, and thereafter crescent after crescent and terrace after terrace were added, resulting in the very attractive Georgian and Regency town of to-day. This development was much stimulated by the fact that Ramsgate was used as a garrison town during the Napoleonic wars, and officers brought their wives to live there. Royalty patronised the place, Queen Victoria used to be brought here by her mother when she was a little girl, George IV the Duke of Clarence resorted here, and Ramsgate was one of the first to be developed of the new fashionable watering places.

Dickens, in his *Sketches by Boz*, describes the animated scene which followed the arrival of the steam packet from London, and W. P. Frith's painting, *Ramsgate Sands*, much reproduced, is a marvellous evocation of the flavour of the period.

But it is Ramsgate as a seaport which interests us. In 1629, 366 tons of shipping were owned in the port, which is not a lot, and the ships were chiefly engaged in the coal trade from the north of England. There was a small pier in Tudor times, improved in the time of Elizabeth I, but it was totally inadequate to serve as a harbour of refuge during storm, and on this particular part of the coast such a harbour was urgently needed.

It might be as well here to discuss the nautical phenomenon that dominates completely this piece of coast, and that is the anchorage or roadstead known as **the Downs**. For the small piece of sea off Ramsgate and Deal, known to sailors from olden days as the Downs, was once the most important and most crowded anchorage in the world. The reason for this is that in square rig days it was very difficult for a sailing ship to sail against the wind anyway, and particularly difficult for her to sail to windward down a narrow channel. So when the prevailing wind was blowing, from the south-west, a ship bound out of London anywhere south would get as far as the Downs and then find herself faced with a long and difficult slog to windward right down the Channel until she reached the broad Atlantic. Ships *could* sail to windward, but it was slow, in-efficient, and hard on men and gear. Many a stubborn skipper who tried to buck the south-west wind in the English Channel found himself slogging and slamming against it for a week or a fortnight, making very little headway, wearing out men and gear, and finally being forced to turn and run before a freshening gale back to the Downs, where he wished fervently he had stayed in the first place.

In the Downs a ship was perfectly sheltered from the south-west wind, the bottom was good holding ground for anchors, and it was an ideal place for ships, bound south out of London, or out of any other port in the Baltic or North Sea for that matter, to lie in comfort waiting for 'a slant' as sailors call it – a slant of wind favourable to their course so that they could steer straight towards their destination and not zig-zag against the wind as a ship has to do when she is tacking. So in sailing ship days a prolonged period of westerly or south-westerly wind would see a great concourse of anchored shipping building up in the Downs and the Small Downs as the area to the north of the true Downs is called. There the ships were safe from all but a freak storm, for the Goodwin Sands gave them at least partial protection if an easterly sprang up, and of course anyway an easterly was what they were waiting for, and provided a ship did not get herself embayed in Pegwell Bay she could slide round the South Foreland if an easterly did spring up and go on her way rejoicing.

But nevertheless, the fact that this anchorage was so very much used meant that shipwrecks were pretty frequent, and it would obviously be a great advantage to have a harbour at Ramsgate into which ships could run under duress.

So in 1750 a harbour was built, but it proved too small and also it soon became choked with sand. The famous engineer John Smeaton was then called in, and between 1787 and 1795 the present harbour was built, mostly with stone from Purbeck, in Dorset. Some of the work was done by French prisoners of war, and the harbour was the first one to be built with the aid of a new invention: the diving bell. Men could actually go to the bottom of the sea and lay the stones in place.

The East Pier was completed in 1814 and is nearly 3,000 feet long. The West Pier is 1,500 feet, and the two piers enclose about 46 acres of water. This immediately became valuable as a harbour of refuge, and it still is one (the present writer has been very glad to run into it out of a north-easter), and the harbour also allowed a big fleet of deep-sea sailing trawlers to develop: a fleet which rivalled those of Lowestoft to the north and Brixham to the west, and which ranged all over the North Sea and the English Channel. This fine fleet of magnificent vessels was dispersed or destroyed in the First World War, the smacks either being sunk by the enemy or forced to shift their base to the West Country, from which they never returned.

Now Ramsgate Harbour is enjoying a great revival of trade. About 40,000 Volkswagen cars come into the port annually, from special transporter ships from Germany, and many British-built cars go out. Like so many of the small harbours Ramsgate is benefiting from the decline of the Port of London owing to bad labour relations, and is increasing its trade in spite of government policy which, since the Rochdale Report came out in 1962, has been to discourage the small ports and concentrate all trade in the very big ones. An attempt to establish container traffic into Ramsgate though is temporarily at a standstill, being hampered by the fact that there is not time during the hour or two each side of high water to load and unload the container ships and get them away while they are still afloat. Perhaps this will be cured by dredging.

Ramsgate has always been a most popular port with yachtsmen, but arrangements have been made for permanent moorings for yachts in the east end of the Inner Harbour, which never dries out, and the gate of which is closed except at high tide. There is from ten to fifteen feet of water in there, and there are floating pontoons against which yachts can be moored so that their owners can get aboard them without getting their feet wet. To moor a yacht costs about £280 a year and there is a waiting list, at the time of writing, of nearly three hundred. There is a school of thought that would increase the yacht marina side of it at the expense of the cargo port. It is an unfortunate aspect of car-importing that a great deal of dry land is required for parking the cars on before they are loaded on the transporter lorries to take them away, and dry land, in Ramsgate Harbour, is in short supply. At the moment the awful sacrilege is being committed of filling in harbour water area to make land for this purpose.

A slightly unfortunate circumstance of the Inner Harbour is that, royal port or no, it has gribble. *Limnoria terebrans* is a marine worm which bores into timber, and timber piles are hauled out of the water here absolutely riddled with it. Gribble does not generally live in our temperate waters, but it is establishing itself in one or two enclosed harbours where perhaps the temperature is higher than the sea outside.

But gribble or no, Ramsgate has a fine harbour and a most pleasant one to sail into, and if yachts are properly painted gribble won't attack them. A pleasant aspect of the harbour are the great brick arches that hold up the cliffside, the arches sheltering great caves which are used as workshops by various nautically-biased industries.

At the west end of this arcade is the most interesting place in Ramsgate: the Fishermen's Chapel. This properly celebrates the marvellous record of life-saving by Ramsgate men. The first lifeboat there, the *Northumberland*, saved 261 lives from 1851 when she was installed to 1865 when another one took her place. The holy alliance with the two steam paddle-tugs that early arrived here, the *Vulcan* and the *Aid*, was responsible for saving hundreds of men from death.

Before the days of motor lifeboats, lifeboats were either rowed or sailed, and although they could go like the clappers down-wind or across the wind they were very slow (like all sailing boats) to windward. To go dead to windward it was quicker to row them, and rowing a few miles into the teeth of a gale was killing work for the crew (often elderly men) and it could be impossible. Thus the arrival of these steam tugs, which could *tow* the lifeboat to windward of a ship in distress, and let her drop down-wind on to her, increased the effectiveness of the lifeboat enormously. The tug might not be able to enter the shallow water in which the ship was wrecked, as the lifeboat could, nor could the clumsy paddle boat come alongside in big breaking seas. The lifeboat though could often carry a line from the tug to the stranded ship so the former could tow the latter off, or at the worst the lifeboat could rescue the men. There are two fine paintings in the Fishermen's Chapel: one of one of the tugs coming from a wreck, and the other of a tug towing the lifeboat out of the harbour mouth into the teeth of a gale. There is a model also of the tug *Aid*. She was built by W. Allsup at the Caledonian Works, Preston, and she reigned for twenty-six years at Ramsgate. She was 126 feet long and 21 feet beam. She had a rudder at her bow as well as aft so that she could manœuvre backward. There is also the model of a sailing trawler: the *Red Ensign*, L.T.180. This was the first ship to use a 'towed skid' for detonating magnetic mines, and she blew the first magnetic mine up in the Second World War off the South Goodwin on the 22nd January, 1940. She helped at the evacuation of Dunkirk, was hit by a bomb in Dover Harbour and again in the Thames Estuary, and she was the last ship to leave Calais before the Germans entered it. She returned to her proper trade of fishing after the war and was lost with all hands off the Longship Sands in the great gale of 1953.

Another item of interest in the chapel is the certificate issued to Charles E. Fish by the Royal National Lifeboat Institution, stating that he did 353 services in the lifeboat in which 887 lives were saved between 1865 and 1891. A Buddhist might wonder what sort of *karma* a man gets for saving 887 lives. And the *pay* of a lifeboatman has always been derisory – never more than a few token shillings. Charlie Fish used to sleep during bad weather in a hammock in a hut at the end of the pier so as to be ready to answer the call of the maroons. A typical service was the one on 5th January, 1881, when the lifeboat was called out to the *Indian Chief*. The boat was towed out into the freezing north-east gale (remember the date) by one of the tugs but by dusk had failed to sight the wreck, but in spite of the fact that the men were soaked in freezing salt spray and rain they decided to stay out all night in the hopes of catching a sight of the wreck in the morning and they crouched down in the bottom of their boat. At daybreak the *Indian Chief* was sighted about three miles away downwind, the lifeboat slipped her tow from the tug and sailed to a point up-wind of the wreck, anchored, and veered out enough cable to drop astern and pick up the eleven survivors who had spent the night lashed to the rigging in the raging gale while the huge seas crashed over the hull of their ship.

On another occasion when the spray was freezing solid on rigging and on men's faces a huge sea swamped the lifeboat and the tow-rope from the tug snapped. The men managed to bail the water out, made sail and picked up their tow again, were towed two miles to windward to where a barquentine was wrecked on the Goodwins, cast off the tow and took the crew off and sailed back to Ramsgate. Before the men had time to go ashore and have a hot drink they were called to sea again to rescue the crew of a sunken collier who were drifting about in their boat.

Charles Fish's predecessor, Coxswain Jarman, didn't do too badly either. In his ten years as coxswain he went out 132 times and saved just under 400 lives.

Ramsgate lifeboat is still very active. In June 1940 she worked thirty hours non-stop ferrying troops from the bomb-blasted beach at Dunkirk to the ships waiting off-shore. Ramsgate itself was the 'briefing port' for the 'little ships': the open fishing boats and life-boats, barges and yachts, that played such a big part in the evacuation. A window in St George's Church commemorates the evacuation, and every year a memorial service is held there.

Ramsgate is still a delightful seaside resort. There are good sands, plenty going on in the harbour to watch, plenty of boats taking anglers out fishing, and the ambience of the old Regency and Victorian town survives Bingo and 'Pop'. The goings-on in Nero's Disco and Tiberius' Casino are nowhere near as decadent as their names might lead one to expect, and you get the best *apfelstrudel* in England in Harrison's Café, on the front.

Above, the highly profitable toll bridge at Sandwich, built in 1755. The Barbican is of the reign of Henry VIII. *Below,* one of the many beautiful houses surviving in Sandwich, a town which made early use of brick for domestic architecture.

Above, the mighty keep of Dover Castle was built in Henry II's time and has been used for military purposes in every war since. *Below,* Ypres Castle at Rye, pronounced Wipers, once the home of John de Ypres, now the town museum. It was built in the reign of Henry III.

CHAPTER 2

Pegwell Bay to Sandwich

Pegwell Bay should be seen at low tide, perhaps from the terrace of that splendid piece of Victoriana, the Belle Vue Inn, when the sands stretch away apparently to infinity and tiny dots, far out, prove to be men digging lug worms for bait. A good man working hard and systematically at this can make a living, and all he needs is a spade and a bucket, so one can truthfully say that no able-bodied man ever need be on the dole in the Isle of Thanet.

Occasionally the silence is broken by an inhuman roar, and a streaking shower of spray out to sea proves to be a hovercraft returning from France. It makes the transition from sea to sand without noticing it, roars across the flats scaring the birds and deafening the worm diggers, and docks itself on the concrete ramp at Hoverlloyd's hoverport. You can get to Calais and back for £3·75 and you don't need a passport.

Hard-by this example of one of the latest forms of transport, up on the low cliff of Tertiary London Clay, is an example of a more primitive vessel altogether: the good ship *Hugin*, which was *rowed* across the North Sea from Denmark in July, 1948. There she sits, 71 feet long and 18 feet in the beam, with a stumpy 40-foot high mast and it is claimed that the ships of her day carried no sail. This I doubt. She was propelled by thirty-two oars, and the fifty-three men who manned the oars were ordinary Danish landlubbers such as doctors and dentists and bricklayers and a prison officer, to describe but a few, and they did it all to mark the 1500th anniversary of the landing of Hengist and Horsa on this spot.

Hengist and Horsa were invited to land on Thanet by the British King Vortigern, in order to help him fight the Picts and Scots who were giving him such trouble by coming across his borders. He had better have dealt with them himself for, as the Venerable Bede put it, they:

> were granted lands in the eastern part of the island on condition that they protected the country: nevertheless their real intention was to subdue it. They engaged the enemy advancing from the north, and having defeated them, sent back news of their success to their homeland, adding that the country was fertile and the Britons cowardly . . .

Horsa, Bede goes on to tell us, got killed fighting these cowardly Britons and was buried in East Kent, where his monument, in Bede's day, still stood. Hengist and Horsa:

were the sons of Wictgils, whose father was Witta, whose father was Wecta, son of Woden, from whose stock sprang the royal house of many provinces.

At all events, the newly arrived English:

devastated the surrounding cities and countryside, extended the conflagration from the eastern to the western shores without opposition and established a stranglehold over nearly all of the doomed island . . . A few wretched survivors captured in the hills were butchered wholesale, and others, desperate with hunger, came out and surrendered to the enemy for food, although they were doomed to lifelong slavery even if they escaped instant massacre.

Of course the Britons were vitiated by four hundred years of Roman domination, during which the Romans were the only ones who practised the trade of bearing arms.

Just where the original Jutes landed cannot of course be known: tradition places it at Ebbsfleet Farm, a mile farther along the shore from where the *Hugin* rests, and this indeed is probable for the invaders – sorry – *guests* – would have kept on up the tidal channel as far as they could go. But who, indeed, can guess where the channel ran in those days? Certainly not where it runs today. These things alter. Nobody knows, either, where St Augustine landed, sent by Pope Gregory after the latter had seen those winsome little boys whom he named angels instead of Angles. He landed in 597. I can scarcely be blamed for quoting Bede again, for he sets the scene so much better than anybody else could:

To the east of Kent lies the large island of Thanet, which by English reckoning is six hundred hides in extent; it is separated from the mainland by a waterway about three furlongs broad called the Wantsum, which joins the sea at either end and is fordable in only two places. It was here that God's servant Augustine landed with companions, who were said to be forty in number.

Bede goes on to describe how the missionaries sent interpreters to King Ethelbert, and how he came to hear them, and, although demurring to be immediately converted to the new religion himself, gave them permission to convert any of his subjects who wanted to be converted, and allowed them to live in Canterbury, then the chief city of his kingdom, which stretched to the Humber.

Minster, three miles inland, was an early result of this Christianisation, and we should go there to see the remains of the fine abbey.

In the middle of the seventh century Queen Ermenburga came from Mercia, where her husband was king, with her three daughters, Mildred, Mildburga and Mildgitha, to claim *weregild*, or blood-money, for two of her younger brothers who had been murdered at the court of King Egbert, in Kent. Ermenburga was, incidentally, the grand-daughter of King Ethelbert, the one converted by St Augustine, and therefore a descendant of Hengist.

King Egbert allowed her for *weregild* as much land as a wild deer could run around in a certain time, and this became the convent lands of Minster, for on the site of the present church here she built a priory. At that time Minster was a natural harbour, for the Wantsum Channel, which cut Thanet off from the rest of England, had not yet silted up, and ships bound for London or out normally made use of it instead of going round the North Foreland.

Mildred, one of the three daughters of the founder, was later beatified, and is the patron saint of Thanet. She was described by Goscelin in 1097 as 'the fairest lily of the English' and 'the jewel of our fathers'.

By 741 the community had grown to seventy nuns and a new and larger convent was built where the present abbey now stands, and it is still a convent and used for the purpose for which it was built. The first building was probably of wood and wattle, of course, and St Mildred's remains were brought here. By this time Minster owned half Thanet, and there are records of ships being built and owned by the convent, and ships taking convent grain to London.

In 753 the Danes began to come, and in 840 they burnt the Abbey to the ground and the abbess and nuns perished in the flames. A small religious house was rebuilt on the site though, and in 1031 some monks came from Canterbury and stole the remains of St Mildred, while their hosts were feasting, and made off with them across the Wantsum, and thus translated the sacred (and highly profitable) relics to Canterbury where one assumes, in one form or another, most of them still are. Actually a bit of them is back at Minster, kept in a reliquary under the altar of the chapel.

Shortly after 1027 the monks built the west wing of the existing building, and this Saxon work is still there. After the Conquest successive Abbots of Canterbury built on to the Minster, and early in the twelfth century the existing Great Hall was built. Excavations in 1929–30 laid open the foundations of a Norman chapel, the semi-circular apse of which is still there to see in the garden south of the Norman hall. About 1413 both the Saxon and the Norman wings were made into two stories, and at the Dissolution in 1538 the chapel and many of the buildings were pulled down, the stone used for building Henry VIII's castles at Deal, and the Minster and its lands passed into secular hands.

In 1928 the Minster, by then an inhabited manor house, was bought, together with ten acres of land, by a man named Senior, and nine years later he allowed a group of Benedictine nuns from Bavaria to come and start a community here. They even managed to get hold of a piece of St Mildred from Deventer, in Holland, where it was taken in 1071.

This small community of nuns, many of them from the British Isles now, as well as from Bavaria, should be taken as a shining example of what women are capable of by supporters of Women's Lib. On twenty acres of land, they produce all the food needed for eighteen people, besides much which they export off the holding. They milk twelve Jerseys, selling most of the milk in the village, they produce their own hay, silage, kale, oats, potatoes, fodder beet and, of course, all their own vegetables and fruit, and enough to sell as well. Besides this they run a small factory producing objects of art. They are pleased to show visitors around the Saxon part of the abbey: they live in the more up-to-date Norman wing.

The fine Norman and Early English parish church is worth going to see, too.

If we work south along the shore from where Hengist and Horsa landed we come to the modern port of **Richborough**, notable chiefly at the moment for its power station. This was built between 1958 and 1963 in order to turn some of the coal from the Kentish coalfield into electricity. But in spite of the fact that Kent has millions of tons of coal, and no oil at all, the decision was made in 1971 to convert the station to oil, and this is what it now burns. Most of the oil is brought from the refineries in the Thames Estuary either by tanker barge or rail tanker. The reason the pipes from the tanker berth are lagged is that the oil, which is residual fuel oil, is like thick treacle, and must be kept warm to make it flow. The bringing of oil by sea is having a beneficial effect on the Port of Richborough incidentally, because it has caused the dredging of the river as far as the power station at least, and the proper marking of the channel. The turbo-alternators require more cooling water than the nearby River Stour can provide, hence the three enormous cooling towers that dominate the landscape.

Farther up-stream on the winding Stour we get to some very strange places indeed. Here are factories, large and small, some of them having their beings in strange old wooden buildings that date from the 1914–18 War. Gradually these old buildings are being replaced by modern factories, the largest being that of Pfizers, who make vaccines and antibiotics, and who alone, we are told, use more water than the town of Ramsgate. There is Petbow's Engineering Works which will deliver custom-built electrical generators ex-works in seven days from receipt of order – surely well outside the traditions of British business! There is a firework factory, where people work in strange little sheds surrounded by blast screens, so that if one blows up the others don't. All this modern industrial development is being encouraged by DATAC, which glories in the full name of Development Areas Treasury Advisory Committee, and is to provide employment for people displaced by the decline of the seaside holiday industry. Britons go abroad more and more nowadays for their holidays, and foreigners coming to England go inland.

And what were the original army-type huts built for? Why, for the famous 'mystery port' of the First World War, and a well-kept mystery it was, too. During that war a large part of the British war effort went through this forgotten port of Richborough and down the little shallow winding mud-hole of the River Stour. At first 255 200-ton barges were used, being shuttled across the Channel by tugs and up the canals to such places as Vendroux, Andruieq and Zeneghem, and over the years not one barge was lost. Then in 1917 it was necessary to send material over to France in greatly increased quantities and train ferries were built to run from Richborough to Calais and Dunkirk, and over a thousand locomotives alone went across the sea from Richborough. Most of the stuff the trains took over was hidden in vast dumps among the sand dunes near Camiers. After the war the train ferries were transferred to Harwich, and Richborough was forgotten again and became derelict. The strictest security about the whole operation was maintained until well after the war was over, for it was thought that the port might have to be used again, and as by now most of the men who worked it are either dead or very old probably little will ever be known about this most vital part of the British war effort.

But in 1938 an almost stranger thing happened to Richborough. The Kitchenor Camp, as it was called, was leased by the Central Council for Jewish Refugees. In February, 1939, the first party of a thousand Jews fleeing from Nazi Germany arrived and by the outbreak of war there were 3,500 of them: a pitiful drop out of a big ocean. They lived there for some time, before being dispersed elsewhere, and it is greatly to the credit of the people of Sandwich that they met with nothing but sympathy and kindness. They were all eventually absorbed into English society. After they had left Richborough the camp was used by 5,000 Free European troops as a transit camp for the remainder of the Second World War.

What is there to see there now? Well, personally I find the old crumbling jetties near the power station very evocative of strange vanished things. Farther up-stream new wharves are being developed, and there is the Richborough Harbour Company, which is trying to revive the little port again. Let us hope that they may succeed, for the more small ports around the coasts of these islands there are the better.

All this land that the Port of Richborough now stands on was sea not so long ago. When the Romans landed all this was water, and ships bound from or to London would go through here and not round the North Foreland: even now sailors call the channel to London inside the Margate Hook Sands the 'Overland Route', and this is in memory of the times when ships taking this channel actually went 'over land', or at least inside the land: the Isle of Thanet. But before the Norman Conquest even monks had already started to *in*, or enclose, the tidal marshes that lay on each side of the Wantsum Channel. In 1038 the Prior of Christchurch at Canterbury mockingly suggested to the Abbot of St Augustine that he *in* land at Minster, and to everybody's amazement he did. He built a sea wall between Cliffsend near Ramsgate and Stonar. Later this was destroyed by the enraged men of Sandwich, who were afraid that their channel was going to be silted up by it, but it was built again and the inning went on. By 1400 nine thousand acres of salt marsh had been inned, right up the Stour as far as Fordwich, near Canterbury. Most of the inning was done by building wooden fences, burying them in earth, then facing the earth bank with a coat of thatch covered by stones mortared together with lime and tar.

Sailors, and the men of Sandwich, claimed that this inning was destroying the channel, and perhaps it was, or maybe anyway the channel was doomed by natural forces. In 1672 the last ship ever to use the Wantsum sailed from London, and in 1750 the new harbour at Ramsgate knocked Sandwich out as a port apparently for good. But in those days, of course, men did not have dredgers.

But before we get to Sandwich, let us cross the water from the Port of Richborough and look at **Richborough Castle**. If we are travelling by land we will have to go through Sandwich to get to it. The best way to go to it is by water, for it was built on the water, and the channel of the Stour flows over part of it: if we could dredge and examine this mud how many coins and Roman relics would we find in it?

For Richborough Castle, or Rutupiae as the Romans called it, is one of the most impressive and interesting Roman remains in Britain. It is thought that the Roman invasion under Claudius of AD 43 landed here. The more famous but less effective landings by Julius Caesar were farther south, of course. But after the troops of Claudius landed, Rutupiae was immediately fortified, became the first Roman base in Britain, and remained the chief port of entry into the country through most of the Roman occupation. It became a major supply depot and big granaries were built there, and about AD 85 much of it was swept away to make room for an enormous marble-faced monument, complete with statues and other ornament, built to honour the Emperor Domitian and his general Agricola for completing the conquest of Britain. Only the foundations of this monument now exist, but they are impressive enough, and one can walk about underneath them for a tunnel was driven by archaeologists searching for artifacts.

In the second century the place was apparently peaceful (it would have been, for the Britons in the neighbourhood had been effectively subjugated and the Angles and Saxons hadn't started to arrive yet) and the fortifications were neglected and unfortified houses were built. Later in the third century a great earthen wall was built, almost certainly as a defence against sea raiders. Shortly after this they were superseded by an enormous stone wall, built by Carausius, the rebel self-made emperor (see p. 46). This wall still stands, and looks as if it will stand for a very long time yet. After Carausius's downfall Rutupiae became a fort of the Saxon Shore, and possibly the headquarters of the Count (Comitus) whose duty it was to defend Britain from the marauding Saxons. We will discuss the origins of these forts more thoroughly when we get to Dover.

Thousands of coins of the late fourth century have been discovered here, indicating a very heavy occupation at that time. But Rutupiae was always important in Roman times, for it guarded the gateway from the rest of the Empire to London. It was a great port of export. The Romans exported from Britain tin, lead, gold, silver, oysters, pearls (presumably from fresh water mussels), hides, grain, beans, bears, hunting dogs and slaves.

As to what is to be seen here now, the ruins are extensive and confusing, but there is a good Ministry of Works leaflet which explains what they all were. With the aid of this and a lot of patience the sightseer may work it all out, but over the centuries one lot of buildings overlaid another in a most confusing fashion. There is an excellent small museum on the site, which gives a good glimpse of Roman military and civilian life.

Strangely the place continued to be occupied after the Romans left, and St Augustine built a chapel here, and the remains of the Saxon building can clearly be seen. On the whole the Anglo-Saxons did not favour re-occupying Roman ruins, but the Jutes seem to have been something of an exception.

And so back we go to Sandwich, which became a great port long after Rutupiae had fallen into the dust. But we cannot even begin to discuss Sandwich until we have discussed the whole bizarre business of the Cinque Ports.

The original **Cinque Ports** (pronounced in a good forthright Norman-English way *sink ports*) were Hastings, Romney, Hythe, Dover and Sandwich. Winchelsea and Rye were quickly added to the league, not as *limbs* but as Cinque Ports in their own right but always called 'The Ancient Towns'.

The origin of the Ports is lost in mystery, but the *purpose* of the institution was simple. It was an arrangement whereby the King of England had ships and men supplied to him for fighting his wars in return for privileges granted by him to the ports supplying the ships. In other words it was a cheap way of having a navy. Edward the Confessor in 1051 gave charters to Sandwich, Dover, Fordwich (high up the Stour near Canterbury and *miles* inland now) and Romney allowing the profits of administering justice provided that they supplied ships and men for his service. According to later charters the Portsmen had the rights of soc and sac, tol and team, blodwit and fledwit, pillory and tumbril, infangentheof and outfangentheof, mundbryce, waives and strays, flotsam, jetsam and ligan. What all these privileges were only a student of law or Old English could tell, but suffice to say they had the rights to wrecks flung up on their shore, and if they didn't like anybody they had a perfect right to fling him over a cliff and frequently did. They were, in fact, little sovereign states. They were freed from taxes and impositions of the central government, kept their own courts, were allowed to engage throughout most of their history in acts of piracy, and in return for these and many other privileges had to provide ships and men for the king's service for a limited period in every year.

Since Edward the Confessor's charter of 1051 Henry II, in 1155, is known to have given a charter to Hastings under which they had to provide him with twenty ships for fifteen days every year. At the coronation of Richard I the Barons of the Cinque Ports carried the canopy over the monarch. This is a privilege (and about the only one) that they still retain. In 1191 Winchelsea and Rye were recognised as full members. In 1278 the Ports got a charter from Edward I, who could never have conquered North Wales without a Cinque Port fleet to supply his armies and protect their seaward flank. At the Battle of Sluys the Portsmen not only slaughtered the enemy, thus giving England control of the English Channel for many decades to come, but even turned on their own side: burning twenty ships from Great Yarmouth so that only three of the fleet from that town escaped. They did this because of the bitter rivalry that existed between the Ports and the men of Yarmouth, over whom the kings had given the Portsmen authority. Every year, at the great herring fair in Yarmouth, the Portsmen sent representatives to control the fair, take dues, hold courts, etc. This arrogance was hated by the Norfolkmen, but they had to suffer it until the seventeenth century, when the Ports finally admitted they were beaten and gave it up. In 1216 the Portsmen joined the French against King John in the latter's wars against the barons.

Letters Patent by Edward III in 1359 laid down that the Ports and their limbs should provide ships according to the following schedule:

La Ville de Hastinges	trois niefs
La Lewee de Pevenesse	une nief
Bolewarethe et Petit Thamme	une nief
Bekesburne en Kent	une nief
Grenéthe en Kent	une nief
La Ville de la Rye	cynk niefs
La Ville de Wynchelse	dys niefs
La Porte de Romenale et le Veu Romenale	qatre niefs
Lyde	une nief
Le Port de Heth	cynk niefs
Le Porte Dovorr	dys et neuf niefs
Folkstan	une nief
La ville de Faveresham	une nief
Le portes de Sandwiz, Stonor, Fordwiz, Dale et Serres	cynk niefs

It will be seen from this that the original five ports had proliferated, but, except for Winchelsea and Rye, the other ports were just 'limbs' of the original five. The usual arrangement was that each ship supplied had to have twenty-one men and a boy, and must work for nothing for the king for fourteen days in every year, after which her services were to be paid for. Hence the kings liked to make their naval campaigns short and sweet.

The Ports held on to their privileges, and were the mainstay of the king's navy, nearly until Tudor times. They had their ups and downs, of course, and were bitterly resented by other English seaports – in Edward II's time they sent a fleet to Fowey to force the Fowey men to 'veil their bonnets' (in other words strike their topsails) when they encountered a Cinque Ports ship at sea. But the Fowey men gave them such a good hiding that they never tried to make Fowey men 'veil their bonnets' again.

When Henry VIII came to the throne it was evident that the day of the Ports was done. Accidents of geography had done for them. Firstly English naval power was shifting westward – it was Westward Ho! and the Ports were badly placed for this trade. The Americas were being opened up, Mediterranean trade was booming, and ships from the West Country were better placed to enter these trades than ones based far up in the Narrow Seas. Also, almost without exception, the Cinque Ports and their limbs were silting up. Sandwich found herself far from the sea up a shallow channel, and Rye, Winchelsea, Romneys New and Old (La Porte de Romenale et le Veu Romenale) were all deserted by the sea. The Ports clung to their empty privileges, such as the right of their 'Barons' to carry the canopy over the sovereign at coronations, and they cling to them now, but their real significance was gone. Dover, alone, retains a real maritime importance, and that because of the great artificial harbour that took the place of the old silted natural one, and because of England's friendship with France not her ancient enmity. The Ports are still proud of their arms:

Per pale azure and gules – three demi lions and demi ships conjoined or and argent.

But back to **Sandwich** itself. Many important events in the history of England happened here. It is said that Wilfrid, after having been consecrated bishop by Bishop Agilbert in France, landed here in 664 on his way to the court of the King of Northumberland. If this is so it will be seen that Sandwich was a port of entry into the country in very early days after the departure of the Romans. In 1006 the Danes under Swein ravaged Sandwich. In 1014 Knut or Canute landed here, and he landed here again the next year, to sail from here northward and make himself King of England. In 1356 the Black Prince landed here after the battle of Poitiers with many French prisoners of noble note.

But by the middle of the fifteenth century the doom of Sandwich as a port was foreseeable. The harbour was beginning to silt up. In 1469 the Hornblower, or Council, sent the Mayor and some of his brethren in a boat along the Wantsum to clear away illegal obstructions such as fish weirs. Sixteen years later every householder, or a substitute provided by him, had to go and dig a new channel for the river, so silted had it become. Sarre Ferry had by then become too shallow for the ferry boat to operate. By 1550 there were only two hundred inhabited houses in the town, compared with eight or nine hundred a hundred years before. Sandwich was suffering the fate that was later to befall the great city of Amsterdam – when grass was said to grow in its streets — its channel was silting up. But the Dutch invented the *krabelaar*, a device worked by tide and wind to harrow and deepen the beds of rivers, and then the *mud-mill*, which was a bucket-dredger driven by horses. The Sandwich men turned this way and then that. They petitioned the king, protested to the Archbishop of Canterbury that his minions were enclosing too many of the tidal marshes, they dug an abortive channel through the sands at the east of the town (the remains of which can still be discerned) but nothing could help them. In 1567 a bridge was built across the Wantsum at Sarre, and it became harder and harder to get a ship alongside the wharfs of Sandwich.

Such is the tenacity of a seaport, however, that Sandwich men continued to own ships long after these had the greatest difficulty in getting into their own harbour. By mid seventeenth century they still had twenty-four ships supplied with cannon and shot and twelve unarmed: a total of about 1,600 tons. In 1645 about five hundred Flemings came over, and trade revived enormously owing to the new skills which these people brought. The weaving started of bays and says and linsey-woolseys. There is still at least one weaver working in the town. Tanning became a big trade, too – and still is: there are three small tanneries.

In 1755 a toll bridge was built across the river at Sandwich to Thanet. In 1903 Edward VII gave the town a charter to charge one shilling per car, or horseless carriage, and this lasts for twenty-four hours. This is still operative, and also 'Every Chariot, Landau Berlin Chaise, Chair, Calash or other vehicle with six horses or other Beasts must pay two shillings and threepence.' The income from the latter source is slight, but so much money is gained from the horseless carriages that the big addition that is currently being built on to the Guild Hall is being paid for by it.

A bypass is planned for the town, which will sweep round to the west of it. This will reduce the money got from tolls but will save the little town from absolute destruction by traffic.

To continue with the sad story of the harbour – in 1825 Rennie came up with a report that a new channel should be dug in from the sea just north of Sandown Castle, and in 1825 Telford had the even more splendid idea to make a great cut slightly to the north of this all the way through Sandwich to Canterbury, Ashford, and then the Medway at Lenham. Nothing came of either idea, and the railways came to destroy all such schemes as the motorways are now destroying the railways.

But in 1845 a tug was brought to the town, both to haul small ships in and out and to dredge the channel. Up until 1966 timber ships were still making their way up to Felton's Yard: now they unload at Ramsgate, and the timber is brought along the already impossibly congested road. But perhaps there is a chance now of a revival. As we saw, oil tankers are already nosing their way up as far as Richborough, and we have Mr Barry Bridgeland getting on with his Richborough Port scheme, and who knows what lies in the future?

Yachts can get up to Sandwich, and the toll bridge will lift to let them go even farther up. At the quay there is ten foot of water at spring's high water and a dubious six and a half foot at neaps. If you go through the bridge there are twelve miles of river with four foot of water, and with twelve foot briggage (that means head-room under a bridge) under the railway. Small boats can get to Fordwich, fifteen miles up, which we have seen was once an important limb of the Cinque Ports.

As to what there is to see nowadays in Sandwich, it is a very lovely little town, with a mixture of medieval, Tudor and Georgian buildings in it. The Guildhall is worth seeing, and has a small but fascinating museum in it which is open when no court is being held. There are some beautiful and indeed important paintings in the hall itself, original charters, and indeed a wealth of antiquarian interest. The Town Sergeant likes showing people around and is himself of interest. The Barbican, by the Toll Bridge, is of the time of Henry VIII, the Fisher Gate, east of this, 1384, and one can walk round the town, almost, on the earth ramparts. There are some fine private houses, Manwood Court is a Dutch-looking brick building, very fine, with the date 1564 on it, and when I last saw it it seemed to be covered with burglar alarms and exhortations to vote for a particular political party. St Bartholomew's Hospital, just off the Dover Road, was founded in 1190 as a hostel for travellers. It has a thirteenth-century chapel. The King's House, near St Mary's Church, has fifteenth-century timber framing hidden by eighteenth-century brick, St Clement's Church has one of the finest Norman towers in Kent, and the cottage in which Tom Paine lived, before his young wife died in childbirth and he moved to America to do quite a lot towards changing the world, is in New Street.

When the bypass has been achieved, and the absolute *persecution* by traffic has ceased in the narrow streets, Sandwich will be an enchanting little place to be.

Where argosies have wooed the breeze,
 The simple sheep are feeding now;
And near and far across the bar
 The ploughman whistles at the plough;
Where once the long waves washed the shore,

Larks from their lowly lodgings soar.
Below the down the stranded town
 Hears far away the rollers beat;
About the wall the seabirds call;
 The salt wind murmurs through the street;
Forlorn the sea's forsaken bride
Awaits the end that shall betide.

John Davidson (1857–1909)

CHAPTER 3

Deal

THE coast to the east of Sandwich is much beset with golf courses: there are no less than three of them, one after the other, two royal and the other a prince's. There is also the **Sandwich Bay Estate** where the rich go to be with the very rich. It is still a pleasant walk along the shore, though, and we reach **Deal** at Sandown Castle, built by Henry VIII as part of his defences to keep the Pope out. The system of fortifications of which this is part was started in 1539, a year after the Pope had excommunicated Henry and preached a crusade against him.

Sandown Castle was designed by an engineer called Stephan von Haschenpurg, a Bohemian. He was Bohemian in more ways than one, for in 1543 Henry sacked him for 'behaving lewdly and spending great treasure to no purpose'. The exact accounts for the building of Sandown are in existence, and it is known that six hundred and thirty men were employed on the site at one period, and that labourers were paid five pence a day, which caused them to strike. Industrial disputes were more easily solved in those days than they are now, and after Sir Edward Ryngley, the man in charge, had sent five strikers to the dungeons at Canterbury and another four to Sandwich Gaol the rest voted to go back to work. Sandown Castle was never attacked by the Pope: it is a measure of the success of fortifications that they should never be attacked, but it was attacked by the Royalists in 1648, in the uprising that followed the defeat of Charles I, and it held out the longest of the three castles at Deal and Walmer against the Parliamentary counter-attack. After the Restoration of Charles II Colonel John Hutchinson was kept here a prisoner before his execution. The sea finally did what the Pope failed to do, and now little remains except a mound of earth. We will get an impression of what Sandown looked like though when we get to Deal Castle.

But we might as well dive straight in at the deep end and describe the circumstances which led to Deal being there at all. Deal came into existence solely to serve the shipping anchored in the Downs (see p. 12). The Downs, as we have seen – that stretch of shallow water between the Goodwin Sands and the shore of Kent – was

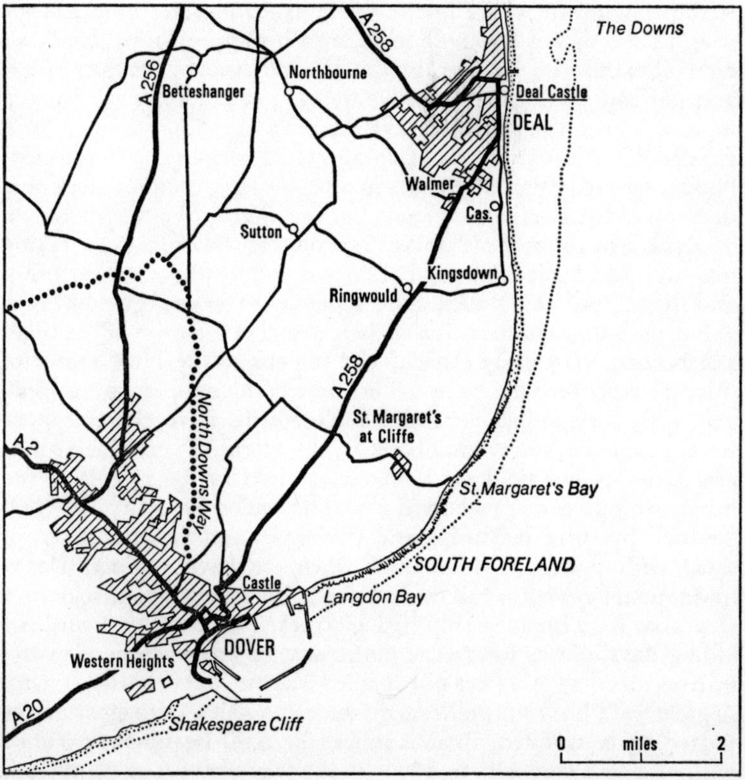

perhaps the most important and crowded roadstead, or anchorage for shipping in the open sea, in the world. As we discussed at great length, so long as the west or south-west wind blew strongly up the Channel shipping would collect in the Downs, waiting for a fair wind to go westward. When an east wind blew up they had, as sailors say, to get the hell out of it, for the Goodwins, although dry at low water, offered no shelter at high and the Downs could quickly become a nasty place to be. Joseph Conrad wrote of hearing: 'upwards of ten score of windlasses spring like one into clanking life in the dead of night, filling the Downs with a panic-struck sound of anchors being torn hurriedly out of the ground at the approach of an easterly wind'.

The literature of sea-travel is full of references to the writer, or his hero, having been stuck in the Downs for weeks if not months.

A ship bound anywhere in the world excepting Northern Europe would have to sail down-Channel, and if the prevailing wind was blowing would be held up in the Downs. And, of course, sailors and passengers, thus held up, wanted to get ashore. They wanted to send mail and receive it, take on fresh supplies, go ashore and get drunk, or just go ashore. Captains were very chary, if outward-bound, about letting any of their own boats go ashore: the crews that rowed them might not come back again. So the longshoremen of Deal reaped a great harvest, acting as floating taxis taking passengers and ships' officers backwards and forwards between ship and shore, and taking out mail, supplies, and fresh provisions.

But the Downs, although a sheltered anchorage most of the time, can become very nasty indeed, and sometimes the great crowd of shipping anchored in them would be caught napping by a freak gale with very serious results. The Goodwins have claimed more wrecks than any other sandbank in the world. There these sands are, a drying-out tidal sandbank lying right in the middle of the busiest shipping channel in the world, and even now, although guarded by three lightships and ten navigational buoys, seven of them with lights on them, and when we have engines, Decca navigational beacons, radar, and the Lord knows what, seldom a year goes by without a ship 'being wrecked on the Goodwins'. In sailing days wrecks were very numerous. As an example of many, in November 1703 a fleet of warships was anchored in the Downs. A great gale blew up and raged for days, anchors dragged, cables parted, ships collided, Rear Admiral Sir Basil Beaumont perished with his ship's company in a hole in the sands known as Abraham's Bosom, the *Restoration*, *Stirling Castle*, *Mary* and *Northumberland* all went to destruction on the sands. In that sort of gale no anchor will hold – no canvas will stand up. Sailing ships can only drive helplessly to leeward until they end up on some shoal somewhere and are very quickly smashed to pieces.

It was in these sorts of times that the Deal *hovellers*, as they were called, showed their mettle. These men kept ships' anchors, some of them weighing several tons, lashed in their boats which were perched up on Deal's steep shingle beach, and when ships in the Downs started to drag their anchors, or part their cables, the hovellers would set the dipping lugsails of their boats, man the oars, and cut the retaining ropes to let the boats swoop down into the great breaking waves – row and claw frantically out through the breakers until they had enough offing to sail, and then, with their boat pitching and tossing under them, perform the hideously dangerous and difficult task of bending a cable from the ship on to

Above, Mermaid Street in Rye. The Mermaid Inn is late fifteenth century. *Left,* Strand Gate at Winchelsea: one of the town's much-battered defences against French attack.

Above left, one of the famous Hastings Luggers waiting for the tide. She is fitted for trawling. *Above right,* the Hastings net shops were built tall and narrow because land was scarce. Many were re-built after a fire in 1961. *Below,* part of the growing and prosperous Rye fishing fleet.

the mighty anchor they carried and heave it overboard to try to save the ship from destruction.

They got well paid for this service, of course, for the masters of the ships were desperate, and it was not a job that just anybody would do. But on occasions such as the gale of 1703, there could be no question of carrying out anchors: it was merely a business of trying to save as many men as possible, and for this there was no monetary reward at all. But the Deal men boasted, and boast still, that none of their number has ever failed to put to sea to save life, and when ignorant landlubbers talk of 'rascally longshoremen' and 'longshore sharks' they ought to consider this. In this particular gale the Deal men not only launched every one of their own boats that could take the sea, but they also went to the Revenue Officers and asked if they could borrow their boats too, for these were by far the best and most suitable boats on the beach. The Revenue men refused, and the fishermen, led by the Mayor of Deal, actually took the boats by force and launched them. Two hundred men were saved altogether, looked after by the Deal people, and the Mayor even had to pay for their passage to London out of his own pocket. The government rewarded the Deal men, in fact, by sending a troop or two of Dragoons along, years later, to burn every one of their boats over a certain size, at the instigation of the Revenue Officers, who accused the Deal men of smuggling. Alas, though, the two hundred men saved (although no doubt *they* were glad of it) were pitifully few, for 1,500 officers and men were drowned and fifteen ships of Her Majesty's Navy and 360 merchant ships were destroyed in that one gale of 1703.

Gales of that intensity are, thank God, infrequent, but whenever any gale blew up, and other men were running into harbour for safety, the Deal men were standing by, ready to carry an anchor to a ship that had been driven on to the sands so that her crew might have a chance to winch themselves off to it, ready to put a pilot on a vessel to guide her to the safety of some harbour, or, as a last resort and when all hopes of a nice fat salvage sum had faded, still and always ready to risk their lives to save the lives of other people. Between 1860 and 1887, during which it happened that a record was kept, *fifty-three* Deal fishermen lost their lives pursuing their calling, and Deal is only a small place after all.

During the Napoleonic wars Deal enjoyed great prosperity. A fleet of warships was almost permanently anchored in the Downs, Deal boats got 7/6d for putting a man aboard a ship and more if there was a gale blowing. Deal was used as the embarkation point for several expeditionary forces, including the disastrous one to

Texel in 1799, and the equally disastrous one to Walcheren in 1809. The returning troops from these fiascos were landed at Deal, including a great many wounded, and the whole town was turned into a great hospital.

Lord Nelson landed at Deal many times, often to dine with Sir William and Lady Hamilton at the Three Kings.

Another advantage to Deal of the Napoleonic wars was the fact that, while the Navy was so busy fighting the French, it had no time to fight the smugglers. A lively trade grew up with blockaded France (after all – the *fishermen* were not at war with each other), bringing into England such goods as the English could not produce themselves and therefore doing much good and not a bit of harm. After the war, though, the government started to hit the smugglers hard. To counter this the Deal men started building the most superb pulling-galleys or *gigs*, some of them eighty feet long, in which they could nip across to France in no time and outpace any Revenue cutter in the world to windward at least. So the government stationed three frigates in the Downs, and after much bloodshed, and the wanton destruction of many fine boats, the smuggling was driven into other channels.

At Deal, of course, there is no harbour, and never has been one, and so Deal boats had to be capable of being hauled up on the beach. The result of this fact, besides the exacting nature of the work the boats had to perform, produced a very specialised boat – the Deal Lugger. The biggest Deal Luggers in the nineteenth century were thirty-eight feet long, twelve-foot three inches beam, and were open boats excepting for a small cubby foreward in which men could huddle to sleep or get away from the weather. For sailing they had to ship from five to six tons of internal ballast (bags of shingle), and with this on board they weighed over twenty tons and could still carry a payload of seventeen tons! Six or seven men were needed to sail them (the dipping lug is not a labour-saving sail) but if they had to row into a gale they would take on as many as twenty. They had three masts with dipping lugs on the fore and main and a standing lug on the mizzen. They were enormously large and heavy vessels to have to beach on steep shingle when big seas were breaking. They would come to the beach head-on and were hauled up it by means of large capstans; they would then be turned round at the top of the beach so as to be ready to run down the steep shingle to hit the waves bow-on, when their great weight would carry them on through the first few lines of breakers until the oars could be made to bite the water or the sails to fill to a slant. Clarke Russel, the marine writer, wrote of them: 'a noble boat, a wonderful structure to encounter Channel weather in, the most weatherly of marine structures'. What a pity that not one has survived, to be an object of awe to succeeding generations.

Smaller boats, relying more on oar than on sail, were the Deal Galleys. These were too light for salvage work, or carrying off anchors, or dredging for lost anchors which was always an important Deal activity (there were plenty to dredge for), but they were used principally for passengers and taking out pilots. They went up to thirty feet long and would pull six oars. Smaller boats still were (and still are) called Punts, although in no way do they resemble what is generally known as a punt. They are very boat-shaped boats.

Pilotage was an important Deal job. Not only were pilots taken out to ships in the Downs to pilot them up London River for example, but also the big luggers used to go 'seeking', as they called it, sailing far down Channel, often beyond the Isle of Wight, in order to put pilots on in-coming vessels. The luggers which sailed the farthest got the prizes. When all the pilots carried had been put aboard ships, the lugger would be sailed home short-handed, often with a man and a small boy. Several luggers were lost in this traffic. One man went down-Channel aboard a ship bound for Australia, with his own little punt hauled up on deck so that he could get in her when abreast the Wight and sail himself home again. Alas the weather was so bad that he dared not launch and was carried all the way to Australia!

In 1881 the Revenue got off Deal's back to some extent, for Deal was downgraded by the Customs from being a 'Port' into being a 'Creek', and the Customs House was turned into a mortuary. Would that all such buildings could be put to such good use.

A reader who wishes to know more about the history of the Deal beach boats would do well to read Edgar Marsh's fine book, *Inshore Craft of Great Britain*, Volume II (David and Charles).

Deal was very much in the front line in both world wars. In the first one the Downs was the Examination Point for all ships, whether British or foreign, passing either way through the Straits of Dover, and between 1915 and 1917 121,707 ships were examined there by the Royal Navy. The purpose of this was, of course, to stop material from being taken to Germany. During all this activity, when an average of a hundred and twenty ships a day were having to anchor and wait to be boarded, only one ship was lost by enemy action inside the Goodwins, and that was the H.M.S. *Niger*, torpedoed while at anchor off Deal Pier. The Deal and Kingsdown lifeboats, aided by many fishing boats, got her crew off safely. She was not, however, the first ship to be torpedoed in the Downs: in the Napoleonic wars the 200-ton *Dorothea* was torpedoed by the French.

On 21st April, 1917, a battle raged in the southern approaches to the Downs which seemed like an echo of wars when fighting wasn't such an impersonal affair. The Destroyer Leaders *Swift* and *Broke* sighted, already very close, five German destroyers which were steaming towards the Downs intent on attacking the shipping there, and if they had not been intercepted they would have wreaked great havoc among the crowded anchorage. The *Broke*, commanded by Commander Evans (subsequently always called 'Evans of the *Broke*') torpedoed one destroyer and rammed another and sank her and then tried to ram a third, but being damaged failed to get to her and had to torpedo her instead. During the first ramming German sailors leapt aboard the *Broke* and had to be repelled by cutlasses.

In the Second World War the Downs Contraband Control was operated again, until the fall of France when the Downs were made untenable by long range guns set up on the French coast. Just south of Deal Castle twin naval six-inch guns were installed and the beach was heavily defended with mines, barbed wire and tank traps, but gaps were left for fishing boats to get through, for the harvest of the sea had to be reaped as usual. Ten Deal fishing boats managed to get to Dunkirk to help with the evacuation and of these only three were lost. Of course, the lifeboats went and they got back again. In January, 1940, a Dutch 350-ton motor coaster was mined and crashed into the pier in her death agonies, Deal Castle had a direct hit from a bomb which destroyed the residential part of the building, and Deal had its share of both bombing and shelling.

But the Downs has played a part in many wars. From here the English sailed across to put the fire ships into the Armada, and in here lay a big fleet of Spanish transports under English protection for this was at a time of friendship between the two nations, and Maaten van Tromp attacked them and sank or captured seventy-seven of them! In the Downs, or nearabouts, was fought the great battle between Blake and van Tromp, and in Deal a special hospital had to be opened afterwards to treat the wounded. Elizabeth Alkin, the forerunner of Florence Nightingale, was in charge of the hospital and she spent her entire personal fortune in running it. The government did eventually allow a shilling a day for feeding the English wounded and sixpence a day for the Dutch, who presumably didn't eat so much.

Deal Pier was reopened on 19th November, 1957, by the Duke of Edinburgh after having been rebuilt after its wartime vicissitudes.

Inland, the Town Hall has a small museum in it. South of the Pier is the Time Ball. This was once connected by electrical telegraph to a similar one at Greenwich Observatory, and at exactly one o'clock each day the ball would crash down its pole so that mariners out in the Downs could check their chronometers. Previously the building had been used as a semaphore station: the first of a chain to London, in the Napoleonic wars, but the Time Ball was installed in 1855. The building is now used as an information office, Marconi's invention of the wireless telegraph having rendered the Time Ball redundant.

Farther south is **Deal Castle**, and this is the best preserved of Henry VIII's three castles in the Downs. These castles were the first English answer to the cannon. They were never put to a conclusive test, and if they had been it is doubtful if they would have stood up to more than a certain amount of battering. By the time they were built fort-building in Italy and southern Europe, where it was further developed, had already moved on to earthen banks which absorb the cannon shot, rather than stone walls which shatter and collapse. Deal Castle, which some say was in the plan of a Tudor rose, had a dry moat intensively covered by frontal fire from small arms fired from a multitude of small embrasures, each fire position with a chimney shaft over it to carry away the smoke from the black powder in use in those days so at least the arquebusier could breathe! Above the small-arms men was the main armament on six massive bastions, and in the middle of this a central keep surrounded by six smaller bastions, or lunettes. There were cannon on these lunettes, and more small-arms men inside them, and cannon on top of the keep. So counting the small arms, there were five tiers of guns one on top of the other and the place was absolutely bristling with firearms. The range of the great cannon has been put at about a mile and a half, which would by no means have given them command of the shipping in the Downs, but which would have made it awkward for an enemy to have landed on Deal beach. These castles have a pretty symmetry, and look formidable, but they wouldn't have stood up to a fraction of the bombardment that the great earthen bastions of Berwick on Tweed, for example, could have taken with little damage.

There is a little museum collection in Deal Castle. The fort inside is like a cross between a maze and a catacomb, and delightful for small children to run about in. They can hardly do it any harm: it was built to stand up to worse than that.

South, on the imaginary border between Deal and Walmer, is the plaque commemorating the landing of Julius Caesar, and it has been proved to most people's satisfaction that Deal or Walmer beach is in fact where that great man did land, although no doubt the shoreline has receded considerably since that time. The plaque was put there to commemorate the two-thousandth anniversary of the landing. At the unveiling ceremony the assembled people sang, we are told, 'Oh God our help in Ages Past', a singularly inappropriate hymn unless you happen to be a Roman.

Caesar made his landing one suspects out of sheer curiosity, but his claim was that the Gauls in Britain had been helping their conquered brothers in Gaul. At all events he sailed from Gessoriacum, supposed to be modern Boulogne, with two legions in eighty sailing transports, on 25th August, 55 BC, but as Caesar was there at the time and we were not we might as well let him tell the story himself:

> I reached Britain with the leading vessels at about nine A.M. and saw the enemy forces standing to arms all along the heights. At this point of the coast precipitous cliffs tower over the water, making it possible to shoot down from above straight on to the beaches. It was certainly not the place to attempt a landing, so we lay to anchor until about three-thirty P.M. waiting for the rest of the fleet. During this interval I summoned my staff and company commanders . . . and told them my plan.
>
> They were warned that, as matters at sea are always uncertain, they must be ready to act immediately when ordered. The meeting ended, both wind and tide being favourable the order was given to weigh anchor, and after moving about eight miles up-Channel the ships were grounded on an open and gently-shelving beach.

Dr Halley, the astronomer, has worked out that on the day Caesar was writing about the moon would have been full, the tides at spring, he would have got to Deal at dead low water and would thus have grounded at least a thousand feet away from the dry sand! Other authorities have claimed that he landed four days before spring tides. The enemy were there to greet them, so galleys had to be sent to outflank them and disperse them by shooting darts at them, the legionaries were reluctant to leap into the water until – as every schoolboy knows – the Standard-bearer of the Tenth Legion called upon the gods, and made the following exemplary speech: 'Leap down Soldiers – unless you wish to betray the Eagle to the enemy. I at any rate shall have performed my duty to the State and my General!'

Of course, the others followed him, a battle started with the protagonists wading deep in the water and Caesar had to order his little 'spy boats' away to give support to his soldiers fighting in the water. One soldier reached some rocks which were dry at low tide (and still are, if they are indeed the rocks now known as 'The Malms' as it is thought they are) and from this vantage laid about him.

Needless to say the disciplined Romans drove away the enemy and secured a beach-head, but the galleys carrying Caesar's cavalry had got blown away by contrary winds and so he could not follow his victory up. Four days later a violent storm damaged many of Caesar's ships, the Britons were still harrying the Romans, and the latter decided to withdraw.

Next year in July, Caesar sailed with no less than five legions, 2,000 Gaulish cavalry and much heavy material including large ballistic machines, all in about eight hundred ships, six hundred of them having been newly built during the previous winter. He sailed from Portus Itius, probably Wissand Bay near Cap Gris-Nez. This time he had an even better taste of the navigational perils of the Narrow Seas, and the tidal waters to which his Mediterranean sailors were quite unaccustomed. A south-westerly breeze gave the fleet steerage-way until about midnight and then failed. The tide continued to carry the fleet eastward, so that it soon far overshot the South Foreland.

The tide carried us right off-course, and at dawn the coast of Britain appeared receding on our port quarter . . .

The Romans were very lucky – and the Britons very unlucky – that the whole fleet was not stranded on the Goodwins. As it was, by dint of furious rowing ('by hard rowing they enabled the heavily laden transports to keep up with the warships . . .') the ships were got back to Deal beach at about midday next day and a landing effected. Again a storm blew up and destroyed and damaged many of the Roman ships which were anchored in the roadstead.

It appeared that a great storm overnight had wrecked nearly all the ships or cast them ashore; the anchors and cables had parted, seamen and pilots had been helpless, and heavy damage had been suffered from collision.

Caesar had to return from his campaignings and cause the ships to be hauled right out of the water (as Deal boats have been ever since), a fortified camp built around them, and repairs to them put in hand. He was then able to fight his way as far as St Albans, but in September he sailed back to Gaul again and did not come back. On the second landing the Britons, forewarned this time, might have given him a very rough time had not one British chief, Arvarwy, completely betrayed them, earning for himself thereafter the name of *Du-bradwr*, which meant in the Gaulish language

'Black traitor', and it means exactly the same thing in the Welsh language today.

It has been postulated that Caesar was not wrecked on the Goodwins because these sands were an island in his day, above water at high tide and populated, and that they were not finally overwhelmed by the sea until the Final Depression in about 1097. There is even a story that they were named Goodwins after the great Earl Godwin, who owned them. Borings have proved that they are just sea-sand, however, for very far down, and there is probably no truth in these intriguing theories.

Leaving Caesar's plaque then, we pass into **Walmer**, and soon come to the lifeboat, perched up on her ways like a fish-eagle waiting to swoop.

Walmer and Deal lifeboats, between them, have as great a record of service as any round the coast, as we might expect seeing that the deadly Goodwins are within easy sight of the shore. Deal and Kingsdown stations were closed in July, 1933, and one big motor lifeboat at Walmer took over.

The records of the two former Deal boats and the Kingsdown boat are awe-inspiring. As one example of hundreds of such occasions all three boats launched on Sunday night, 19th November, 1916, to go the aid of the Italian steamer *Val Salice*, bound for Italy from Sunderland with 4,000 tons of coal. The Kingsdown boat made what in local parlance is a 'dry launch'. That is – after she had made her rush down the steep beach and hit the water – she was flung back by a great wave and swamped. Such a launch is indeed anything but dry, but having made it, no boat can get away from the beach until she has been hauled up again, drained of water, and turned round. The North Deal boat was luckier and came back at 3 a.m. with thirty Italian sailors on board. No sooner were the saved men landed than the boat had to put to sea again to the United States steamer *Sibiria*, 3,535 tons, ashore on the Goodwins. Deal Number Two boat had tried to reach her but had got badly damaged by the seas and had to return. The Kingsdown boat, although damaged by her 'dry launch', was launched again and managed to come home with fifty-two Americans. She beached at 2 a.m. on *Tuesday* with them. There were some changes of crew during the forty-eight hours during which these boats were working non-stop to save the lives of total strangers, but at least one man, William Hoile Junior, was noticed as having had twenty-four hours in one of the boats, constantly either rowing or sailing an open boat in what was, by all contemporary accounts, a formidable gale.

Many were the big successes, such as when the North Deal boat, helped by the Ramsgate boat towed by her tug, took off ninety-six sailors from the U.S.S. *Piave* of New Jersey, wrecked on the Goodwins, but at other times there were hours of heart-breaking toil with little to show for it, as when it took the Deal boat *Charles Dibdin* three hours to reach the Esthonian three-masted schooner *Toogo*, which had been driven on to the Goodwins by a hurricane-force easterly, only for the lifeboat to cruise for hours amid the wreckage, her crew hearing at one time piteous cries for help, and finally to pick only two men up out of the water. The rest, including the captain's wife, who was aboard, were all lost, excepting for one man picked up later almost miraculously by a steamer. On that service once again the lifeboat had to launch again immediately she got home, and as there was no time for a change of crew the already exhausted men took *six hours* to row against the gale to the Goodwins. They had the reward of saving, however, three men from where they had lashed themselves to the rigging of the ketch *Corinthian*. They had been there for sixteen hours, however, and one of them was dead.

In the severe winter of 1940, during the Second World War, the *Charles Dibdin* launched twenty-six times in four months and saved forty-five lives. The next year, while cruising the farther edge of the Goodwins during a service, one of the crew, Jim Rich, actually died aboard the boat from exposure, which shows that service even in the sophisticated modern motor lifeboat is not a bed of roses.

And what of the little boats that the crew of the modern Walmer lifeboat still have to earn a living in? Well, they are typical Deal 'Punts', much like the Punts of sailing days, none of them very large, and there are a large number of them. The principal trade of most of them nowadays is taking angling parties out fishing. The angling off Deal is good, and these fine little boats are kept at a high standard of safety and efficiency by the voluntary efforts of the fishermen's own organisation. The Board of Trade inspectors accept their findings completely. So far, among these fishing party boats, there has never been a serious accident. Of the boats that go commercial fishing (as opposed to taking angling parties) there was one boat trawling when I last went there, the rest were long lining (putting out lines of about a mile long with a thousand hooks on each line) or trammel netting. The trammel net is gaining popularity on this coast, which is a little hard to explain, because in the West Country it has been almost entirely superseded by the new ray net, or tangle net. The latter is a single net of very fine man-made fibre that sinks to the bottom and simply tangles up anything that creeps or swims into it. The trammel is three nets, all hung together on one head-rope but with separate foot-ropes. The two outer nets are fine mesh – the middle one large-mesh. A fish swimming into it pokes a pocket of the first net he hits through one of the big meshes of the inside net and thus pockets himself. A few men at Deal and Walmer still shoot some lobster pots, over wrecks off Walmer.

Most of these Punts have transom or lute sterns, which we will describe when we get to Hastings. It is notable that those with elliptical sterns are all registered at Rye. There was one Hastings Lugger on the beach in 1973 – the *Janie B* (RX 257). She had not then been to sea for many months and was badly drying out, which is a great shame.

To change the subject dramatically, a man named Bunyan in Deal is said to have a fine collection of old microscopes.

Walmer Castle should not be missed, for its state apartments, for from the early eighteenth century it has been the official residence of the Lords Warden of the Cinque Ports. William Pitt, Lord Liverpool, the Duke of Wellington, and Lord Granville made it their permanent homes and Wellington died there. Before he did Queen Victoria and the Prince Consort visited him. W. H. Smith was Lord Warden in 1891 and left many pictures and ornaments in the place, but it is the presence of the great Duke of Wellington that is all-pervading. One room, in fact, is crammed with Wellingtonia from the collection of T. H. Lucas, and Wellington's bedroom is preserved exactly as it was when he died in it, the old shabby armchair in which he died still standing where it was when it was painted with the great old man dying in it by a contemporary artist, and the Duke's camp bed, in which he always slept whether at home or on his campaigns, still by the wall. The room gives the impression of a fine simplicity and austerity. The last words which the Duke was heard to utter were not romantic perhaps, but at least they were practical. They were: 'Send for an apothecary.'

At Deal is the Royal Marines School of Music, which makes a splendid sound at concerts and marches-past. Deal has extensive barracks and a long connection with the military. Cobbett, who hated the military above most other 'tax-eaters' as he called them wrote:

Deal is a most villainous place. It is full of filthy-looking people. Great desolation of abomination has been going on here; tremendous barracks, partly pulled down and partly tumbling down, and partly occupied by soldiers. Everything seems to be upon the perish. I was glad to hurry along through it, and to leave its inns and public houses to be occupied by the tarred, and trousered, and blue-and-buff crew whose very vicinage I always detest.

He should have looked out the gallant crews of the Luggers and the Galleys and the Punts. He would have found something he could have admired among them.

CHAPTER 4

Kingsdown to Dover

INLAND from Deal is a large coalmine. **Betteshanger** was inaugurated on 19th May, 1924. The Kent coalfield was started in 1913, after borings had proved the prognostications of the geologists right. It is a difficult field, with many geological faults, friable coal and poor drainage, but eight million pounds were spent on it in post-nationalisation modernisation. Betteshanger has fourteen seams of coal proven, eleven of which are good enough to be workable, and the coal is of good quality, being semi-anthracitic and suitable for steam-raising. The first miners were brought from the North and Midlands, but have merged now with the local population.

Deal and Walmer are on low-lying ground – in fact most of the modern parts were built by the fishermen on a shingle bank flung up by the sea, Old Deal being well inland like other villages along this coast so as to be hidden from pirates. But as we progress southwards the land begins to rise. **Kingsdown**, now practically a part of the Walmer-Deal complex, is also the seaward extension of an old village built inland: **Ringwould**, which was, astonishingly enough, a limb of the Cinque Ports.

A bracing walk along the top of the cliffs, past the Obelisk put up in 1921 to the Dover Patrol, brings us to **St Margaret's at Cliffe**. St Margaret's was also built inland some way from the edge of the cliff, and there is a fine and grand church built at about the time of Henry II, very late and rich Norman. On no account miss the unique west doorway, nor the fine chancel arch. This church was both bombed and shelled during the Second World War because there were two long-range guns mounted just near it busy shelling the German-occupied coast and these attracted counter-battery fire.

Up in the top village is a most pleasant pub, the Cliffe Tavern, where there is in winter a good fire and at all times good sandwiches. Down on the shore is the Coastguard, once the Green Man, rebuilt with beach flints after destruction by enemy action. This pub can boast the loudest juke box in the United Kingdom, and some of the action of the *Scarlet Pimpernel* stories was set here. Just to the east of the houses down on the beach was a big cliff fall in March, 1973, interesting for the fossils of the chalk in the sundered mass, but beware further falls, and beware getting cut off by the tide, which comes right up to the foot of the vertical chalk cliffs here. Noel Coward used to live in one of the houses down on the beach here, Peter Ustinov lived in an old coastguard lookout on the cliff to the westward, and a fairly elderly seafaring gentleman still earns a living from fishing from the beach here, and acts as adviser in all nautical matters to many millionaires.

Up on the cliff again we are on the **South Foreland** itself, where the North Sea turns into the English Channel, and here are many old gun emplacements and other fortifications of many wars. Marconi made early experiments from one of the two lighthouses here. Down below the vertical cliffs the five-masted square-rigger *Preussen*, the biggest sailing ship in the world, went ashore in a sinking condition after having been rammed by the London Brighton and South Coast Railway turbine steamer *Brighton IV* off Beachy Head. The captain of the *Brighton IV* lost his ticket and committed suicide.

Like all seaports **Dover** is best first seen from the sea, but if you do approach it by land the best course is this cliff-top walk from the eastward. From these high cliffs the harbour and then the eastern part of the town unfold dramatically. Cobbett, in 1821, approached the town from the west, on his horse, and, as usual, his description will never be bettered:

> The valley that runs down from Folkestone is, when it gets to Dover, crossed by another valley that runs down from Canterbury, or, at least, from the Canterbury direction. It is in the gorge of this cross valley that Dover is built. The two chalk hills jut out into the sea, and the water that comes up between them forms a harbour for this ancient, most interesting, and beautiful place. On the hill to the north stands the castle of Dover, which is fortified in the ancient manner, except on the sea side, where it has the steep *Cliff* for a fortification. On the south side of the town the hill is, I believe, rather more lofty than on the north side; and here is that cliff which is described by Shakespeare in the play of *King Lear*. It is fearfully steep, certainly. Very nearly perpendicular for a considerable distance. The grass grows well, to the very tip of the cliff; and you see cows and sheep grazing there with as much unconcern as if grazing in the bottom of a valley.

Dover, being the Gateway of England and one of the most interesting places around our coasts, has a very interesting history, a history which is almost a history of England herself.

Before Julius Caesar sailed by it, put off from landing by the sight of all those warriors shouting defiance at him from the cliff-tops, Dover was undoubtedly a port of entry for people from the mainland. No doubt the *Belgi*, who had partially conquered Britain when the Romans arrived, by means of the great technical superiority of their heavy wheeled ploughs and their chariots, landed at Dover. There was a good natural harbour there in those days, for the River Dour (from the Welsh *Dwr* – water) flowed out at a wide mouth into the sea, and left – in that spectacular cleft in the high chalk cliffs – a good harbour. As this was the nearest harbour to Europe, and in fact within easy sight of it, it was the natural port of entry into the country. The modern Market Place is built over where the natural harbour once was, and the poor old Dour has to creep shamefully along underground in noisome tunnels, where it is not running between concrete walls like an open sewer. A most dishonoured stream.

The Romans, although they landed first at Deal, soon made Dover one of their two chief ports, the other being Richborough Castle. To guide their pilots across the Narrow Seas at night they built two lighthouses, or *phari* as they called them, one on the Western Heights, now mostly knocked down, and the other still standing at the west end of the Saxon chapel within the walls of Dover Castle. Throughout the centuries many bits and pieces of Roman work have been discovered, but it was left to the Archaeological Rescue Corps to come up with solid discoveries, and they have done this because of the threat of the new York Street diversion, currently being built to carry traffic around the centre of the town. This made it necessary to knock down many buildings, and so the Rescue Corps was able to excavate where no excavation was possible before, and they have laid open the foundations of what was probably the chief Roman naval base in Britain, built in the second century, with superimposed on it a third century Fort of the Saxon Shore – one of the string of nine such forts built from Suffolk to Hampshire, with counterparts over on the French coast.

There is a theory, put forward by Donald A. White of Wisconsin in 1961, that these forts were not built, as was thought, by the Romans to keep the Barbarian out, but by the Barbarian to keep the Romans out, and far-fetched as this sounds it is probably true. For in AD 284 one Carausius, a Belgian sailor, was promoted to high rank in the Roman Navy by Diocletian, and told to keep the Saxon pirates away. Carausius turned this job to good account by letting the pirates go ashore and raid and then pouncing on them when they sailed away, seizing the stolen goods for himself. Ordered on the carpet by his superior Maximian to explain this behaviour he

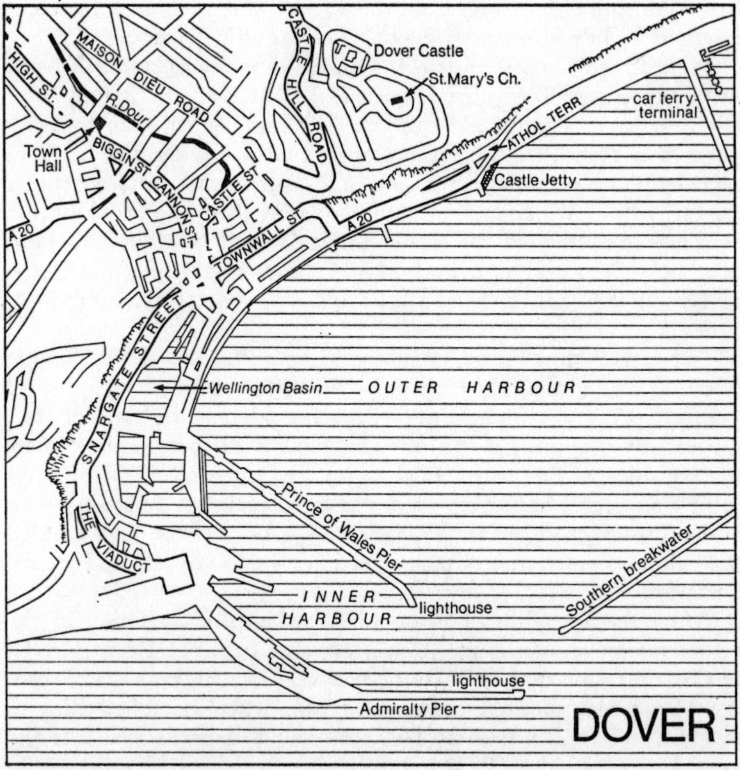

declined to come, but rebelled against Maximian, seized the whole of Britain and Northern and Western Gaul, made himself Emperor with the grand title of Marcus Aurelius Mauseaeus Carausius, and built this impressive string of coastal forts. He built them to keep the Romans out, not the Saxons. But in 293 his possessions in Gaul fell to the Emperor Constantius Chlorus, Carausius himself was murdered by his own Finance Minister Allectus, Allectus was defeated by a Roman army which landed in Hampshire, west of the westernmost fort, and thus outflanked him, and Rome again ruled Britain, and went on doing so until the legions were recalled at the beginning of the fifth century. But after the defeat of the rebels Carausius's forts were retained, and improved, and put under the command of an officer named *Comes litoris Saxonica per Britannium*, or the 'Count of the Saxon Shore'. This gentleman ultimately controlled, besides the nine great forts, a string of watch towers from Yorkshire right round to the Bristol Channel, and he commanded mobile forces ashore as well as the ships at sea.

William the Conqueror had the sense not to try to land at Dover, but he took care to capture it a week after he landed. He may have felt that he had more right to the Castle at Dover than to other parts of England, for the chroniclers tell us that Harold of England especially made it over to him in that disastrous oath he swore under duress while a prisoner of William's in Normandy. Anyway, William strengthened the castle, made Odo of Bayeux – his half-brother – its custodian, and at onc time Hugh de Montford – and from then on, as a fortress, the Castle went from strength to strength.

The Constable of the Castle was *de facto* Warden of the Cinque Ports. William certainly took over the custom from the English of granting privileges to the Cinque Ports in exchange for 'ship service'. Dover was required, in his day, to furnish, at forty days' notice, twenty ships at the town's own charge for a period of fifteen days in any one year, and every ship was to be manned by twenty men and a grommet. The latter article was a boy. If the king needed the ships for more than fifteen days in any one year he had to pay for them.

When the Dauphin of France landed, at the invitation of the rebellious barons, in King John's days, he besieged Dover Castle, but by that time that fortification was very strong. Hugh de Burgh, the Constable, shouted defiance at him when he asked him to yield: 'Never will I yield to French aliens this castle which is the very key of England!' De Burgh was very nearly reduced to surrendering, but reinforcements under Sir Stephen de Pencestre managed to get through to him through Earl Godwin's sallyport and the garrison managed to hold out. Louis the Dauphin drew off. But next year, in 1217, he sailed again from Calais with eighty-six ships. He was met at sea by the Cinque Ports' fleet, which got to windward of him and released on the breeze a great quantity of quicklime – the forerunner of chemical warfare. With the French thus blinded the English fleet ran downwind, and with much ramming, and cutting of halliards so that sails came down at a run, and archery, and boarding, the French were signally defeated, a hundred and twenty-five knights were captured, over a thousand other ranks, and one of the leaders, Eustace the Monk, had his head cut off.

In 1242 the Portsmen had a serious naval reverse though. Henry III foolishly gave them permission to raid the French coast, with the result that the French came across, raided their ports, and more or less mewed them up in harbour for several years. In 1295 the

French burnt and pillaged Dover. There was pretty constant enmity between the French and English seamen for centuries.

The Portsmen took sides in the Barons' wars, and when Prince Edward (later Edward I) wanted to reduce their arrogance he called in the men of Great Yarmouth to do it. The Cinque Portsmen had long held all sorts of powers and privileges over the Yarmouth men, so the latter were very happy to sail in and settle old scores. But when Edward became king he let bygones be bygones and relied heavily on the Portsmen for help in his Welsh wars.

There has never been a time when Dover, as a harbour, was not important. After the murder of Thomas à Becket a great trade in pilgrims grew up from the Continent to his shrine at Canterbury, very similar, no doubt, to the sea traffic that now exists between Africa and Medina. Henry V was brought back, dead, in great splendour, from France through Dover. Henry VIII came here often, and sailed from here to the Field of the Cloth of Gold. Charles I met his bride here, and afterwards sadly sent her away into exile from Dover: Charles II landed here in triumph at the Restoration, closely observed by the observant Mr Pepys. In peace and war there was a constant coming and going between England and the Continent through Dover.

The story of the development of the 'Dover Packets', the little ships that have plied backwards and forwards between Dover and France since Neolithic days (although they weren't always called packets) is one of continual technical development, badly set back now and then by deteriorating harbour conditions. Thus in 1629 the port owned thirty-six ships totalling 2,063 tons, while in 1701 there were only seven ships totalling 415 tons. The reason for this, apart from the French wars, was the silting-up of the harbour due to the inexorable eastward drift in the Channel which we shall discuss when we get to Lydd. When John Evelyn crossed the Channel on 12th June, 1649, and again on 13th July, 1650 on both occasions he was chased by privateers, so there were other disabilities besides the eastward drift. In 1720 the building of much faster Dover packets had begun, and from then until 1820 the development of very fast sailing craft suitable for this short but rough sea passage went on fast. Most of them were built in Dover. It got so that sailing packets were sailing from Dover to Calais in three and a quarter hours.

But in 1820 the death-knell of these fine little sailing ships was sounded by the *Rob Roy* a steamship, ninety tons and thirty horsepower. By 1823 the Post Office was sending mails not under sail but in the *Spitfire*, eighty-three foot long, forty horsepower. In 1830 the S.S. *Firefly* crossed in three hours. In 1846 the S.S. *Onyx* did it in one hour twenty-five minutes. Hovercraft don't do it *so* much faster.

There were strange experiments. In 1875 the *Castalia* took to sea. She was twin-hulled for stability but people were *still* seasick and she was not a success. In 1875 there was the *Bessemer*, with her saloon slung in gimbals so that the delicate passengers didn't roll with the ship. Gimballed saloon or no she crashed into the West Pier at Calais and that was the end of *her*. In 1936 train ferries started, and they now take about one hour twenty minutes, just five minutes faster than the *Onyx* in 1846, but in the *Onyx*'s days passengers weren't subjected to hours of delay by the Customs and Immigration authorities.

The story of the harbour itself is the story of man's constant fight against the eastward drift.

The Dour Estuary, which had been the harbour in Roman days, gradually silted up, and the little ships of the day were forced to land on the open beach as the fishing boats still do at Deal and Hastings to-day. In 1495 one John Clerk built a pier into the sea which at first seemed so successful that mariners gave the harbour it formed the name Paradise (after a similar one at Calais). But alas the deadly eastward drift did its work. Shingle driven eastward by this phenomenon came round the end of Clerk's breakwater and silted up his paradisial harbour. Dover citizens used to be called out by beat of drum to dig the shingle away, but no matter how hard they dug the shingle beat them. Ships were reduced to landing on the open beach again. A report of 1581 put it: 'By experience it has always been found that as the peere was built out so the bankes of beache allso began to growe, and lay farder out as the peere was farder built.'

It was a local man named Digges who at least started to solve this problem, in the late sixteenth century, by building an inner harbour which he called the Great Pent. This impounded water at high tide and let it surge out at low tide so as to scour the new outer harbour which he had built to the east of Clerk's wall. The Great Pent was eventually turned into the existing Wellington Dock.

By Charles II the port was sadly decayed and silted again, and Dover was in poverty. All during the eighteenth century plan after plan was prepared for improving the harbour, but none acted upon. The fact was, and is, that you couldn't find a more naturally unsuitable place for a harbour than Dover, and yet a harbour there had to be because of the great geographical importance of the place. It was not until 1830 that men had the power and knowledge required to build a true harbour in this most exposed place.

Then, successively, the old Great Pent was turned into the Wellington Dock, the floating Granville Dock was completed in 1874 (a floating dock is a dock into which vessels can only go at high tide, thereafter to be impounded by a gate which keeps the water in so that they float at all stages of the tide), by 1850 the Admiralty Pier, which had been started in 1847 as the successor to Clerk's Pier, was carried below the line of true tide which at last minimised the silting problem, by 1871 it had been extended to a length of two thousand feet at a cost of two million pounds, in 1892 the Prince of Wales Pier was started. It eventually cost £600,000. In 1909 the Prince of Wales, later George V, opened the completed harbour much as it is to-day: a harbour capable of sheltering the entire Royal Navy. If you sail into it for shelter though don't think you're going to have a peaceful night at anchor in the six hundred acres of the Outer Harbour. I used to scuttle for what we used to call the 'Submarine Dock', now called the Camber, but you can't go there, it's beset by ferries. Most yachts lie nowadays in the Wellington Dock, where there is always sixteen feet of water. Yachts by the way may only use the eastern entrance to the Outer Harbour: the western being reserved for bigger ships.

Dover now handles three times as many passengers every year as any other port in the United Kingdom (nearly six million of them a year in fact) and this may possibly be more than any other port in the world. There is roll-on roll-off for a hundred-thousand road haulage vehicles to clutter up our roads and shake down our villages (nine-tenths of their loads could – and should – go to other ports about the country by sea), there are train ferries, hovercraft, and drive-on car ferries for over a million cars a year.

Over all this trade and activity there hangs a shadow.

The first plan for a Channel tunnel was by Albert Mathieu in 1802. He wanted artificial islands in mid-Channel with shafts going down from them to the tunnel for ventilation, and underground staging-posts for horses to be changed and rested. The whole thing was to be lit by candles in elegant chandeliers. Napoleon approved this idea but the English didn't. In 1833 there was a serious scheme for a submerged tube by Thomé de Gamond, who plunged 108 feet down to the bottom of the Channel with buttered lint over his ears to keep the water out, a bag of flints to sink him, and an inflated pig's bladder to bring him up again. In 1856 the same intrepid man came up with another plan for a tunnel with air shafts. He pointed out that the Varne sandbank has only fifteen feet of water over it at low spring tide.

In 1872 the English Channel Tunnel Company was formed, and

started making borings, but ran into financial trouble. In 1880 William Low, the engineer, and Sir Edward Watkin, the manager, sunk a seventy-four-foot shaft down below Abbot's Cliff, between Dover and Folkestone, and began to drive a seven-foot tunnel towards France. On the other side the French Tunnel Company sank a shaft two hundred and eighty feet deep. Sir Edward sank another shaft to the east of the first. He predicted that in 1882 the tunnels would hole through. He planned for complete trains to be lifted up a giant vertical shaft by hydraulic power. There are photographs, possibly unique, of Sir Edward's shaft-heads, and the men who sank the shafts, in the possession of the landlord of the Chequers Inn at West Hougham.

Alas, Sir Edward and his engineer ran out of money, and also there was great hostility for the tunnel idea in high quarters. Gladstone opposed it, Queen Victoria eventually turned against it, and people like Tennyson, Browning, Huxley and Cardinal Newman signed a petition against it. Britain was an island, and they wanted to keep her so.

To rally public support Sir Edward began giving bizarre champagne parties below the Channel to 'people of the best fashion', lowering them 163 feet in a skip and then having these elegant ladies and gentlemen pushed along his tunnel in rock trolleys by his miners to a special banqueting chamber that he had had hewed out of the chalk. When the War Office opposed the tunnel on security grounds Sir Edward proposed arrangements for flooding it, filling it with hot steam, filling it with shingle, or blowing it up. But the War Office still said no. Poor Sir Edward went on tunnelling away illegally until 1894, and then gave it up.

In 1907 and 1913 new proposals were made, but all turned down. In 1918 Marshal Foch said that the existence of a tunnel would have shortened the war by two years, by allowing supplies and troops to flow through. In 1924 the issue was raised again, with Ramsey Macdonald, Balfour, Asquith, Lloyd George and Baldwin ranged against it. In 1929 the idea was turned down in the Commons by only seven votes though. In 1948 Sir Herbert Walker, then Chairman of the still-existing Channel Tunnel Company, persuaded Parliament to set up a study group. In 1956 Americans became interested, also the Suez Canal Company, which after all didn't have much else to do, and in 1957 the English and French companies set up *Technical Studies Incorporated*, which has spent £500,000 on research. In August, 1964, they set up a team of scientists in Dover Castle, and in September trial borings were being made in the Channel. Now, September, 1973, the Government has given approval and work should start in eighteen months. The tunnel will be thirty-two miles, twenty-three of them submarine.

The current idea in most favour is to have twin working tunnels with a smaller service tunnel between them and that a train would leave each end every four minutes, going a hundred miles an hour, and that the air pressure thus caused would be relieved by cross-cuts every 250 yards between the two main tunnels. Four thousand two hundred people and 1,800 vehicles could be carried like this each way every hour. But such estimates vary from day to day.

Obviously if all these people and all these vehicles were debouched on to the roads of England (or France for that matter) in one place the result would be even more awful pollution and dislocation than occurs at present. But if trains were loaded and unloaded at a variety of points far inland – right up in the Midlands and North and even Scotland – the result could be a great diminution of traffic and congestion. If the railways of both countries accepted the challenge of a tunnel imaginatively, and if their governments supported them, an enormous improvement could be made to our environment.

The alternative to a tunnel was to have been a bridge and (perhaps for not entirely altruistic reasons) the steel industries of both England and France lobbied hard for this. A fairly late estimate is that a tunnel would cost £700 million while a bridge would cost £1800 million, but a bridge would be capable of carrying ten thousand vehicles an hour in each direction. They would travel on their own wheels, juggernauts and all, and it does not take a genius to see that the impact they would have on the rural areas into which they debouched would be awful.

One thing is certain. Neither bridge nor tunnel would do the Port of Dover any good.

Other, even stranger, manners of crossing the English Channel:

Balloons. Only two years after the first man-carrying balloon rose into the air Monsieur Pierre Blanchard and Dr John Jeffries arrived at Dover, on 5th December, 1784, Dr Jeffries, an American, with the money and M. Blanchard with the balloon. Placing the balloon in Dover Castle they proceeded to quarrel violently. Jeffries actually hired a press-gang of Jack Tars at one stage of the quarrel to go into the castle and take the balloon away by force, but the Governor of the castle shut the gates against them. The matter was eventually brought about by the two aeronauts, and on 7th January, 1785, the wind being NNW., the balloon was inflated until she was ninety-four feet in circumference, and away she went. When she was five miles from the French coast she was nearly down to the water and the balloonists had to throw away nearly everything they had – including the gallant Blanchard's *trousers*! Up they went again, after this sacrifice, and they made a landing twelve miles inland from the French coast. Jeffries related later that he was 'soon well mounted and had a fine gallop of seven miles'. We are not told what happened to *his* trousers. The 'boat' of the balloon rests in Calais Museum.

In 1963, on 13th April, Yost and Piccard Junior flew from near Dover to Gravelines in three-and-a-half hours in a hot air balloon.

Airships. On 5th November, 1910, a gentleman left Wormwood Scrubs (from *outside* the prison) in an airship. He landed at two o'clock in the morning next day at Douai, having travelled 170 miles, and the French Customs demanded £30 deposit on his dirigible.

Aeroplanes. Louis Blériot's eleventh aeroplane was twenty-six feet six inches long with a wing-span of twenty-five feet seven-and-a-half inches, she weighed 661 pounds all up and fuel, and she had a three-cylinder Anzani engine of from twenty-two to twenty-five horsepower.

Although he had a badly injured ankle from a recent crash, Blériot hobbled out to his plane near Calais and took off at 4.41 a.m. on 25th July, 1909, got carried eastward by the westerly wind just as Julius Caesar had done on his second expedition, altered course and made up his westing again, and landed at Dover Castle. A British Customs Officer wrote him down in his book as 'Master of a Monoplane'. The shape of his aeroplane, cast in granite, beside a tricolour windsock, marks the spot where he landed.

Kites. Samuel Franklin Cody, not to be confused with Buffalo Bill although he dressed up like him, set off from Calais at 8 p.m., 7th November, 1903, in a fourteen-foot boat pulled along by a kite. He landed at Dover at 8 a.m. next day.

Inflated Rubber Suits. In 1875 Captain Boyton, U.S.A., launched himself into the Channel in an inflated rubber suit and propelled himself towards France with a paddle and a small sail. A boat accompanied him carrying a crate of carrier pigeons. During the voyage twenty-nine 'quaint messages' were sent back to Folkestone by the carrier pigeons. I wish I knew what they were.

Gliders. In 1931 a Canadian opera singer named Lissant Beardmere took off from Lympne in a glider towed by an aeroplane. He cast off over England at 12,000 feet, and landed at St Inglevert, near Boulogne, half an hour later. The very next day Herr R. Kroufield crossed the Channel by glider both ways. The first soaring flight – i.e. not power-towed to take off – was by G. H. Stephenson on 22nd April, 1939. He was launched from Dunstable at three in the afternoon intending to go to a party in Reigate. At 6 p.m. he telephoned his host to say that he couldn't come. He was in France.

Hovercraft. First crossing 1959.

Swimming. At 12.26 p.m. on 24th August, 1875, a twenty-seven-year-old ship's officer named Captain Matthew Webb covered himself with porpoise oil and launched himself off the end of the Admiralty Pier at Dover into the last of the ebb. He wore no goggles, ate nothing on the swim but drank beer and tried to sip cod liver oil, which made him sick, and he knew only inefficient strokes such as the side-stroke and the breast-stroke. He touched bottom on the other side, completely exhausted, at 10.41 the next day, having covered in his tide-driven course at least fifty miles. He refused to be made a hero of, and all he could be got to say by reporters was: 'I went into the water determined either to reach the other side or sink. All I can say is that I kept plugging at it and it was a terrible hard job towards the end. But I was determined not to give up as long as I had strength to move a limb.' It was *thirty-six years* before the next person succeeded in swimming the Channel.

Coracle. Denzyl Davies of Cenarth and Bernard Thomas of Llechryd crossed the Channel on Tuesday, 28th August, 1973, in fourteen and a half hours, landing at Cap Gris Nez. They were not the first people to cross the English Channel in a coracle, but they are probably the first to do it for about two thousand years.

Dover in the two world wars was perhaps the most important place in England. In the first war the Dover Patrol operated from here. This was a fleet mostly of steam trawlers and drifters that laid and serviced a minefield that ran all the way from the South Goodwins to Dunkirk and effectively cut off the Channel from the North Sea for the enemy, and that swept German mines, and that did a great deal to keep the Narrow Seas open to the British and closed to the Germans. Many of the little ships were armed with nothing bigger than a rifle, and many were lost. Dover was used intensively during the First World War. Half a million wounded men were landed there. In the Second World War 366,000 men were landed from Dunkirk, most of them at Dover. We can still see the mouths of strange tunnels and caves up in the chalk cliffs, and to work out and date all the gun emplacements, shelters and entrenchments in the cliffs and on them would be a formidable task. Big guns kept up a constant fire on the French coast during most of the Second World War and the Germans replied in kind, making this place aptly called Hell Fire Corner or Hell's Corner.

As to what to see in Dover in more peaceful times, the Town Hall is very fine with its great Maison Dieu Hall, a restored thirteenth-century hostel for pilgrims. It was founded in 1203 by the Hubert de Burgh who so gallantly defied the Dauphin in Dover Castle. Large numbers of pilgrims from the Continent on their way to Canterbury must have lodged here, and also English pilgrims outward-bound for the shrine of St James of Compostella. Many wounded and destitute soldiers and sailors from the French wars were lodged here, too, in the Middle Ages. The Hall that we now see is supposed to have been rebuilt in 1253. It is much restored but still impressive.

There is a small but beautiful and interesting museum in the Town Hall. One of the many items of local interest is a hoard of coins: Scots, Irish, English, French, Low Countries and Italian, dug up in 1955 when a trench was being dug in Market Street. The hoard is supposed to have been buried on 2nd August, 1295, when fifty French ships and galleys, with ten thousand men, sacked and burnt much of Dover. Presumably the owner didn't live to dig his gold up again, but what a light it throws on the trade of those early days!

St Mary's Church is fine Norman and Early English, and well worth looking at. There are large galleries in it for the seating of the august and important. The Cinque Ports pilots once had their own gallery, but this has been pulled down, but their successors, the Pilots of Trinity House, sometimes now sit, for official ceremonies, in the South Gallery.

St Edmund's Chapel is a tiny but beautiful building consecrated on 30th March, 1253, by St Richard of Chichester, to St Edmund. St Richard's bowels were buried in it and the cist they were buried in is still there to see. Mass is said here every Saturday morning at ten o'clock.

The beautiful second-century Roman 'Painted House', recently discovered just outside the walls of the long-lost Fort of the Saxon Shore, is to be preserved and exposed to the public. It rivals many a house in Pompeii, and should not be missed on any account.

Dover College was St Martin's Priory (Benedictine) and is now private, but one can get permission sometimes to see the Refectory, which is twelfth century and one of the largest Norman buildings in the country: the interior is a hundred feet long. There are traces of ancient paintings.

St Radigund's Abbey, inland, was enormous, built in the twelfth and thirteenth centuries, now almost totally pulled down. It was founded in 1292 directly from Prémontré. It is a good place to go on a moonlight night, when the rhododendrons are in bloom.

Dover Castle I am not going to attempt to describe. It is incomparably the finest and most interesting military building in England, and it cannot be more than glanced at in less than a full day.

There was certainly an Iron Age fort on this splendidly defensible position, the Romans built one of their two Dover *phari* here, and it still stands as not only the earliest Roman building in this country but also the most complete. The Saxons built a church hard by it, of Roman material, St Mary-in-Castro, one of the most important Saxon buildings in England. What we see is probably of about AD 1000. The weird mosaic work in the chancel and nave was put there in 1888, and Sir Gilbert Scott also had a good go at the building in 1860, but it is surprising what a lot of Saxon work survived these visitations. The Saxons also had a castle here, and as we have seen, poor old Harold, when a prince, was forced to promise to give William the castle if he ever became king. The latter, after he had got it, immediately set about improving it. But the mighty keep was built in Henry II's reign and cost that monarch a large part of his revenues for many years. Most of the building was done in the 1180s. It is a grand and magnificent building, walls twenty feet thick, two fine Norman chapels, fascinating galleries running under the battlements, great halls much truncated by the construction in 1800 of superb brick vaults of enormous thickness to support the great guns of the period, a big collection of arms of various periods, a model of the Battle of Waterloo, and a well now 250 feet deep but once much deeper. How interesting it would be to dig it again to its former depth and sift carefully through the material that must be contained within it. There are tunnels still in existence dug by the French attackers of 1216, and a marvellous system of subterranean passages serving redoubts thrown out from the main castle walls at various later periods.

Dover Castle was in continuous military use and occupation from Saxon times until after the Second World War. In 1958 this occupation came to an end and it was handed over to the Ministry of Works. The last great military use was when it was used for the headquarters of Operation Dynamo, the withdrawal of the British Army from Dunkirk in 1940. It would even to-day be a formidable fortress: it would take plenty of medium or heavy artillery bombardment to reduce those enormous walls.

But the whole castle is magnificent, and part of its interest is to observe how it was constantly used, and brought up to date, right up to and including the Second World War, when it was heavily armed and very much a fighting fortress. There is a good booklet about it on sale within, by Mr Allen Brown, and here is no place to try to rival it. On no account miss the moving *graffiti* inscribed so carefully and well by French prisoners of war who were once confined within the keep. These speak somehow for all poor devils shut up within thick walls.

There is much that is ugly in the Dover of the motor car age, but a man must be hard to please who does not also find much that is romantic and beautiful. To stand in Atholl Terrace, for example, on a fine summer night, and look upwards over the roofs of the mellow Georgian houses (miraculously spared by both Hitler and town councillors) and see the vast sculptured chalk cliffs looming up above their roofs, is to be transported right out of this ugly petrol-reeking world.

CHAPTER 5

Western Heights to Romney Marsh

THE **Western Heights** of Dover were once crowned with the companion *pharos* to the one we inspected at Dover Castle. Near here was sometimes held the Court of Shepway of the Cinque Ports, where the Barons met to discuss their affairs, and where the Lords Warden used to be installed in office.

But at one time these Western Heights were turned into one of the strongest fortifications ever built. The Rock of Gibraltar could not have been more impregnable. No doubt when Napoleon was rampaging about on the other side of the Channel Dover had to be defended; but really John Newman, in Pevsner's *Buildings of England*, is very near the mark when he writes of: 'the maniacal scale and thoroughness of this C 19 equivalent of a hydrogen-bomb stockpile' becoming 'oppressively apparent' as we explore it.

Started in 1793 the gigantic excavations and edifications went on until 1814 when peace broke out, but were resumed again in the 1850s when Palmerston and his government again took fright at the thought of the French. The idea was that a substantial part of the British Army, in the event of an invasion, should remain behind the enemy beleaguered in this fort and the mightily strengthened Dover Castle over the valley, and allow the Grand Army to march on towards London or wherever it would. The enemy's line of communication could then have been cut. But as neither I, nor anybody else, could possibly better it, I must give William Cobbett's account of these fortifications:

I went to see, with my own eyes, something of the sort of means that had been made use of to squander away countless millions of money. Here is a hill containing, probably a couple of square miles or more hollowed out like a honeycomb. Here are line upon line, trench upon trench, cavern upon cavern, bomb-proof upon bomb-proof; in short the very sight convinces you that either madness the most humiliating, or profligacy the most scandalous must have been at work here for years. The question that every man of sense asks is: What reason had you to suppose that the *French would ever come to this hill* to attack it, while the rest of the country was so much more easy to assail? However, let any man of good plain understanding go and look at the works that have here been performed and that are now

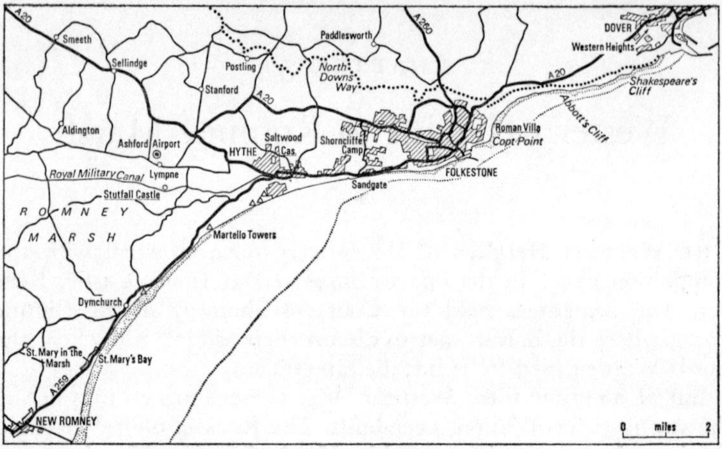

tumbling into ruin. Let him ask what this cavern was for; what that ditch was for; what this tank was for; and why all these horrible holes and hiding places at the expense of millions and millions? Let this scene be brought and placed under the eyes of the people of England, and let them be told that Pitt and Dundas and Perceval had these things done to prevent the country from being conquered; with voice unanimous the nation would instantly exclaim: Let the French or the devil take us, rather than let us resort to means of defence like these. This is, perhaps, the only set of fortifications in the world ever framed for mere *hiding*. There is no appearance of any intention to annoy an enemy. It is a parcel of holes made in a hill, to hide Englishmen from Frenchmen. Just as if the Frenchmen would come to this hill! Just as if they would not go (if they came at all) and land in Romney Marsh, or in Pevensey Level, or anywhere else, rather than come to this hill; rather than come to crawl up Shakespeare's Cliff. All the way along the coast, from this very hill to Portsmouth; or pretty near all the way, is a flat. What the devil should they come to this hill for, then? And when you ask this question, they tell you that it is to leave an army here *behind* the French, after they have marched into the country! And for a purpose like this, and withal, so scandalously disgraceful, more brick and stone have been buried in this hill than would go to build a neat new cottage for every labouring man in the counties of Kent and of Sussex!

The citadel of this mighty ants' nest is now one of Her Majesty's Borstals, so we are not allowed to see it unless we come foul of the law. But if we make our way down to the waterfront again and then climb up the steep hill on to the Heights – 'there is a cliff whose high and bending head looks fearfully on the confined deep'. In other words we are on top of Shakespeare's Cliff and about four hundred feet above the sea. Although perhaps King Lear was not to know it the chalk immediately below us is nodular Upper Chalk with Flints, below this Middle Chalk, below this Bottom Chalk on Marl, and Grey Chalk with Gault and Greensand below the lot. In the Upper Chalk are sharks' teeth, ventriculites, micrasters and sponges, oysters, ammonites and reptilian remains. As we go lower we find corals. Down in the Gault, better seen at the base of the cliffs farther west, are many Gault fossils.

The Gault was laid down in a huge delta that covered South East England and the English Channel some hundred and thirty million years ago. As the sea encroached up the estuary, sand began to be laid down instead of mud, and this formed the origin of our Greensand. About a hundred million years ago the sea became deep enough and extensive enough for the chalk to be laid down, at a rate of about a foot in thirty thousand years. The limey ooze that formed the chalk was composed mostly of the skeletal remains of microscopic algae called Coccoliths, Foraminifera and also the shells of shellfish. The reason why the chalk is so white and pure is that the land areas surrounding the chalk sea were low and the climate was arid. Thus very little silt and mud got carried into the sea to contaminate the falling limey skeletons. Most of the visible fossils were laid down during those times when a temporary uplift raised the earth's crust in the area, so that the sea became shallower and better for the deposition of fossils. The Great Chalk Sea lasted for a very long time indeed, hence the enormous thickness of the deposit.

As we proceed west we can find ways down to the foot of the cliffs, and this is well worth doing, for here, in what is known as the Warren, the underlying Gault Clay, being impervious to the water that has seeped down through the pervious chalk, has acted as a slide, and the great cliffs have slipped and foundered to leave the sort of broken landscape that we find in the Beast Cliff of Yorkshire or the Undercliff near Lyme Regis. Here are fossils of the Gault and an interesting primeval world of living plants and animals. The railway runs along the bottom of this wilderness, before it disappears into tunnels at each end, and it obviously gives the railway engineers something to think about as the cliffs keep on slipping and sliding and the sea keeps nibbling away at the bottom. The reason why the Dover cliffs do not slip and slide, farther east, is that there the Gault clay is well below sea-level and therefore is not cut away by the waves, which come up against the smooth hard chalk instead.

Folkestone is a very respectable seaside resort. If we approach it along the cliffs from the east we come to the site of a Roman villa, probably built in the second century and rebuilt in the fourth. Three hundred years of peaceful occupation by a succession of exiled Romans, their families, and their slaves. Near here are Martello towers, which we shall discuss when we get to Hythe.

Copt Point is a considerable rocky promontory and it is a little difficult to see why Folkestone Harbour was not built north of this instead of where it is.

Folkestone was a limb of the Cinque Ports and supplied one ship for Dover's quota. Under Edward III it got a corporation. The French, helped by the Scots, burned it down in 1378, by the seventeenth and eighteenth centuries it was at a very low ebb (Defoe called it 'a miserable fishing town') for the sea had encroached on the land, spoiled what harbour there was, and in 1766 an Act of Parliament was passed to allow the town to charge a duty on coal brought in for the repair of the harbour. At that time there were only about five or six freights in a year though, mostly coal, and the ships had to land on the open beach and in fine weather.

The great moment came when in June 1853 the South Eastern Railway arrived, after which Folkestone boomed ahead as a seaside resort, and also the railway company developed the harbour.

The harbour is still no great shakes, and certainly no harbour to run to in time of need. To run for it in an easterly and at low tide would be to say goodbye to your boat. The Outer Harbour is dredged to seventeen feet but affords no shelter from the east and is very busy with cross-Channel shipping. The Inner Harbour dries out, although it has plenty of water at high spring tides. A small fleet of decked fishing boats use the Inner Harbour, and catch quite a lot of fish, many of which are sold at excellent fish stalls along the Stade at fair prices. For some reason or other Folkestone fishermen are known to their brethren in other ports as Sap-drinkers! Folkestone is a good place for the boat-owner who knows it and is used to its vagaries. If you can get under the railway bridge you can lie in a sort of inner-Inner Harbour, and there you are quite safe, at least from the sea.

The cross-Channel port was developed in 1972 as a drive-on drive-off port for cars and lorries for Boulogne, Calais and Ostend, and a million passengers go through it every year.

The parish church at Folkestone is large, medieval, with a perfectly lovely sanctuary of the early thirteenth century, and an appalling reredos of 1885. In the seventh century a nunnery was founded at Folkestone by Eanswythe, the granddaughter of King Ethelbert. This, and a Saxon abbey that followed it, were destroyed by the Danes. A Benedictine abbey was then founded by one of Edward the Confessor's Norman cronies (that too-holy man did a lot towards paving the way for the Norman conquest by encouraging this sort of infiltration). The Norman parish church was burnt in 1216, and it was then that the lovely chancel was built.

As for the rest of the town, the old fishing quarter with its narrow steep streets is still picturesque. Most of the town is heavily Victorian. Trinity House has built a big very modern-looking pilot station at Folkestone, with a positively futuristic look-out tower. From this operate fast forty-foot cutters capable of doing twenty knots for taking pilots out to ships bound for Gravesend, or for taking pilots off outward-bounders. This arrangement has replaced the pilotage that used to operate from Dungeness.

The Leas are famous. These are landscaped cliffs west of the harbour, and their existence is due to the fact that the North Downs, the truncated end of which forms the white cliffs of Dover, trend away from the coast at Dover Hill, and the Lower Greensand which is beneath them is revealed. It is this soft sandstone that forms these cliffs, vertical in places where there happens to be a vertical cleavage, gently sloping at others, and porous and well drained. The great dome, or anticline, of chalk which once joined the North Downs to the South has been completely cut away by the weather, to expose the Greensand beneath.

Sandgate is a nineteenth-century little town. One of Henry VIII's great forts, such as the ones at Deal and Walmer, was built here about 1539, turned into a sort of glorified Martello Tower in the Napoleonic wars by being lowered and strengthened to seaward, and now the sea is busy carrying what is left of the romantic ruin away. I can remember it being much larger when I was a boy. H. G. Wells lived at Spade House, which he had built in the eighteen-nineties. Radnor Cliff House, along Lower Sandgate Road, is occasionally open to visitors. Shorncliffe Camps are enormous, and were built in Napoleonic times and were especial subjects of Cobbett's wrath:

> Here has been the squandering! Here has been the pauper-making work! Here we see some of the causes that are now sending some farmers to the workhouse and driving others to flee the country or cut their throats!

Cobbett would be sad to see that the barracks are still flourishing.

The Prince's Parade runs straight and – let us be honest – dull to **Hythe**. Here the Lower Greensand *cuesta* that we met at Folkestone Leas does what the chalk of the North Downs did the other side of Folkestone – it veers off to the north away from the coast. It is here called the Hythe Beds of Kentish Ragstone. Hythe was built on the face of the *cuesta* as it leaves the coast, and undoubtedly the shingle of Palmarsh, now used for firing ranges by the School of Small Arms, has been deposited there by the sea since Hythe was first built. The sea deserted Hythe, as it did so many other ports along this coast. Hythe, now inland, once sent eleven ships to fight the Armada. Hythe itself is an extension of **Saltwood**: when it was named it was certainly just considered as the *hythe*, or quay, of Saltwood, but long ago the tail wagged the dog. It was Hythe, though, that became one of the original Cinque Ports, and the town has the oldest Cinque Port charter in existence, one of Edward I of 1298, and this merely confirms older privileges.

Hythe is now nothing of a port at all: the creek that once brought ships in as far as West Hythe, and in Roman times to Lympne (although there is controversy about this) was blocked by shingle in the time of Henry III. Leland, in Elizabeth I's time (she gave Hythe a charter), says that there was only a small channel or gut, which ran within the shore for nearly a mile eastward from Hythe towards Folkestone, where small vessels could come with safety; but the encroaching shingle has now filled even that and now the great seawall keeps both ships and sea out, apparently for ever. But Hythe suffered much in the past, from enemy raids, storm, flood, fire and silting. A writer of about 1570 stated that the town used to stretch for two miles and had four parish churches but by his time most of it had gone. In spite of all sorts of theories by all sorts of people I doubt if anybody has the faintest idea what this coast looked like even as late as late medieval times. In Blaeu's map of 1624 Hythe still had an inlet from the sea with two islets in it. Hythe was important enough for Philippe IV of Spain to detach five galleys to attend to it when he invaded the Sussex coast with three hundred ships. The Hythe men pretended to flee, then turned and did great slaughter, captured one galley and drove off the rest.

In Victorian times the town grew, ugly enough, down towards the sea on the new shingle, and in this century it has grown again, up along the *cuesta*, or cliff, both east and west of the great church, so that retired people and others can live with an exalted view of the sea.

The church of St Leonard at Hythe is one of the great churches of Kent, although it was once but a chapel of ease of Saltwood.

But the fact that Hythe was a Cinque Port, and thus very prosperous, made it necessary and possible to build a great church. It has been called a 'herring church', much as the great churches of West Suffolk are called 'wool churches'. The latter were paid for by wool, Hythe was paid for by herring, for a great deal of the port's prosperity was due to the East Anglian herring fishery in which, to the chagrin of Great Yarmouth men, they had been given something of a monopoly. Great building went on here in the early thirteenth century, when the fine chancel was built – high above the modest Norman nave and leaving a processional way below. The Early English crypt is gruesomely full of bones. Eight hundred thigh bones and 590 skulls were carefully examined in 1910, by somebody with more of a stomach for that sort of thing than the present writer, and pronounced to be of the fourteenth and fifteenth centuries, and carefully stacked away again for the edification of posterity: either to give us a healthy sense of impermanence, or else complacence in the knowledge that we, at least, are still walking about.

Saltwood has a castle, very romantic, once the home of the archbishops of Canterbury, and the story is that the four knights who so reprehensibly murdered Thomas à Becket plotted their deed here. The castle was substantially rebuilt about 1160, in 1885 turned into a dwelling which it still is, but there is plenty of the old castle left and it is well worth going to see. The fourteenth-century gatehouse is the main residential part, and there is a great hall. It is visitable on weekend afternoons during the school holidays, and there are guided tours.

Hythe should be held up as an example to all canal-side towns, including Birmingham. Instead of concealing its canal behind hideous fences or advertisement hoardings and using it as a rubbish dump, and then being surprised when children get drowned in it, Hythe has opened its canal right up, kept it clean, beautifully landscaped it, put fish in it, duck on it, and rowing skiffs by the side of it for people to hire, and made it a most delightful feature of the town. It is most unlikely that any children will get drowned here – it is too populous a place. You can hire a skiff and row four and a half miles and back, over well-dredged and well-cared-for water. Every two years there is a Water Carnival, which one can find out about by writing to the Hon. Secretary, Venetian Fête Committee, Hythe, Kent. Every city councillor from every city that has a canal running through it should be forced to come to Hythe to see what can be done.

Here might be the place to discuss the whole subject of the

Royal Military Canal. In 1804, when the great Napoleon scare was on, it was decided to construct a defensive moat, or canal, which would cut off the Dungeness Peninsula from the rest of England. So this canal was dug, under the supervision of Colonel Twiss with Rennie as engineer, and William Cobbett said of it: 'Here is a canal . . . made for the length of thirty miles (from Hythe, in Kent, to Rye, in Sussex), to *keep out the French*; for those armies who had so often crossed the Rhine and the Danube, were to be kept out by a canal, made by Pitt, thirty feet wide at the most!'

Whether it would have been of any military value is a matter of great doubt. Certainly it had gun emplacements every quarter of a mile along it, and kinks in it at intervals of a cannon-shot so that every part of it could be enfiladed, but linear defences have ever been ineffective, and the best form of defence has always been attack, and soon the attacks of Nelson on the Nile and Trafalgar, and of Wellington in the Peninsula, rendered all such defences redundant. In 1806 somebody had the good sense to stock the canal with tench. If some more good sense were shown the whole canal would be dredged and opened for navigation. The Rother is already being forced open again by local enthusiasts and this canal would make a fine extension of its cruising waters. After all if this South Coast is not for recreation what is it for?

Back to Hythe Beach we find the vestigial remains of the great Cinque Port fleet which used to sail off to Great Yarmouth every autumn to the Herring Fair: three or four full-time fishermen who haul their boats up the beach with winches, and who go trawling. One of their boats, the *Mollyrose* of J. and W. Griggs, actually has Decca navigation, and to pay for this has to fish very professionally. These boats are the traditional boats of this coast, the heirs of the old Luggers, and we shall discuss the type fully when we reach Hastings. For the rest, in Hythe, model-lovers will like the shop containing Antique Models opposite the police station in Prospect Road, and all railway-lovers will go for the Romney, Hythe and Dymchurch Light Railway, which we shall discuss when we get to New Romney.

From now on we shall see more and more of those strange erections, the Martello Towers. There were seventy-four of these, within gunshot of each other most of them, built in and after 1806, all the way along the coast from the Solent to Aldeburgh in Suffolk. They were each about thirty-foot high and armed with a swivel gun and two howitzers. They were very well built of brick, three-storied, with the entrance high off the ground so they would be difficult to assail. They were planned by the Colonel Twiss who was responsible for the Royal Military Canal, and a Captain Ford, and their name was taken from a similar tower in Corsica, called Torre della Mortello, which had successfully resisted a British attack in 1794. They were never put to the test, but the fact that so many are still standing, in such good condition, testifies to the quality of their workmanship. A recent book, *Martello Towers*, by Sheila Sutcliffe, gives a good account of them.

Before we leave Hythe we should make a journey two or three miles inland, either by boat along the canal or walking along the towpath, to **Lympne**, pronounced, all simply, Lim. This may not be on the coast but it *was* on the coast, and was a very important port in Roman times, and the site of one of the forts of the Saxon Shore.

The ruins of the Roman fort, which was called Lemanis, is now called Stutfall Castle, apparently because the Jutes who came along after the Romans called the place *Stout Wale*, or strong fortress, and it is believed that they occupied it for a while. The name Lympne is said to come from the Welsh word for *elm*, but as this is, and was in Roman days, *llwyfen*, and Lympne was originally spelled Limne, surely it is more likely that it derived from Lemanis? Where the mysterious silent 'p' came from I cannot find out: certainly Hasted, in his *History of Kent* of 1790, called it Limne, and so did other early writers.

At all events it was an important place in Roman times, when a good tidal creek took ships right up to its walls. The Romans probably had a watch tower up on top of the cliff, like their watch towers at Whitby and Ravenscar and many other places. There is a Roman road, called Stone Street, running straight towards Canterbury. When somebody excavated at Stutfall Castle in 1850 he found a broken altar with an inscription on it stating that Aufidius Pantera, Prefect of the British Fleet (i.e. the Roman fleet in Britain) had dedicated the altar to some god. The ruins of this once-great fortress are on slipping Weald Clay at the foot of the escarpment, and it has been suggested that the Romans had to abandon it, around AD 370, and that they built another fortress on top of the cliff. Local people will tell you that Stutfall Castle was originally built on top of the cliff but has slipped down to the bottom. This I do not believe.

The Romans left, and the Jutes came in, and became the English, and went on using Lemanis as a port, and in 892, according to Asser (a Pembrokeshire man who became King Alfred's historian), a huge Danish army landed in 250 ships near Lympne and overran the countryside before being put to flight by the English.

By the time the Normans came the River Limene, Lympne's harbour, was already choked with shingle. As we shall see in due course the Romans had inned (walled from the sea) what is now most of Romney Marsh, and this may have been partially responsible. Now there is absolutely nothing on ground or map to show where the once-busy River Limene was. Some people believe that it ran into the sea at New Romney.

With the Normans came a new stage of Lympne's history, for it belonged to the Archbishopric of Canterbury, which gave it to the Archdeaconry of the see, the incumbents of which built first an abbey and then a luxurious residence. The archdeacons, departing a little perhaps from their Master's injunction to turn the other cheek, then proceeded to fortify it, so that by 1536 Leland was able to say of it that it was 'lyke a Castelet embatelyd'.

In time the castle came into secular hands, and it is now part of a big private house, open to the public April to October on Wednesdays, Sundays and Bank Holidays in the afternoon, and from June to September every day and all day except Mondays. You can get tea there and lunch parties if you order them. It is a splendid place, with fine sweeping views over the old sea-bed that is now Romney Marsh, and the real sea beyond, and France beyond that. It is fitting that – built on the site of a Roman watch tower – it has been a watch tower ever since. It was used so in the last two world wars, and a small thing from the first that gave one person at least amusement was the *graffito* of the Devil wearing a *pickelhaube*, or German spiked helmet. Fortunately the present owners have had the good taste not to destroy the 1914 concrete erection on top of the medieval tower. After all it is as much a part of history as the tower is. There is a most splendidly written illustrated guide to be bought within: a model of its kind.

The church of St Stephen, just next door, is fine too, and the broken masonry that is all that is left of Lemanis, down at the foot of the cliff, is worth visiting if you can get there alone.

And although Lympne may not any more be a seaport, such is the strange continuity of Man's affairs that it is still a port. Over the road is Lympne Airport, called now for some ridiculous reason Ashford Airport (it is nowhere near Ashford), from which *Skyways International* operates its flying machines, and it is a pleasant and friendly sort of airline to travel with.

There is one more thing to mention about the tiny vestigial place of Lympne, and that is the origin of the cross on the main road called

Shepway Cross. Shepway means the way to the ships. This was one of the places (we have seen another on the Western Heights near Dover) at which the Barons of the Cinque Ports used to meet to discuss their affairs, for it will be realised – *they could not meet in one of the Ports* for this would be acknowledging that port's supremacy over the others. Leland wrote: 'the Lord of the Cinque Ports kepeth his principal Court a lyde by East fro Lymnehill'.

Dymchurch crouches behind its mighty sea-wall, a wall first built by the Romans too in the new-drained Romney Marsh and now so raised and strengthened – first by Rennie during the Napoleonic wars, then by the River Board after the 1953 tidal surge – that it rivals some of the great Dutch sea-dykes such as the one at Walcheren. The need for this great sea defence is caused by the fact that the accretion of shingle at Dungeness, and the efforts that are being made to *retain* shingle all along the shore to the west, are starving the coast from Dymchurch to Hythe of shingle. Incidentally there is sand at places here, at low tide, and a good place for digging lug worms for bait, and razor fish for bait and food. A way to catch razor fish is to walk backwards over the sand and watch where small spurts of water come out of holes where you have walked (the pressure of your weight alarms the fish). You then push a 'razor spear' – a thin iron rod with small barbs near the point – into the hole. The razor fish closes on the spear and you pull him out. Boiled, he is delicious. As for the wily lug – he makes two holes, one with a 'worm-cast' on it and the other about a foot away, the 'breathing hole'. You must shove your spade *between* these two holes to get your lug. To dig below the worm-cast, as the uninformed always do, is to dig in vain.

But to more terrestrial matters. Dymchurch has a fine Norman church, with lovely detail in it, it also has the Silver Waves Holiday Camp, and New Hall, which was new in the fifteenth century (actually it looks mostly eighteenth century now), which was important as the *Court of the Lords, Bailiffs and Jurats of the Romney Marsh.* These important gentlemen sat here to arrange for the drainage of the Marsh and for its defence against the sea, and they sat here for the last time on 5th September, 1951, and now they sit somewhere else, for ours is an age in which nothing seems right unless it is new. Well, the Lords, Bailiffs and Jurats managed to keep the sea out since the Romans first drained it by sitting in Dymchurch New Hall (there was an older Hall that got burnt down in the fifteenth century) and it is to be supposed that they will keep it out no better now that they sit somewhere else.

St Mary in the Marsh has a smashing church.

The history of this peninsula formed by Romney Marsh, Walland Marsh, and Dungeness, is extremely interesting. When the Romans came what is now called Romney Marsh was an area of saltings covered by the sea at high tide. They drained this by inning it with the Rhee Wall, which is now the high road from Appledore to Romney. Thus the land to the south-west of the Rhee Wall, which is now called Walland Marsh and is not Romney Marsh at all, was never drained by the Romans and in their day was still covered by the sea. They completed the other side of the triangle of the Romney Marsh inning by building the sea-wall along which we have been walking.

The deposition far out into the open sea of this deltaic land is made possible by a shield of sea-borne shingle that advances before it towards the south, and this phenomenon we will discuss when we come to Lydd. But the land itself has been subject to many changes. During the Neolithic Depression, before 6000 BC, the land sank so that the sea was deep over what is now Romney Marsh. In the ensuing Forest Uplift as it has been called, from 6000 BC to 3000 BC, the land, according to C. J. Gilbert, F.G.S., rose about thirty feet, the present marshlands rose from the waves and forests grew on them. The fossils of these forests have been found off Winchelsea Beach and Pett Level. There was a second depression from 3000 to 1500 BC, the forests were overwhelmed, the beach was driven progressively inland, and then all was submerged and buried in silt brought down by the rivers. Borings in the Marsh find moor log (old fossilised oak trees) from five to fifteen feet underground, and even as deep as twenty-five feet in Pett Level.

The next uplift, called the Roman Uplift, went on until about AD 500, and brought the Marsh – heightened as it was by all the silt that had been deposited on it during the last Depression – above the sea again, and it was this Uplift that enabled the Romans to in Romney Marsh. After this has come what has been called the Final Depression (which, of course, is most unlikely to be final) and this is still going on. The land has been sinking in relation to the sea (or the sea has been rising in relation to the land – nobody can tell which it is) about six inches in every century, and it is so sinking now. But in the eleventh and twelfth centuries inning was going on apace, and Thomas à Becket, amongst other ecclesiastical land-owners, did great drainings to the west of the Rhee Wall, in what is now called Walland Marsh.

Now as for the *land* thus inned, it is some of the finest, and fattest, in the world. Some of it compares well with the Black Fens of East Anglia, Leland called it: 'a marvellous rank ground for fedyng of catel' and it still is. Most Marsh farmers to-day believe that it had always been grassland before being ploughed up during the Second World War. Cobbett, however, when he rode through it in 1823, saw vast fields of wheat, and remarked that it was some of the best wheat he had ever seen: well over five quarters to the acre (and that was before sulphate of ammonia was ever heard of). Cobbett's five quarters were forty bushels, a good crop any time. He said of the sheep: 'They are called Romney Marsh sheep. Very pretty and large. The wethers, when fat, weigh about twelve stone, or one hundred pounds.' I make twelve stone 168 pounds, but that is what Cobbett said.

These Romney Marsh sheep are now world-famous, having spread as far as Australia, South America, South Africa, Russia, and a score of other countries. They are much used for crossing with the Merino and lighter breeds to put some weight and mutton on the cross. They are (as anything that lives out of doors on the Marsh during the winter has to be) extremely hardy. Probably of Flemish origin, they are large and have coarse long wool. As Cobbett says: 'the faces of these sheep are white; and, indeed, the whole sheep is as white as a piece of writing paper. The wool does not appear dirty and oily as that of other sheep.'

Cobbett went on: 'This place is another proof of my old observation: *rich land* and *poor labourers*. From the window of the house in which I could scarcely get a rasher of bacon, and not an egg, I saw numberless flocks and herds fattening, and the fields loaded with corn!'

The shepherds on the Marsh are still called *Lookers*, and have a wealth of traditions of their own. The present writer, as a young man at Wye College, had the honour to assist one of them in a humble capacity during one lambing season, and obtained some insight into a profession perhaps even older than the one that is generally called 'the oldest profession in the world'. Living out on the lonely marsh generally miles away from their masters the lookers are men of great independence. The land can in places fat ten sheep to the acre, but there is great, and as yet unexplained, diversity in grazing capacity of the Marsh. In the Second World War the government caused much of the Marsh to be ploughed up. Enormous crops were got off it, and some of it is still under the plough. There is even a bulb-growing industry now, started by a 'Yellowbelly', or Lincolnshire man, who moved down here recently to find a land much like his own.

The Lincolnshire farmers got the name 'Yellowbelly' from the fact that they used to contract the shaking ague that stalked their marshes. In Romney Marsh this same ague was called 'The Bailiff of the Marshes', and people hung charms from their necks, on them written:

Three days shiver
Three days shake
Make me well for Jesu's sake.

Happily, there is no ague now.

CHAPTER 6

New Romney to Camber

IF we are in a horseless carriage we will be well advised not to attempt the track that leads to Littlestone, behind the sea-wall. Very sensibly this is kept rough to discourage horseless carriages and would that half the lanes of England could be. At **Littlestone-on-Sea** we come to a grandiose water tower of 1890, in case anybody should wonder what it is, and a tiny town of quite substantial villas built at about that time, too. Farther along we get **Greatstone-on-Sea**, and this wasn't planned and laid out as was Littlestone, but just appeared, and is a jumble of bungalows, probably quite fun to live in if you like having a marsh behind you and the sea in front of you.

New Romney, of which these two places are seaward extensions, was new in Saxon times perhaps, for then it was built as a more or less planned town. It was almost certainly then on the eastern bank of an inlet of the sea that came in between where Littlestone and Greatstone now are, and this was the mouth of the River Rother. From this estuary the Romans dug a hundred-foot canal, on the seaward, or south-west side, of the Rhee Wall. But in 1287 a most dramatic thing happened: there was a terrible gale and monstrous waves hurled masses of mud and shingle through New Romney, burying houses and churches – and what is more – inns – and the mark of the floods can still be seen, it is said, on the pillars of the surviving church. And – lo – when the gale subsided a fearful thing was observed. The River Rother no longer flowed out into its old estuary at New Romney but it flowed out at Rye, and there it has flowed out ever since.

Before this disaster New Romney was an important place, a Cinque Port, ships used to moor to rings in the wall of St Nicholas (the existing church), and the ship-owners and merchants were prosperous. It was then that St Nicholas Church was built, massive Norman, enlarged eastward in the fourteenth century. This church was spared from the awful visitation of the Victorians by the then brand-new Society for the Protection of Ancient Buildings – J. O. Scott had already started his horrid trade and had begun to pull down the Norman work when the Society stopped him, thus

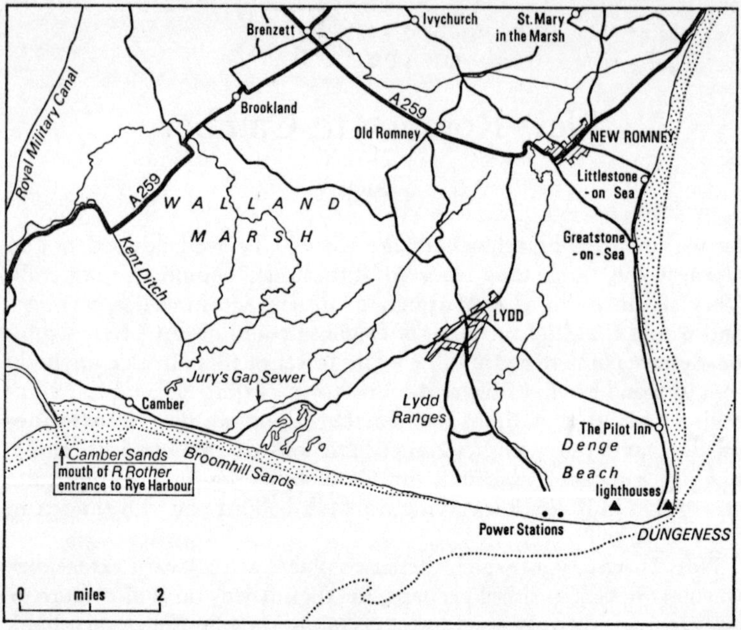

proving that if sensitive people care enough they can outwit even architects, parsons, and Chairmen of Parish Councils.

At all events New Romney clung on to some sort of harbour even after the Rother had deserted it, and no longer kept its depth by scouring it out. And the town tried to cling to the dignity of being a Cinque Port, and, with Lydd, even used to charter ships from other ports to send to the king's service rather than lose its privileges. But the fight had to be a losing one, and by the fifteenth century New Romney was nothing of a port at all.

New Romney became a prosperous enough little town, though, for agricultural prosperity from the newly reclaimed marshes replaced mercantile, and even now it gives an impression of dignified affluence. Many of the Marsh graziers live in Lydd and New Romney, in decent Georgian houses, rather than out on the windy flats. Like all the seaside places along this coast New Romney had a great record of smuggling, and no doubt the *owlers* as smuggling gentlemen were called added greatly to its prosperity. Not only goods were smuggled but people too: one Farmer Hunt, who lived just to seaward of the town, used to charge a guinea a night for accommodating Jacobites, who landed on the lonely beach here on secret missions from the exiled James II. Strangely the tradition of human smuggling still goes on. If you see police cars ranging about the coast here at night (as you frequently do) you will probably be right to guess that they are looking for illegal immigrants.

Old Romney, inland a couple of miles along the Rhee Wall, was probably a port, too, but as the harbour silted up so trade moved nearer the sea. It has an enormous church for what is a tiny place – just a few farmhouses. A couple of miles inland again is **Ivychurch** with another enormous church, with a pub on one side of it, a farmhouse on the other, and practically nothing else. Assuredly the population of the Marsh must have been vastly greater in medieval times than it is now, and indeed intensively farmed by men and not machines it could still support a hundred times its present population.

Now we will talk of that strange phenomenon: the *Romney, Hythe and Dymchurch Light Railway.* This was the creation of two racing motorists of the nineteen-twenties: Captain J. E. P. Howey and Count Zborowski. The count, alas, killed himself at his expensive sport but the captain pressed on alone, won a concession from the Southern Railway, built the Duke of York's Bridge over the Royal Military Canal, built fourteen miles of fifteen-inch gauge, built a fine collection of locomotives and rolling stock, and opened the line in 1927. It now goes from Hythe to Dungeness. The locomotives are perfect scale historical models, one-third down, the trains are fitted with vacuum brakes, and all summer a full service is operated which is patronised by some three hundred thousand people a year. In the last war an armoured train used to patrol the line. At New Romney are the workshops, a museum of models, and a place where you can get tea.

Lydd was a limb of the Cinque Port New Romney, and it was once on the River Rother, too: in fact in Roman times Lydd was on an island in the mouth of that river. The river shifted from Lydd to New Romney in fact, before it made its spectacular move over to Rye.

Lydd was given a charter by King Eadbright in 741, so it is not new. In 774 King Offa made grants of land near Lydd to Christchurch, Canterbury. The church is large and fine, and extremely interesting. In the north-west corner is some rough masonry that some people have dated so incredibly early as the fifth century: in other words it was built before the Romans departed. This may or may not be, but it seems well possible that this masonry was put here before St Augustine reached these shores. This predominantly Early English church, with a splendid Perpendicular tower, is called the Cathedral of the Marshes and rightly so. The tower is 132 feet high and the church 200 feet long and it has fine detail. Lydd is now a pleasant town, where wealthy Marsh sheep-masters live out their quiet lives, while their faithful lookers, far out on the marshes, actually look after the sheep. Lydd has been the terminus of two important links with the Continent: one, Pluto, a submarine pipe-line which took petrol to fuel the Allied armies after the invasion in the last war, and the other, still operative, the electric cable which takes current to France at such times as they need it more than we do, and brings it back when the position is reversed.

It is instructive to walk to **Dungeness**, particularly if you are a botanist, because the land over which you walk, or shingle rather, has been laid down in successive waves, and thus the farther we go south-east the newer the land and therefore the more newly established the flora. The best way to make the journey, in fact, is to go first to Dungeness and then walk inland towards Lydd. You will then see how soil, plants, and indeed the whole biosphere alters from the time the clean-washed shingle is flung out of the sea, first for many a decade to be drenched by sea-spray in gales, until the time when the receding sea has left it well inland, soil has been built up upon it, and it carries a rich flora and fauna. On the *fulls* nearest the sea you might find a little lichen only. Farther inland perhaps some sea-purslane and sea-beet, sea-kale comes next (you can cook it and eat it but don't – it has a hard time hanging on to life anyway), then, farther inland yet, the sea-dock, sea-campion, the sea-pea that hares love so, the fine yellow-horned poppy. Farther back still tough grasses become apparent, and legumes such as clover and birds-foot trefoil: in fact a whole rich flora. Here is that highly complex living thing – a soil – being progressively formed before our eyes. There are perhaps 1,500 years of development between the farthest-flung of the sea-sprayed fulls to the more comfortable but crowded ones inland.

Incidentally, if you haven't stuck to the boring road and are making this walk you may soon get second thoughts about it all. Walking through shingle is laborious work. The locals *used* to use things they called *back-stays* for walking over shingle: miniature skis that fitted on the boots. As a boy I used *plashers* on the Essex and Suffolk mudflats for the same reason – to stop you sinking in. I don't think anybody uses such things now – and very few people have heard of them.

The *Flora of Kent*, by Francis Rose, lists the many plants we can find on this walk, and Walter Murray's *Romney Marsh* is useful for the layman, although it does not show how to identify the plants listed. May and June are considered the best months for flowers here.

We can see as we go how the retreating sea left ridges, called *fulls* locally, of shingle (shingle is always called *beach* about here) on top of the old peaty clay down below. This clay was forest during the 'Forest Uplift' when all this land was well above the sea, before it was immersed during the Depression that started some 3000 BC. The reason *why* all this shingle has been deposited, and why the Ness is even to-day retreating eastward, is still controversial, but for my money the problem has been solved very satisfactorily by W. V. Lewis's article in the *Geographical Journal*: 'The Formation of Dungeness Foreland'. Earlier theories were the facile ones that the tide flows harder (a trifle) from the west than from the east in the English Channel, or that opposing flood tides meet here – the one up-Channel and the one down-North Sea – and, meeting, dump their loads at Dungeness.

Mr Lewis pointed out that they don't *have* loads of shingle to dump. No tidal currents that the tides can send hereabouts can lift a single pebble off the bottom. This is an easily observable fact. What is happening in fact is that the *waves* move the shingle (as any paddling infant may observe), and the prevailing wind in the Channel is south-west, and the waves generated by this knock and roll the shingle eastward. In any south-west wind we can see them doing it. Now there are north-east winds, too, and they have the effect of pushing *back* the shingle so knocked along by the south-west winds, and the two winds, thus mutually opposing, shape the shingle into the symmetrical point we see. Why don't the *south-east* winds undo all this good work by knocking the Ness away or flattening it? Why, because they only have a short *fetch* as sailors say, they only have the short stretch across the narrow Channel from France and thus they don't have time to build up waves of any consequence. In other words the only two winds with any effect are the ones that roar either up – or down Channel. This same phenomenon – of a pointed nose of shingle being built out from the shore – can be seen in other parts of the world beside Dungeness – and always where there is more land a short distance over the sea in the direction in which the ness is pointing. In other words the Ness is shaped by the big waves that come either up or down the long narrow channel – and not by the little waves that only have a short fetch across it. Why the exact position of Dungeness is where it is is a complicated matter, and Mr Lewis deals with it, to my satisfaction at least, but it had to be somewhere – and here it is. The Ness is advancing towards the east, at from eight to ten inches a year, although Mr Lewis claims that in one year alone, 1931, it went east by twenty yards.

And so we get to Dungeness itself, and its lighthouses and power stations and all the rest of it and, thank God, the Pilot Inn and another very good pub, too, which I have many times been in but the name of which I can't remember. And not so long ago pilots used to land at the Pilot Inn, having brought ships down from London River, and either go back to London by car or board another ship. Now, as we have seen, they work from Folkestone instead. The beach near the Pilot Inn is a lovely dry steep beach to land on in a westerly wind, but not so good in an easterly, and that's why they gave it up.

There have been four lighthouses at Dungeness. Because the headland is extending to sea all the time it is occasionally necessary to build a new one. The first that we know of was built by Sir Edward Howard, who had a licence to do it in 1615, when it was claimed that a thousand men were drowned every year owing to the lack of it. Howard was empowered to levy a penny a ton on all shipping passing in sight of it. During the dreadful reign of James I it had to be extinguished owing to pirates. Nothing of Howard's lighthouse now remains. The second lighthouse had a plaque on it which read:

> This lighthouse was erected by Thomas William Coke Esq: of Holkham House in the County of Norfolk instead of the old lighthouse which originally stood 540 yards to the northward and which by means of the land increasing from the Violence of the Sea became useless to Navigation A.D. 1792. Distant from the Sea 100 yards at low water.

Actually Samuel Wyatt built it even if Coke of Norfolk paid for it. This plaque, by the way, is now on the third lighthouse, having been moved there when the latter was built to preserve it. The stump of the second lighthouse has been made into the house that still houses the lighthouse keepers.

A third lighthouse was built in 1904, 143 feet high. This had to be superseded when the nuclear power station was built, because the latter obscured it. So the fourth one was built in 1960, by Ronald Ward and Partners, and it is the latest thing in *phari*, built of pre-stressed concrete rings, not battered in shape in that charming way that lighthouses have always been before but in fact swelling out at the top into a sort of bulb and with an intriguing spiral ramp at the bottom of it leading to a door high up, far out of the reach of Father Neptune. But how long will it be before the sea inexorably retreats even farther and yet another lighthouse has to be built? Or is this retreat going to have a term set to it? The ten fathom line is only a few yards off the Ness and an angler can easily cast his hook into thirty feet at high water. It seems impossible to believe that the eastward drift of shingle can fill up all that great hole, and, after all, the tides have got to have somewhere to run. Maybe the Ness has grown as far as it will grow.

Now we come to the objects that we must have been aware of during all our sojourns in the Marsh country, and these are the two mighty power stations, *Dungeness A* and *Dungeness B*. *A* was commissioned in 1965 and produced 550 megawatts. This is very simply done by bringing together a sufficient quantity of natural uranium and surrounding it with graphite. Neutrons are flung out of some of the uranium atoms at a high speed (ten thousand miles per second) and are slowed down to a mere thousand miles per second by passing through the graphite. At that slow speed, when they are bounced back into the uranium, they are capable of hitting other uranium atoms and releasing more neutrons and thus starting a chain reaction – a reaction that produces heat. In order to control the speed of this reaction (which would become awkward if it got out of hand) boron rods can be inserted into the mass of uranium and graphite. The boron has the power of absorbing free neutrons, sopping them up as it were. This it does and slows down the reaction. Thus by pushing the boron rods right in the reaction can be stopped, or it can be speeded up by pulling them out. Thus the reactors at *Dungeness A* are simply spherical vessels containing uranium rods inserted in graphite, with an arrangement for pushing boron rods into the mass as far as is necessary. The heat produced is collected by blowing carbon dioxide gas at high speed through holes in the graphite and transferring the heat to water in boilers (six per reactor) and using the steam thus produced to drive turbo-alternators in the good old fashioned way. Some of the *wastes* of this process will still be dangerously radioactive for hundreds of millenia.

Dungeness B is under construction at the time of writing, by a large force of gentlemen, most of whom come from across the Irish Sea, and this will be bigger still: bigger in terms of power that is, although the buildings will be smaller in size. It will produce 1,200 megawatts. Parties are conducted around the power stations on Wednesdays. Apply at any local electricity showroom.

The power station buildings, although vast, are not uncomely. It is the overhead power cables that are unforgivable. In certain country, among great mountains, for example, pylons can enhance the view. In this dead flat – and once so beautiful – Marsh they can only vulgarise and destroy it.

One amusingly typical facet of this power station building at Dungeness is that the engineers, secure in their metropolitan superiority, refused to take any advice from the local fishermen, and built their power stations very close to the south-west shore. They underestimated the speed of coastal recession here, and so now the C.E.G.B. is spending many thousands a year running a fleet of lorries and a bucket-crane loading shingle from the east of the Ness and carrying it round to the west and there dumping it. The owner of the foreshore from which it is loaded, who happens to be the Mayor of Lydd at the time of writing, receives payment for this shingle at so much a yard, and as the supply is inexhaustible (for, of course, the sea brings it straight back again) and the *need* is inexhaustible, and he doesn't have to lift a finger himself, he is on to a very good thing.

Now the bungalows that dot along the shore north of Dungeness, and arouse the ire of the ignorant, are the nicest things about the place and long may they remain. They are the homes of the gallant men who man the Dungeness lifeboat, which has made so many rescues, and who, when not on lifeboat service, make a hard and honest living at that hard and honest occupation – fishing. We see their boats hauled up to power winches on the steep shingle beach, or being launched down the beach on *trows* (greased baulks of timber) or coming home to the beach – often accompanied by big breakers – to be hove out, all four tons of them, by the winches. There is one thirty-footer, but most of them are twenty-eight. They have steps built into their stems so that the mate can climb aboard after they have been launched, for they are launched stern-first, unlike the lifeboat, which is turned round after she has been beached so as to be ready to swoop down to hit the breakers head-on. They trawl for plaice, and get plenty, and not a few soles, and whelks are quite a good crop. When the south-easter blows hard they dare not go off, for the breakers would fling them back and damage the boats, and then the fishermen wish they had a proper harbour to work from.

As for the bungalows in which they live, these are far back from the shore now, although once they were on it. This is because of the accretion of the shingle. You have only to look at the lifeboat house, now long-abandoned while the lifeboat sits in the open over a hundred yards to seaward of it, to realise how quickly the sea is retiring here. But the saddest thing about these fishermen's bungalows is that – although they built them – they are not their own. They belong to the same man who gets all the money from the C.E.G.B. for the shingle. He only has to give a man three months'

Above, Friston church, ancient and beautiful, but like many Sussex churches restored by the Victorians. *Left,* the Martello Tower at Pevensey, one of the many built to keep Napoleon out.

The Belle Toute Lighthouse, built 1831, at the foot of 536 foot high Beachy Head.

notice and he can drive him out of his house and make him pull it down. He is a humane man and surely won't, but there is something very wrong about the fact that he could if he wanted to. These fishermen are the *real* Dungeness men, and if this wild, wind-scoured barren wilderness belongs to anyone it belongs to them.

The Royal Society for the Protection of Birds owns 1,300 acres of Denge Beach, the wilderness to the north of the power stations. The society only managed to get this land through the foresight of one man: R. B. Burrowes, who spent his own fortune buying odd bits of it to save it from either the army or from speculators. It is now a fascinating area, and big enough to lose oneself in: one of the few wild places left in England. The wilderness to the west was all gobbled up by the army years ago, and is fenced in, and used for firing ranges. Farther west still, near Jury's Gap Sewer, we see a dummy town, looking something like those Wild West towns of Hollywood that are nothing more than façades. This was built in 1973 to train soldiers for street fighting, an activity that more and more of them have to engage in.

Camber is a weird little place. Once it was the home of hardy men who caught fish in *keddle nets*. These were net weirs, about fifty feet long, set up on stakes at right-angles to the shore, with pounds or traps locally called *bythes* at the seaward ends of them. They dried right out at low water and the fishermen simply walked down the sand and took the stranded fish out. We still see thousands of similar devices in the tideless Baltic, but those, of course, never dry out. Once on the Camber and Broomhill Sands there were fifty of these engines, and their owners were wildfowlers, eel-catchers, and smugglers in their spare time – *Marsh-pilots* many of them were called, for they piloted the bands of smugglers over the intricate marshes.

Now Camber is given over to many bungalows and Pontins Chalet Camp, and caters exclusively for that insatiable craving of the very young human – simply lots and lots and lots of *sand*. Even grown-ups use the sand here sometimes – for the sands are much used for sand-yacht racing.

CHAPTER 7

Rye

WHAT is delightful about **Rye** is that it is not just 'an historical old town' preserved to be gaped at by tourists and to be the home of retired people or weekenders, but very much a living, thriving seaport and market town. The weekenders are there, of course, and so are the tourists, but there still seems to be room for boat-builders, fishermen, bricklayers and carpenters, and if you go into the big bar room of the Pipemakers' Arms you will find a lively company of working people, with not a honker in sight. The fishermen, and other people who work on the water or by it, are inclined to use the Ypres Castle, up the steep steps near the Gun Garden.

The seafarers of Rye, called by their brethren elsewhere the *Mudlarks*, have a long history. Named Rye in Saxon times because it was an island (it stands on the very end of one of those ridges of high land of the Weald known as the Forest Ridges, but the sea had cut the end off, as it were, and made an island of it), it was very early a port, at first only a Cinque Port 'member' of Hastings (was there a subtle difference between a 'member' and a 'limb'?), but in the fourteenth century it was created a Head Port in its own right, attached to nobody. Winchelsea had the same distinction conferred on it. The two ports were named in the king's charter as 'our Antient Townes' and 'Antient Townes' they still are: they cling to the distinctive title. The development of Rye and Winchelsea through the early Middle Ages is shown by the fact that in the twelfth century Hastings contributed twenty ships to the king's fleet and of these, two were from Rye and two from Winchelsea. By 1229 Hastings alone sent six while Winchelsea sent ten and Rye five.

But the Cinque Ports declined, as much owing to the westward drive of trade with the opening up of the Americas and Mediterranean as to the eastward drift of the shingle that blocked their harbours, and their naval strength declined, too, until their ancient honours were empty ones, such as carrying the canopy over the monarch at coronations. The last ship service was at the time of the Armada, when all the Cinque Ports together could only scrape up five ships and a pinnace. The main power then was from the West

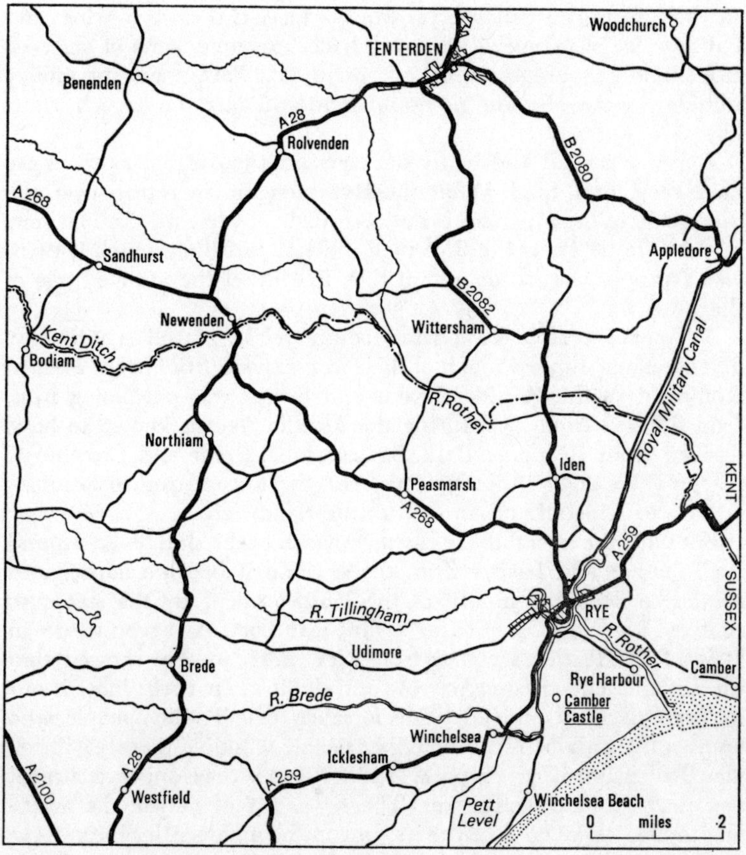

Country. Rye provided one of the ships that fought the Armada, and this was of sixty tons burthen, had a crew of fifty-eight, mounted two brass guns, two fowlers, fifteen calivers and fifteen muskets. She was victualled with 2,500 biscuits, 300 nail of beef, 100 salt fish, two hundredweight of bacon, one hundredweight of butter, one hundredweight of cheese and no less than fourteen tuns of beer. With all that beer under their belts the Mudlarks must have fought lustily, but they probably needed it with all that salt tack.

Rye as it stands is largely the result of the rebuilding after 1377. For in that year the French, tired of the never-ending bellicosity of the Cinque Ports mariners, came over and sacked Rye very thoroughly; burning the town, damaging the church and stealing the bells from it, stealing – yet worse – forty-two casks of wine, and killing a lot of people. Rye struck back, executed some of her own citizens to encourage the others, petitioned Parliament for money to build town walls, and no doubt went and gave the French what-for.

Rye was sacked and badly damaged in 1339, 1365, 1377, as we have seen, and 1448. What the Rye men did in return over the other side of the Channel is not recorded. But like all the mariners of the Cinque Ports the Rye men did not care very much if there was a proper war on or not: if they felt like it they started one of their own.

The port was always important commercially as well as militarily. The Romans shipped much of their iron exports from it, for even in Roman days the Weald of Kent and Sussex was producing iron. Iron shipped from Rye during the Middle Ages is known to have derived from Beauport Park, Sedlescombe, Brede and Crowhurst. In the years 1632 and 1633 Rye sent 394 tons of iron to London, 99 tons to King's Lynn and 30 tons to Sandwich.

But with the inexorable eastward march of the shingle Rye found itself farther and farther from the sea and it became harder and harder to keep the mouth of the Rother open. By the sixteenth century Rye was classified as a fifth-rate port. A survey made in 1562 of the Rother's course from Newenden to Rye showed that the channel had become narrow and shallow. In 1618: 'now is our harbour decayed and all trade forsaken us!' To-day people who know a little about Rye (including people who live there!) will tell you 'Rye is finished as a port!' In fact Rye is developing as a port, and may develop further yet. There was a recession in the seventeenth and eighteenth centuries, but in the nineteenth century Rye was a flourishing port. At the beginning of that century there were several fast forty-ton sloops sailing a regular packet service to London besides a small fleet of larger vessels. We know, for example, that the brig *William*, 108 tons, built Rye 1815, master Captain Samuel Vidler, crossed to New York with a load of emigrants in seventy-one days. This brig was eventually lost off Holy Island, Northumberland, in December, 1851. In 1865 there were fifty-six merchant ships registered at Rye, although several of them were owned by people who lived at Hastings. Rye had become a considerable ship-building place. Hoad Brothers, Hessel and Holmes, Mills and Sons, G. and T. Smith, were all building ships or barges, and a traveller to Rye in 1855 saw seven ships a-building all between 200 and 300 tons. The Smiths built many sailing barges. In case there are readers who are not familiar with the East Coast, who might take this word 'barge' to mean a river barge, or confuse it with the 'narrow boat' or 'monkey boat' of the narrow canal system (the one with the roses and castles painted on it, which is not a barge at all but a boat), I may here explain that the East Coast sailing barge was one of the finest sea-going ships ever evolved. Carrying from a hundred and thirty to over four hundred tons of cargo they traded all over the North Sea and English Channel and some of them even crossed the Atlantic under sail. They were only called *barges* because they were flat-bottomed so they could get into shallow harbours such as Rye. Smiths built the grand old boomie barge *Martinet* that eventually foundered in Hollesley Bay in 1941 after having been shaken up by a German bomb. Captain 'Bob' Roberts wrote a fine description of her last hours in his book, *The Last of the Sailormen.* He was her mate at the time. Rye was the most considerable barge port on the south coast. The spritty *Olive May* was the last barge to be owned there.

Hessel and Holmes built the *Madeira Pet,* a wine and fruit schooner of 83 tons, 97 feet long, 18 feet beam. She was launched by Don Miguel, Pretender to the throne of Portugal. In 1857, while in Guernsey ownership, she became the first ship ever to sail from Europe to Chicago! She sailed there from Liverpool, with 240 tons of cutlery, earthenware, paints, glassware and chinaware, and she loaded 4,000 cured cattle hides back, together with a barrel of cured whitefish as a present for Queen Victoria! Her arrival in Chicago, so far from the sea, caused great celebrations in that city.

In the middle of the nineteenth century plenty of these fruiterers and wine carriers were owned in Rye. They were very fast schooners, driven hard by small crews of hard men. Many a time a fruiterer has left London, reached the Downs at a time of south-west wind, sailed straight through the fleet of merchant shipping anchored there waiting for the wind to change, loaded in the Mediterranean, and sailed home to find the same ships still waiting in the Downs! These handy little schooners with their fore-and-aft rig, fine lines, and liveliness on the helm, could be driven against the wind like modern ocean-racing yachts. If steam had not come to knock them out – who knows how sailing ships might not have developed?

By the turn of the century, although far fewer ships were owned in Rye, the harbour was still working about two hundred cargoes a year. These were mostly coal in, corn out, Dutch cheese in, Sussex oak trees out. Much of this trade, though, was carried in West Country schooners. But in the First World War trade declined to nothing, and after the war it took a long time for trade to build up again. The first cargo in – a load of roadstone from Ostend in the sailing barge *Alde* – came soon after 1918, by 1933 there were from seventy to eighty cargoes in a year, mostly in barges. Rye owned then about ten big ketch or 'boomie' barges and several 'sprittties': the former carried about two hundred tons, the latter around a hundred and thirty. By the beginning of the Second World War there was still a brisk barge trade into Rye, but the war killed it stone dead. At 'D' Day Rye harbour was reserved as a bolt-hole for a part of the invasion fleet if such were needed. Fortunately it was not.

But now, wonder of wonders, and in spite of the Rochdale Report, which recommended the running down of all small ports, Rye is building itself up as a commercial port again. Alsford Wharf, down-river, is taking up to eighty ships a year, and, of course, such figures, to compare with the number of ships using a port in the past, are misleading, as ships are far bigger nowadays. The largest to come to Alsford so far was 800 tons. Ships of 160 feet long and 12 feet 6 inch draught are the largest that can come in comfortably. The Rye Harbour Board seems to hold the sensible view that, with ships, bigger does not always mean better. A multiplicity of smaller ships spreads the work-load of a port. A few large ones puts a strain on plant and people. A regular trade comes in from St Valériy-sur-Somme with multi-sawn and wired timber, and fertiliser and other bulk imports are developing. Trade is increasing, and the Harbour Master is getting a smart new office east of the river, there is a shipping broker's office in the town, and Rye is coming into her own as a port again. With the Common Market, and the seizing-up of the Port of London, many such small ports can have a good future.

As for ship building, Mr Harry Philips is still going strong, and his son has just taken over the business, making the fourth generation to work the yard. They build the traditional Sussex Lugger for fishermen all along the Sussex and South Kent coast, and they have also started a new enterprise of fitting-out steel hard-chine forward-deck-house hulls imported from Holland. These little vessels are ideal for single-handed or double-handed trawling from small harbours and it is to be feared that they will knock out the traditional vessels, which look so much nicer. Another yard is turning out hard-chine glass fibre general-purpose boats, and yet another yard ply-wood ones. But Mr Harry Philips is undisputed King of the Waterfront (and every waterfront has to have one!) and amongst his other activities he is playing a big part in forcing open the inland navigations again.

Inland navigation from Rye was once important, and there was even a serious scheme, in about 1800, of joining with a canal the Rother and the Medway. This came to nothing, which was just as well, because experience has shown that canals joining two seaports, unless there is much traffic to be picked up on the way, could seldom compete with sea traffic.

But, as it was, Rye bargemen (we are talking about *river* bargemen now – not sea-going sailing vessels) could get up to **Bodiam** (where is a great castle to go and see) with twenty-seven tons. Vidler & Co., the chief barge-owner, had a coal and ballast depot at **Newenden**. On the River Brede barges could get as far as **Brede**. On the Royal Military Canal they could get as far as Hythe, and **Appledore** and **Tenterden** were both ports.

In living memory there were twenty barges working the Rye system of inland navigations. An important trade was going down to the mouth of the Rother and loading shingle (or 'beach' as it was called) to take to places up-stream. Two men could load twenty-five tons in the five hours of lowest tide. Some of this was put aboard sea-going ships or barges for places as far away as Scotland. Coal loaded from ships to take up-country was another important trade, much of it to go to fire the hop kilns. The barges were about fifty feet long, and they set either a spritsail or a gunter-lug sail – the latter in local parlance called a *monk*. Like Norfolk wherries these barges could sail themselves off a lee bank. The mast was mounted in a tabernacle and could be dropped easily for shooting bridges. Horses were not used, but much bow-hauling was done by the men themselves, or the barges were poled along by thirty-foot quants. In fine weather the Vidler barges would sometimes even venture out to sea (as the Broads wherries indeed sometimes did) and they would load sandstone at Fairlight. The Rye bargemen were a race apart. But as the years went on, and motor lorries became the curse they are to-day, the young men would not take to the barges. The old ones clung on, loving the life, and knowing not what else to do. I have been told that as they got old they got cunning. When taking shingle to Bodiam the load would be measured by the waterline of the barge. Not wishing to load more shingle than they had to (it was hard work) the old men used to let in bilge water to push the waterline down. They would then arrive at Bodiam at three in the morning and be unloaded before the purchaser of the shingle was out of bed.

The last barge to trade was the *Primrose*, owned by Ellis Brothers, the builders' merchants. Her sad remains can still be seen, with those of several others, cast away on the saltings, on the west bank of the Rother half way down to Rye Harbour. One I measured there was 54 feet long by 12 feet wide, with fine lines fore and aft, an open hold with bulkheads fore and aft, strakes spiked with iron.

Another local trade was carried out by what were known as the 'boulder boats'. There were about forty of these, each perhaps 30 feet long, lug-rigged, and they all went herring drifting every autumn. But the rest of the year they sailed down to the 'main' (the open sea) and laid themselves alongside the open beaches to load 'blue boulders' or flints. These they sailed back to Rye Harbour and loaded into schooners or ketches that carried most of them to Runcorn, in Cheshire, for transhipment into narrow boats to be carried to the potteries on the Trent and Mersey Canal. There they were ground up as a constituent of pottery. Mr Harry Philips told me that they never used to clench the roves (rivets) of these boats. Unclenched the roves could 'draw' a little, allowing the planks to give a little when the boats were being bashed by the surf when heavily loaded with boulders. If they clenched them the roves would break or drag out of the wood and the boat would come to pieces.

As for the care of the Rye navigations in recent years, the Catchment Board took over in 1940, and the new Water Resources Board ground into action on April Fool's Day, 1964. These authorities did one half of their job well – to drain the marshes. The other, equally important, part of their duties they have failed lamentably in: to keep open the navigations. But public pressure is mounting to force them to do this part of their job and the day may come – why not? – when we shall see vessels sailing from Rye to Hythe again – and up to Bodiam. Only recently protests caused the removal of the low bailey bridge on the Iden–Wittersham Road over the Rother, opening the river to Newenden.

Rye has always been a fishing port, and is one now. In the last of the sailing days there were about forty fifty-to-sixty-foot sailing trawlers fishing from the port, like some of the smaller Brixham and Lowestoft trawlers. The Smith Brothers built many of them, and the last one they built was trunnel-fastened: that is, stuck together with wooden pins, not metal ones. Before 1914 a small fleet of steam trawlers had begun to fish from Rye. One of them, the *Margaret*, was sunk with all hands by enemy action on 16th December, 1916.

Now there are some twenty or thirty small motor boats, most of them decked, some of them with forward wheel-houses, some beam trawling but most otter trawling. Beam trawling (see *Companion Guide to the Coast of South-West England*) is coming back again, after having dropped out of fashion with the invention of the otter trawl some fifty years ago. The development by the Dutch and Belgians of twin-boom fishing (towing two trawls from two booms guyed out from each side of the vessel), and with the use of very heavy chains for ground ropes which actually plough the fish out of the bottom of the sea, is making many a trawlerman think again about the otter trawl. The beam trawling with heavy ground chains is doing great damage to the fisheries, but as long as it is profitable, and allowed, fishermen will keep going over to it.

There is one boat fishing full time out of Rye for scallops, with the use of dredges. These are heavy rakes which plough deeply. But there are also some fishermen who employ scallop dredges with trawl nets attached to them, ostensibly to catch scallops but really to catch soles. This practice again is damaging the grounds. But there are scallops there, and a good trade for them. There are also *queens*, a smaller shellfish but just as delicious. These are eagerly bought by the Americans but in England there is no sale for them, and if caught they are thrown back. The English are conservative eaters.

Trawling out of Rye is not a bed of roses. Plenty of shot-down doodlebugs litter the seabed, countless aero-engines, wrecks, and at least three submarines. All these foul the nets and do great damage, and nets are expensive to replace. A boat with Decca navigation can avoid them, but this is expensive. Many fishermen here use trammel nets. Some put a length of drift net on the end of the trammels – to catch cod. For some reason or other (the Arctic getting colder?) cod have been coming farther south in recent years, and in winter plenty are being caught in the Channel. Before the war this was rare.

In 1964, after eleven years of negotiations during the tedious course of which many a south coast fisherman was driven out of his livelihood, Britain at last nerved herself enough to establish a twelve mile limit. The effect of this was to raise the value of the English catch from £17½ million in 1964 to £30 million in 1970. At last commercial fishing in the English Channel had become profitable again. There are, of course, virtually no fish left at all on the French side of the Channel. The French have an insatiable appetite for fish, the Mediterranean has long been fished out, and they have never developed distant-water trawling as the British have done. So they have been doing to the English side of the Channel what they had long ago done to their own side, trawled intensively with 50 millimetre mesh nets (the English are limited to 70 mm and over), and coming in great fleets, which scoured up and down just outside the three mile limit when there was one, and unaccountably disappeared from view as soon as darkness fell – for some reason they would show no lights. Often a dozen big French trawlers would come into Rye Harbour to shelter together from bad weather. With the establishment of the twelve mile limit some of this has been stopped. There is still poaching, of course, but it is poaching farther away. Sometimes, the Rye men complain, there will be a raid of big French and Belgian trawlers that will simply mop up the inshore ground in a night or two, leaving the local men who fish in small boats nothing to catch for many months. Under the terms of Britain's entry into the Common Market the time is to come when our inshore grounds will be thrown open to unrestricted fishing by foreigners again, and this will, if it happens, simply put an end to the fishing communities in such places as Rye altogether. The position is very simple. No English fisherman wants to go over to the French side of the Channel to fish. There are no fish there. Every French fisherman wants to come across to the English side, where the grounds have been to some extent conserved.

But back to dry land again. What is there for us to see in Rye? Well, the little town itself is very picturesque, with narrow and in some places cobbled streets, and nearly all of the town should be turned into a pedestrian precinct straight away. Without cars it would be a paradise, and whatever inconvenience the residents might suffer with having to walk a hundred yards or so to their automobiles would be compensated a hundred times over by other factors. But as it is, it is a splendid little place, fine in the winter when there are not too many strangers about.

The church is beautiful and idiosyncratic, built mostly between 1400 and 1500 because the French had burnt the older church down. There is one town gate left, built 1340, before the big French raid. There is a fine old gabled brick grammar school built about 1636 – it is thought by Flemish craftsmen. The Mermaid Inn is just a bit too famous, but as far as the fabric goes deservedly so. The cellar is thought to be thirteenth century, the rest of the building late fifteenth century. It is really a wow. There is a good little booklet you can get from the Rye Museum called *The Inns of Rye*. The *Official Guide*, by the way, is excellent, unlike ninety-nine out of a hundred of these usually so fatuous publications. Don't miss the Water House, or Cistern, built 1735 and a masterpiece of the cistern-builder's art. The Museum is in Ypres Castle. This is pronounced Wipers Castle, and was called Ypres because the town sold it, in one of its periods of penury, to a man called John de Ypres as a dwelling house. The town bought it back in 1518, after it had been through several hands, and it is now used as a courthouse and museum. It was built in the reign of Henry III, when there was a dire need to defend the town, and was then called Badding's Tower. The Museum is small but very interesting, and its setting is beautiful. There is a model of an old Rother barge, another of a Rye sailing trawler, much Cinque Port regalia, a fine baker's oven of about 1870 – just to mention a few of the things that particularly interest me. Also here are the Customs of Rye, as codified in the reign of Edward III, which begin:

This byn the usages of the Comynaltye of the towne of Rye used ther of tyme out of minde which mens mindes cannot think the contrarye.

There are many fine-looking shops in Rye, perhaps the most notable being the butcher's in the High Street. There is Fletcher's House, now a coffee house, once a vicarage and home of John Fletcher, the dramatist of Shakespeare's time. Fletcher wrote:

Drink to-day, and drown all sorrow,
You shall perhaps not do it to-morrow:
Best, while you have it, use your breath;
There is no drinking after death.

Wine works the heart up, wakes the wit,
There is no cure 'gainst age but it:
It helps the headache, cough, and tisic,
And is for all diseases physic.

Then let us swill, boys, for our health;
Who drinks well, loves the commonwealth.
And he that will to bed go sober
Falls with the leaf still in October.

A Master Fletcher, in the reign of Henry VIII, was one of the pioneers of the fore-and-aft rig in England.

Lamb House, rebuilt in the 1720s, was the home of the novelist Henry James from 1897 to his death. The Rye Pottery is well worth a visit and there are several smaller studio potteries. At the bottom of Mermaid Street at the corner on the left as you look downhill is a private house which was once the Borough Arms Inn, and before that the London Trader, the latter name from the little packet boats that kept Rye in touch with the great world. But Rye is full of fine old buildings. The magnificent weather-boarded warehouses, and the lovely stone one, down by the quay, are justly famous.

But the best thing to do about Rye is just go there, off-season, and wander aimlessly round its beautiful streets, and try to imagine what they looked like in the sixteenth century. November the Fifth is a good time to go, and end up on the Town Salts down by the

Rother, where they have a mighty good bonfire and eat roast bloaters.

It is pleasant to sail or walk down the Rother to **Rye Harbour**, which is a village of its own and quite distinct from the 'Antient Towne'. We pass, on the west bank on the way down, the works of Westlake and Company, where, surprisingly enough, research is carried out into the *breathing of engines*. Then there is a works wherein is carried out some strange alchemy that turns old sump oil back into clean oil again. Then a tar works. Then the big timber yard at Alsford where we may see a ship lying discharging timber or other goods. Then we pass a strange little church which has the sort of monument in its churchyard to which we have become quite horribly accustomed in our peregrination around the coasts of Britain. This one has an inscription on it:

> To the memory of the seventeen brave men, the crew of the *Mary Stanford*, Lifeboat, who perished in a heavy gale while gallantly responding to the call for help of the S.S. *Alice* of Riga on the morning of the 15th of November 1928.

Seventeen men must have formed a very large part of the male population of this tiny place, brave or otherwise.

There is a nice little beer house the name of which I can never remember, then we come to the big pub, the Conqueror, where can be had many a grand evening with vigorous singing of a Saturday night. The landlord and landlady are local people (how unusual nowadays!) and the landlord runs a boat which takes parties of fishermen out. There is no proper lifeboat at Rye now, but there is an inflatable rescue boat.

Over the river, where we cannot get unless we swim or have a boat, is the harbour master's new office and some new *ablutions* put up for the convenience of yachtsmen. There is a long staging there to which one can tie up, and dry out, and thereafter find it very awkward to get across the muddy river to the pub, or anywhere else for that matter. One can run up-river to Rye on the tide in a yacht, but once there, there is very little room for you. Rye ought to *make* room. This would be very easy, for, after all, there are many miles of river and canal above Rye, all of which would float a yacht. The present yacht mooring is very inconvenient – it is, quite simply, on the wrong side of the river.

There have been several suggestions about this yacht mooring business. One is to break through into one of the big gravel-pits, fit lock gates, and make yet another 'marina'. Another is to dredge out the west bank of the river just below Rye Harbour and make this into a fish landing, with a new road for fish lorries, and then to allow yachts to lie at the stagings up at the Town Salts where the fishing boats now lie. Although at first sight this looks like kicking fishermen out in favour of yachties there would in fact be a big advantage to the fishermen in it, for they would have two hours more time to fish on each tide, the water being deeper down there. It is sad that most of the Rye fishermen do not own their own boats. These are owned by landlubbers (people will tell you 'film stars and the like of that') who do it as an investment in what is a very profitable industry. Working for somebody else the fishermen are able just to sign on at 'the Labour' if they don't feel like going to sea. But one can imagine the sort of fleet and shore facilities the Dutch or Hanoverians would make of it in a place so well situated for the fisheries as Rye. Rye Bay is a good trawling ground, and Rye is a long way from the next possible harbour.

Over the other side, on the east bank, was once the *Rye and Camber Tramway*, along which small trains hauled by steam locomotives used to take passengers to Camber Sands some half a dozen times a day during the summer right up to the Second World War. The Navy took it over and that finished it. On the west side, too, there was a tramway for carrying shingle from the great pits inland to be cast into huge concrete blocks for the building of Dover Harbour.

If you keep on down the west bank of the river you come to the pier which protects the mouth of the river and here, generally, there is a dragline scooping up shingle and putting it into motor lorries. This work goes on endlessly to keep the eastward drift from blocking the harbour mouth. Surprisingly, instead of just dumping the shingle to the east of the harbour mouth and thus losing it for ever (it would be taken on eastward) the lorries carry it west again, and dump it over the wall at Pett Level, for the eastward drift to carry it inexorably back to the harbour mouth again. The reason for this apparently strange behaviour by the Kent River Board (I know this is Sussex) is that they find it necessary to protect the Pett Level wall from attack by the sea, and the supply of shingle coming from the westward seems to be inadequate for this purpose. Can it be because every *other* place is trying to preserve its shingle too? Sea defences are preventing new shingle from being made, for they are preventing the cliffs from collapsing and thus providing the material. At all events the River Board finds it expedient to dredge this shingle out of the mouth of the Rother and truck it back to where it came from – to the westward – and dump it there again. Thus, so long as they can go on meeting the cost of a dragline and a fleet of tippers, they can keep their harbour mouth clear *and* protect the wall of the Pett Level.

On the end of the pier is a flashing light beacon, and when there is a fog it makes the most monotonous whistle. It knows when there is a fog because a laser beam from the harbour master's office shines on it and when this is cut off the whistle begins to whistle. Unfortunately anything else intervening starts the whistle, too – a passing ship, for example, and when I last saw it the whistle was being started and stopped by hand.

There is a fine round walk from here along the shore to Winchelsea Beach then inland to Winchelsea and back via Camber Castle (not to be confused with Camber Sands). Or, more interesting for naturalists, from the Harbour Village along a footpath beside the great flooded shingle pits that were dug to build Dover Castle. There is a nature reserve between these pits and the sea, and it is a good place to study the botany of the shingle ridges, to watch birds, and also to observe the formation of the ridges or 'fulls', and realise how they have been successively built up, full by full, by the retreating sea. It would be interesting to find a method of dating each one. No doubt the sea will go on receding, and Rye will get farther and farther away from it; but so long as the mouth of the river can be kept open by dredging, Rye can develop as she should develop: into a fine little port with a good fishing fleet and a good commercial trade. The town should give precedence to industries with a marine bias: either those producing marine goods, such as boat building, or else industries depending on sea-borne trade. It would be sad if Rye just became a dormitory for rich Londoners, or, worse, just a nondescript mess of 'light industry'. Rye should stand or fall as a port, as she has done for the last twelve hundred years.

Camber Castle, standing forlorn in the marshes half-way to Winchelsea and nowhere near Camber, has been deserted by the sea and is now the foster child of the Ministry of the Environment. It was built about 1540, one of Henry VIII's new gun-forts to keep the Pope out (it cost the king's subjects £23,000) and when built it was within a stone's throw of the sea. Now it is nearly a mile and a half inland. In Elizabeth's time it was armed with one cannon, two curtal cannons, one demi-cannon, one culverin, two demi-culverins and two sucres. It was never attacked or defended.

There are plenty of beautiful things to see about Rye. **Appledore** is a charming village, once a port, and there the raiding Danes built their fortified base to protect their 250 ships when they raided England in 829. In 1380 the French got as far inland as this and burnt the village and the church. The present church is large and fine – Cobbett remarked (in 1823) that it was large enough to hold three thousand people but there were not five hundred people in the village old enough to go to church. On 19th January, 1901, a peal of Grandsire Triples was rung on the bells of Appledore.

Appledore is on the Royal Military Canal and was a port and will be one again. There is a stone on the canal, just where the Kent Ditch runs into it half-way back to Rye, which has the date 1806 cut in it, the date the canal was dug. Incidentally the canal was given up by the military in 1930, but refortified in 1940 with rather feeble little pill-boxes. One is inclined to recall Cobbett's words about the armies that crossed the Rhine and the Danube being stopped by a thirty-foot ditch!

Peasmarch has an astonishingly beautiful Norman and Early English church. **Brookland** also has a superb church, with a most strange and rare detached belfry and an unbelievably beautiful font.

There was a famous battle near Brookland between smugglers and government narks on the night of 11th February, 1821. Several on both sides got shot. The Marsh was a famous 'owling' or smuggling ground. The lookers (shepherds) and wildfowlers used to act as 'Marsh pilots' and lead the owlers through the maze of drains and ditches where the preventive men could not follow them. The whole countryside was on the side of the 'free traders', who were only bringing in goods that the English could not produce for themselves and therefore were doing nobody out of a living. They were simply making small luxuries, like tea, silk and brandy, available to poorer people. They were only anticipating the Common Market after all. Kipling, as usual, got it just right when he imagined a mother's admonishment to her child:

> Five and twenty ponies
> Trotting through the dark –
> Brandy for the Parson,
> 'Baccy for the clerk –
> Laces for a lady, letters for a spy,
> Watch the wall, my darling, while the Gentlemen go by!

According to Holinshed on 1st October, 1250, at the old town of **Winchelsea**: 'the moon, upon her change appearing red and swelled, began to show tokens of the great tempest of wind that followed, which was so huge and mightie, both by land and sea, that hath not been lightlie knowne, and seldom, or rather never, heard of by men then alive. The sea, forced contrarie to his natural course, flowed twice without ebbing, yielding such a rooring that the same was heard (not without great wonder) a far distance from the shore . . .' Those of us who remember the great tidal surge in the North Sea in 1952–3, with its accompanying gale, may find this description very familiar. Holinshed goes on: 'At Winchelsea beside other hurte that was doone, in bridges, milles, breakes and banks, there were three hundred houses and some churches drowned with the high rising of the water course.'

And in 1287 came the final blow: another great storm which swept Winchelsea away altogether. So completely did it go that nobody now even knows where it once stood, although there has been plenty of conjecture. The original Winchelsea was an important place, and a great port in its day – important enough to have a royal mint in it in AD 959. Edward I took a personal interest in it (he even had to attack it once, after the Battle of Evesham, for then it was held by de Montford's men). But he himself ordered the displaced burghers to build a new town, where Winchelsea still is, and this was an early example of town planning, like Newborough in Anglesey, and New Buckenham in Norfolk. The streets were laid out in a grid plan, like New York, and you can see that it was once much larger than it is now – you have only to walk the distance from the New Gate to the nearest existing house to realise this. The town wall, now all gone but for two gates, once contained ninety acres. It is probable that the town, as planned, was never completed.

But it was a considerable town, and when Elizabeth I came through it she called it 'Little London'. But Evelyn, in 1652 when he was waiting at Rye for his wife to come from the Continent, walked over 'to survey the ruins of Winchelsea, that ancient Cinque Port, which by the remains of ruins, and ancient streets, and public structures, discovers it to have been formerly a considerable and large city. There are to be seen vast caves and vaults, walls and towers, ruins of a monastery, and a sumptuous church in which are some handsome monuments, especially of the Templars, buried just in the manner of those in the Temple of London . . .' He then goes on to say that the place was full of ruins and rubbish. And, before that, at a Royal Enquiry of 1587: 'no ships, captains, or mariners belong to this town, but only one sailor named William Bucstan.'

Henry James, writing of Rye and Winchelsea (we have seen he lived at Rye) called them 'the two small ghosts of the Cinque Ports family, the pair of blighted hill-towns that were once sea-towns and that now draw out their days in dim after-sense of a mere indulged and encouraged picturesqueness.' It is typical of James that he failed to notice even the fifty-odd ships that were registered in Rye

Above, the Royal Pavilion at Brighton, designed by John Nash in 1815 for the Prince Regent. *Below,* Worthing grew under the patronage of Princess Amelia, the Prince Regent's younger sister.

Above, the church at Bosham in which Harold of England prayed before sailing to Normandy. The bow of a Dutch *Lemmerak* in the foreground. *Below*, sailing in the splendid natural tidal waters of Chichester Harbour, at West Itchenor.

when he lived there. Such things were just not within the range of his vision.

And now even the 'indulged and encouraged picturesqueness' has deserted Winchelsea, in my eyes at least. The houses, although each one is built on the foundations of a medieval house or of several perhaps, are just large rich-men's houses, most of them built without taste during the last seventy years. To find old Winchelsea you have to go down into the cellars, for many a modern house has a fine vaulted cellar of the fourteenth century underneath it – a good one to view is at Manna Plat, in Mill Road, where you can see it while having *refection* – and very nice, too.

Presumably Winchelsea became popular with the London rich too soon, and so tidily the ruins were swept away and large ugly 'gentlemen's residences' built instead. If it had happened now more care would have been taken to preserve the old.

The great thing to see in modern Winchelsea is the church which is superbly beautiful. I believe that nobody could enter this building without being moved, but I will spare the reader a description because there is a good church guide. But the light flooding in from the windows, designed by Douglas Strachan after the First World War (and whatever one may think of the glass of these windows the fourteenth-century tracery is superb), the marvellous tombs – both against the north wall and the south – the slender pillars and fine proportions of the arcades – the whole strange ambience of the building – all this combines to make entry into Winchelsea Church an aesthetic experience of a high order. Among the riot of blue glass in the windows is a memorial to the lifeboat crew of Rye that was overturned in 1928. The look of downright *fear* that the artist has put into the eyes of the lifeboatmen shows an insight into the real nature of this work that many of us, perhaps, do not have.

For the rest in the town, the old Court House is now a museum open in the summer. The modern house called The Friars is built from old stone. Squire Weston and his brother lived here, and were the origins of Thackeray's *Dennis Duval*. Tower Cottage, just by Strand Gate, used to be the home of Ellen Terry. Pipewell, or the Land Gate, was rebuilt in 1405 after the French had knocked it down. At New Gate the French were admitted by a traitor in 1380, whereupon they slaughtered most of the inhabitants and sacked the town. The French were always raiding the place: there is still a Dead Man's Lane, named after a fracas in 1357.

The Battle of *L'Espagnols-sur-Mer* was fought off here in 1350, and Froissart's account of it makes war sound a delight. King Edward III and the Prince of Wales sailed forth with the Cinque Ports fleet – 'the king dressed in a black jake of velvet, and wore upon his head a cap of black beaver which well became him.' The King was gay and ordered his minstrels to strike up. But a man from the masthead cried: 'Ho, I spy a ship, and it appears to me to be a Spaniard.' The minstrels were silenced and the King asked if there were more than one. The watch cried: 'Yes – I see two, three, four – so many that – God help me – I cannot count them!' When the two fleets began to near each other the King said to his Sailing Master: ' "Lay me alongside the Spaniard who is bearing down upon us, for I would have a tilt with him." The King's ship was large and stiff; otherwise she would have been sunk, for the enemy was a great one, and the shock of their meeting was like the crash of a torrent or tempest; the rebound caused the castle in the King's ship to encounter that of the Spaniard; so that the mast of the latter was broken, and all the castle fell with it into the sea, when they were drowned.'

The Spaniards lost fourteen ships and the rest fled. 'The King ordered trumpets to sound the retreat and made for England.' The fleet anchored off Winchelsea a little after nightfall, and the King and Princes: 'took horses in the town and rode to the mansion where the Queen was . . . and passed the night in revelry with the ladies, conversing of arms and armour.' Because of his victory gold coins were struck describing Edward III as 'Avenger of Merchants' and 'King of the Sea'.

But now the sounds that we hear at Winchelsea are not the distant roar of cannon nor the revelry of kings, but the purr of lawnmowers on large and velvety lawns behind high walls. Here from the tile-hung walls on their plinths of ancient stone the patrician inhabitants gaze out over the marshes below: the marshes over which the sea once raged that destroyed old Winchelsea, and they feel themselves quite secure from the invasion of that sea again, and also perhaps from the other sea from which they have taken refuge: the sea of bungalows, bingo halls and caravans that washes remorselessly along the shore of the English Channel. And incidentally makes a valuable contribution to the rates.

CHAPTER 8

Winchelsea Beach to Hastings

WINCHELSEA BEACH has more of interest than a casual inspection might suggest. Even the Ship Inn, which is a modern building of no great architectural distinction, is the heir to a fine and magnificent public house, built right on the sea-wall itself, the old Ship Inn, four hundred years old and with a huge cellar for storing smuggled goods. Steve Donoghue, the famous jockey, used to drink deep here, as did Gracie Fields, Henry Savage, the author (who used to live in a Gypsy caravan nearby), and many another 'personality' of the 1920s. Mr Jim Hickman, who has been known to come into the new Ship, has photographs of what the old Ship looked like, and indeed it was a noble building with a splendid veranda and – although it nearly stood in the sea itself – it had a range of stables to *seaward* of it! Mr Hickman was born there, and can remember when people lived in the two cottages nearby. They used to go line-fishing and shrimping along the shore. They would peg out long lines on the beach at low tide and wait for the tide to cover them and then visit them at low tide again.

But – *sic transit gloria mundi!* The day came, or at least the night, when, with the *Daily Mail* there to take photographs, the top of the predicted high spring tide carried half the pub away. The landlord and the customers, who were quite cut-off from the mainland of England (and incidentally from its silly licensing laws), went on lifting their glasses in the other half, while listening to the roar of the waves and the crash of falling masonry, and went on drinking deep indeed until morning came and revealed the desolation about them. The landlord continued to serve drinks in what was left of the pub for several months, until the brewers had built him another one, which is where we are drinking now. There is a plaque on the new sea-wall on the site of the old inn (a hundred yards or so beyond the last caravan site going west) which marks the melancholy spot, so that we can stand there, moist of eye and hat in hand, and think for a few moments of those devoted boozers. We may compare the history of the Old and New Ship with the history of Winchelsea itself. But the sea is encroaching here where it is receding elsewhere. Martello Towers built here in 1805 are now half a mile out to sea (there is nothing left of them) and out there, too, are petrified forests.

Another plaque, just to seaward of the little road that runs straight to the sea from the funny little church, marks the entrance to Smeaton's new Rye Harbour. This was built, to Smeaton's design, between 1761 and 1787. It had a mouth to the sea thirty yards wide and then a deep wide canal straight to Rye. But the sea wouldn't have it. Shingle piled up remorselessly, the Rother would insist on breaking out where it is now, and all that is left to see are the remains of two hundred years old piers of timber and this plaque that the River Board has, with rare sensitivity, put here to mark the spot. Obviously Smeaton had the idea that if the Rother and the Brede could be made to run out by the same mouth at this point their scouring would keep a harbour clear.

Now in the days when the old Ship Inn bit the dust the sea was kept out of the **Pett Levels** by a wooden barrier with a clay wall backing it up on the landward side. The great new wall that protects these levels is a very different matter. There is a fence of continuous steel piling driven deep into the soil, buried now inside an earth wall, with a massive concrete-block apron on the seaward side, a concrete coping on top, and even a concrete apron on the land side where erosion might take place. There are wooden groins running out into the shingle in front, but most of these are bereft of planking and so do no good. Maybe the River Board's method of constant dumping renders these unnecessary. Maybe the current price of timber has something to do with it. Ramps run up the back of the wall at intervals so that the shingle lorries can get up for dumping. The wall is very high and strong, but still the sea overtops it at times. It is to be raised two feet in the near future. And if the Final Depression of the geophysicists goes on it will have to be raised more yet. Along the way to Pett there is a rather grandiose plaque to Colonel Body, D.S.O., O.B.E., D.L., J.P., Chairman of the Rother and Jury's Gut Catchment Board.

All of the Pett Level was flooded by military policy in 1940 (it is a poor method of defence that defends good land by destroying it). When the sluices were opened, though, it was several months before the sea could be got to come in. The flooded marshlands became a temporary haven for water birds, and a coastguard, Reg Cooke, made a close study of them. He still lives at Pett and is a good ornithologist. The three big spoil pits behind the wall now (from which the earth for the wall was taken) are a bird reserve, but disappointingly poor in varieties.

Cliff End, near Pett, is a fascinating place. The Marsham Sewer (an open waterway – not a sewer in the sanitary-man sense) runs

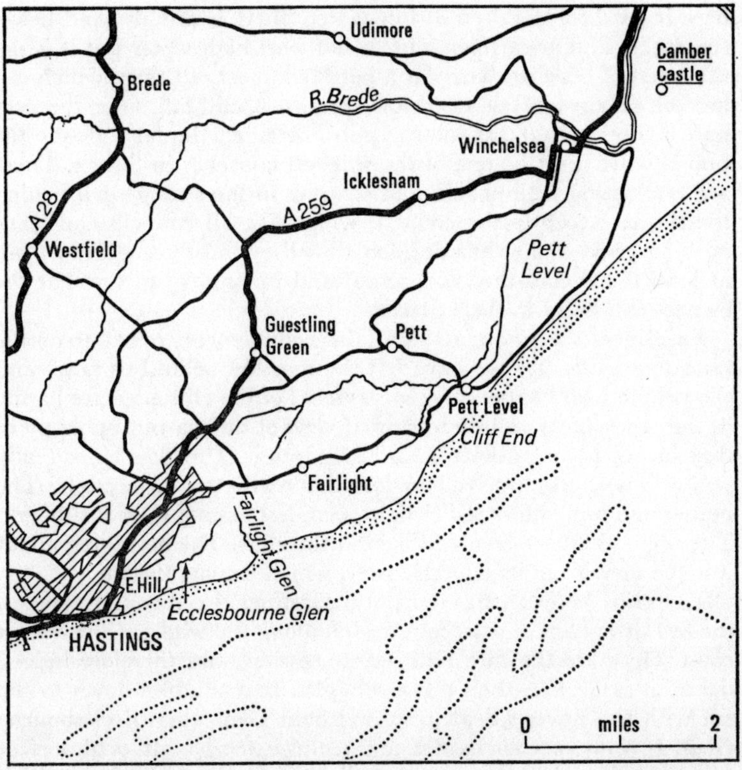

through a picturesque valley between sandstone escarpments before flowing into the Royal Military Canal, which should be opened up to here for navigation. There is a nice little Beach Club up behind the seawall, with some small boats in front of it in which several local men go part-time fishing. The club has a motor-winch for hauling boats up the beach. If you sail into Cliff End and beach beware rocks which are strewn along the shore, but there are two conspicuous white houses as shore marks each side of the bulldozed channel and the club mast is between the two of them. Sail straight into the mast at right-angles to the shore. Local men like to launch or land within two hours each side of high water to avoid the rocks, which are then well covered. There is good conger fishing among the rocks, one local man puts a few lobster pots out, and the members of the club are a very friendly lot of people.

The Smugglers, hard by, is a very good pub indeed. The shore here is good for children at low water (there is muddy sand below the rocks) and good for adults to bathe at high water but it is not the safest of beaches. There is a petrified forest out there which can be seen (I am told) at dead low springs. A cliff-fall, after the very hard winter of 1963, shook the pub like an earthquake. Beside the pub is what must be one of the smallest churches in Sussex. There are fascinating little shacks and shanties in the strange dell behind the shore. Recently the council, which like all councils can leave nothing good alone, has decided that they must come down, but at least it has had the good sense (and humanity) to say that the owners can build in their places.

Fairlight is a strange residential seaside resort perched up on the sandstone cliffs (for we have left the marshes behind us now) and the people who happen to own stretches of the cliff edge are happy in that they have an uninterrupted view of the sea but unhappy in that bits of their gardens keep falling into it. The Cow Head really was a cow shed, and its Hay-loft Bar really was a hay loft. The houses and bungalows of Fairlight seem lost among their shrubbery. The original village is inland behind the cliffs. The best thing about it is the view from its church tower, which is magnificent.

The cliffs between Fairlight and Hastings are beautiful: one of the few little gaps of wild country left along the whole of the Sussex coast. Here are the Fire Hills, gorse-covered and therefore indeed liable to catch fire, then the lovely glen that tumbles down to the sea with the Lover's Seat in it: Fairlight Glen, then Ecclesbourne Glen. It is all very enchanted and seems extensive although in fact it is a small area. Then we eventually come to East Hill from which we look straight down on **Hastings**. It is a dramatic way to come upon a town. And one of the most pleasing components of this view is the group of well-kept allotments across the valley below – surely the urban scene has nothing better to offer the sight than this?

The **Old Town** of Hastings is as beautiful and interesting as any piece of townscape in Britain. The **New Town** of Hastings was described by Henry James as 'very grey and sober and English'. 'Hastings,' he went on, 'and St Leonards' with their long, warm sea-front and their multitude of small cheap comforts and conveniences, offer a kind of *résumé* of middle-class English civilisation and of advantages of which it would ill become an American to make light.' There was, he wrote: 'four or five miles of lodging-houses and hotels staring at the sea across a parade adorned with hand-organs and German bands, with nursemaids and British babies, with ladies and gentlemen of leisure – looking rather

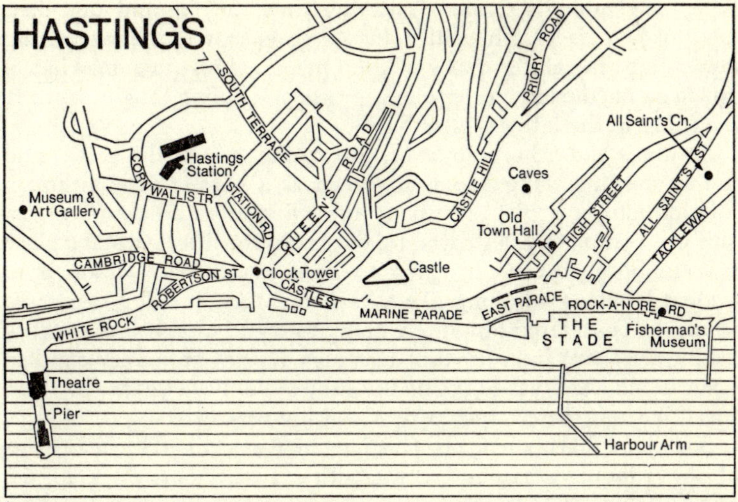

embarrassed with it and trying rather unsuccessfully to get rid of it – this is the great feature which Brighton and Hastings have in common.' Well, some of them get rid of their leisure now by roaring up and down the front in their motor cars to the danger of other peoples' life and limb. But we shall confine ourselves to discussing the Old Town and the Stade, or fishermen's quarter, which was, of course, well outside of James's field of vision.

Hastings has a long and distinguished maritime history, and in Anglo-Saxon times appears to have been something of a county of its own for we read several times of the men of Kent, Sussex and Hastings, such as when the men from these three entities unsuccessfully resisted Offa's army. A glance at the map shows that Hastings was happily cut off from the rest of England by what were then the impenetrable swamps of Romney Marsh on one side the Pevensey Levels on the other, and the uninhabited clay forests of the Weald to the north.

In 1147 a Cinque Ports fleet sailed to Lisbon to help drive out the Moors and a Hastings man named Gilbert was made the first Bishop of Lisbon. One wonders if he was a member of the Winkle Club. In 1149 Hastings was important enough to get a charter from King Stephen. In 1201 King John came here and issued his Ordinance of the Sea, which declared quite unequivocally that England was top dog on the oceans and that all foreign vessels should 'stryke and vail their bonnets' on meeting any ship in the

King of England's service (meaning that they should dip their top sails). This custom still holds good, except that now we dip our ensigns in salute to any of the Queen's ships (in somewhat of an excess of courtesy perhaps in the case of a sailing dinghy saluting a battleship the latter salutes back).

Hastings had a harbour once, just to the west of the castle, and the astonishing thing about this town as a port is that, although this harbour was blocked up by the shingle in the *twelfth century* and was completely destroyed by the sea in the fifteenth – the place has stubbornly gone on trying to be a port! And, although at present bereft of anything like a harbour at all, it still is a port. It would be considered absolutely crazy to try to establish the sort of fishing fleet and industry that Hastings has got on a very exposed open beach. And yet – just because seven hundred years ago there was a harbour here – such a fleet and industry exist.

Somehow, harbour or no, Hastings managed to go on being one of the Cinque Ports and contributing twenty-one ships to the King's Navy. In 1339 the French, having burnt Portsmouth, came and burnt Hastings as well. The Ports' fleet soon put this right by burning Boulogne, but, of course, this didn't rebuild Hastings any more than it did Portsmouth. In 1343 the town, weakened so much by the visit of the French, could only contribute one ship to the king's expedition to Brittany, but in 1347 she managed to scrape up five for the Siege of Calais, but one of these had to be quickly bought for the occasion from Winchelsea – a former limb of Hastings herself!

In 1377 Hastings got burnt down again, and this really was the end of Hastings as an effective naval port. She did manage to send one ship to fight the Armada – quite a big ship, too – the *Anna Bonaventure*, seventy tons, crew of forty-nine, and eleven fishing boats to act as tenders for her. Hastings was still desperately trying to restore her harbour. In 1562 a sum of money was raised to build a harbour but unfortunately someone made off with it. In 1597 some sort of a harbour was achieved after three years' hard work but a south-east gale on top of a high spring tide overthrew it. In 1635 a quotation was made for the building of a new harbour in the lee of the White Rock but nothing came of it. A great storm of 1656 destroyed what was left of the Elizabethan pier. In 1806 John Rennie drew up plans for a harbour but these were turned down. In 1837 William Cubitt, the man who piled all those dreary acres of grey buildings on the London clay, wanted to build a harbour for £150,000 but nothing came of it. In 1890 a Hastings Harbour Act was passed and by 1897 a stone wall was built, the sad broken remains of which give the fishing landing a little shelter still to-day. The fishermen drive their boats through the gaps in it torn by the sea. The refusal of a completely land-lubber council in this enormously wealthy seaside resort to spare £3,000 a year for its upkeep caused the harbour to collapse. The wall had one good effect, though. Its broken remains caused an enormous amount of 'beach' to collect in its lee (that is to the east of it – its lee from the eastward drift) and this has made an extensive area of dry beach for the fishermen to haul their boats up on. For Hastings is nothing but a beaching port still.

There is a new scheme, though, that looks like succeeding, and that is to make a nine acre yacht harbour, using the Castle Rocks, which run parallel with the shore, for the foundations of part of it, and joining this wall to the shore at White Rock, dredging to eight feet at low tide (Hastings has a rise-and-fall of twenty-four feet at springs – the highest on the south coast). There is no harbour of refuge for small boats between Rye (which is difficult) and Shoreham, so a harbour here would be very welcome to cruising yachtsmen. An argument against such a yacht harbour is that an enormous new yacht harbour is already being built at Brighton, but not everybody wants to moor his yacht in a floating city (which this will be), there seems to be no limit to the demand for mooring space in the south-east, Hastings would be a port of call for hundreds of yachts, and the thing could do nothing but good. It would be roughly where the ancient Cinque Port harbour once was, and it would make Hastings into a true port again. Who knows – if fuel-oil goes up in price a few more points – Hastings may be a commercial port again.

Hastings, with extraordinary tenacity, managed to operate a fleet of trading vessels right into the seventies of the nineteenth century, although there was absolutely nowhere for them to be kept at Hastings in safety. But sizeable merchantmen were built on Hastings beach and launched into the open sea. Many an old print or painting shows them – often several being built at once. Ships were built there up to 170 tons, which is a great size for the open beach. One ship was built even bigger than this – and a strange vessel she was, too: the *New Moon*, built for Lord Willoughby d'Eresby in 1860 by George Tutt and his son Fred. This one-off job was 220 tons, 136 feet overall, she drew 5 feet 6 inches forward and 11 foot aft. Her main deck was only nine inches above the water but she was fitted with air compartments like a lifeboat so she couldn't fill and sink. She was clinker built and her mainsail alone had a thousand feet of canvas. She was very fast – in any sort of wind at all she would make twelve or thirteen knots. She was built as a racing yacht and was very successful.

Many of the ships built on Hastings beach were for 'away', but there was always a fleet of locally owned ships. These were employed generally in carrying coal from the north to Hastings, or for carrying local produce to London or other cities. In the lack of a harbour the loaded coal ships were driven up on to the beach at high tide, and when the tide had left them carts would come alongside and the coal would be 'whipped' or 'jumped' out of the ships into the carts. The process of 'whipping out' was that the coal would be shovelled into a chaldron down in the hold, a whip (that is a single rope passed through a single pulley block slung on a yard-arm) was made fast to the chaldron at one end and to perhaps a dozen 'cats' tails' at the other. As many men as there were cats' tails jumped up on to a wooden staging on deck – each man grasped a cat's tail – and they would all jump off the staging together. Their combined weight would cause the chaldron to rise, whereupon it would be swung to one side and its contents shot into a wooden shoot which carried the coal to the waiting cart below. There are many contemporary paintings showing this operation being performed at Hastings.

Many of these little colliers carried on this trade for many decades. Perhaps the best known was the *Pelican*, 100 tons, built and owned locally. She reigned from 1838 to 1879, or forty-one years. This may not seem a long reign for a collier (150 years is not unheard of) but when one thinks that every voyage she would have to be driven ashore on the open beach fully loaded, certainly to pound on the stony sand or shingle if there was any sea, and then take the risk (and it was *always* a risk) of getting off again, it will be realised that this is exceptional.

The *Pelican* was marvellously lucky (another way of saying she had a good skipper!). Her master's name was Captain James Dunk. On one occasion she managed to land coal at Hastings on four successive Saturdays – having had to go each time to Seaham Harbour, in County Durham, to fetch it! She started life as a brig but in the 1870s was altered to a brigantine. She only carried a crew of four – and they had to help unload. She would not have been lost when she was, in 1879, but that a disgruntled person, never discovered, had partially severed the warp that ran out to an off-shore anchor with a knife and when she tried to haul herself off the beach, in an on-shore wind, the rope broke and she was driven ashore and that finished her.

There were many disasters. Any large ship driving ashore on an open beach is at risk, for her master can never be sure what the weather is going to be like when he wishes to haul himself off again. Of course, an anchor would be dropped from the stern as she sailed in for her to haul herself out to again but if an on-shore gale sprang up, with big seas breaking on the beach, no anchor in the world would hold while the ship was being windlassed off to it. The ship would be thrown broadside back on the beach and would break up. Just after Christmas, 1838, for example, four ships were ashore at Hastings and had not only discharged but had loaded cargoes for away, when the wind shot round from north to south-west and came in a gale. The *William Pitt*, loaded with old iron and sixty-five quarters of oats and wheat, was flung ashore, holed, and water-logged. The *Sussex*, a sloop with 160 quarters of corn on board for London, was to windward of the others and set sail and tried to claw off. But her jib carried away, she got into stays and fouled the other ships, she anchored, but in the evening had to cut and run ashore to save the lives of her crew. The *Queen Victoria*, a brig of 99 tons, was flung ashore. And another ship was lost. All the ships were total wrecks but nobody was drowned for the fishermen formed a living chain into the sea and got everybody to safety.

Examples of other Hastings-built ships were the *Wanderer*, 92 tons, 62 feet long, launched 1840, and the fruit schooner *Isabel*, 152 tons, built for J. and J. Adams, of Pudding Lane, London, for the Mediterranean trade.

As for fishing, Hastings has had a fishing industry certainly since coracle days, and – quite amazingly for a port without a harbour – is one of the top landing-ports for inshore fishing boats now. As the place has simply no *natural* advantage as a fishing port this must be simply because there is a strong fishing community here, which has remained stalwart and unbroken since the days when there *was* a harbour. And they don't show any signs of giving up either. The crews have a large proportion of young men and boys in them, and little boys nip off to sea whenever they can get away from school, and when they leave school go fishing with their fathers as a matter of course. This is the more surprising in a big modern town like Hastings, with plenty of better-paid and much easier work ashore.

As one travels round the coast from the north-east of England, down the east coast, one observes constant changes in the type of boats that operate off open beaches. The Northumberland, County Durham and Yorkshire coble is a long narrow low rakish vessel, very heavily built, with a deep sharp forefoot for parting the waves when she is launched bow-first, and a low flat after section for running easily on to the beach when she comes to the land stern-on. She is as unlike the Hastings Lugger as a boat could be and still be a boat, and yet she does the same job. In north Norfolk we find the Sheringham and Cromer Crabbers and the Wells Whelkers. These are quite different from either. Very lightly built 'like a basket', with narrow strakes on fine timbers, double-ended, they allow themselves to be driven sideways on to the beach when they land, their crews giving them a list towards the land so they are thrown over on one bilge and the waves break harmlessly against their bottoms – knocking them up the beach with each wave. A tractor hauls them to safety.

From Winterton round to Deal we get the 'punt', not anything like a punt, but a short, beamy, full-bilged boat, heavily built, with a wide transom stern. Anything but 'rakish'. She comes to the beach head-on and is hauled up by a winch.

But once round into the English Channel we come to a different sort of vessel altogether. Perhaps Hythe is the first place where we see them (although there was *one* at Deal when I was last there). This is a very beamy, full-bilged, long-keel boat, enormously high out of the water – a great *lump* of a boat, with very full apple bows and a lute stern in the older boats and an elliptical stern in the newer. In either case the stern overhangs greatly and has great *lift*, for these boats are both launched and landed with their sterns facing the seas. The beaches from which they work are almost without exception steep, and a coble-type vessel would plunge straight down into the water launched from such a beach. The great *lift* of the Lugger stern prevents this from happening. The enormous freeboard and the great high bulwarks give these boats a medieval appearance. One feels that they have changed little since William the Conqueror came over in a ship very like one. So high out of the water are they that steps have to be let into their high vertical stems for the last man to climb aboard when they are being launched. As far as *speed* goes the coble, either under sail or power, would leave them standing. It would be a race between a race-horse and a cart-horse. But they are very seaworthy, practically unswampable and uncapsizable, will come to the beach in extreme conditions, will carry a big load, and are large stable fishing platforms. And this type, with modifications, obtains right along the south coast until we get to Cornwall, and there there are so many harbours that beach boats are no longer required.

The modern Hastings Lugger (not a lugger at all, of course, nowadays, but a motor boat) is about thirty-two feet long, gross tonnage eight to twelve tons, has a diesel engine from 50 to 100 horsepower, is fitted with a 'fish-finder' (echo sounder), ship-to-shore radio telephone, pulls an otter trawl, is worked by two men with a 'boy-ashore' – the latter generally an elderly man who is quite necessary to have the winch running when the boat comes in to land and the hook down by the water's edge (speed may be vital then if there is a big sea running – the boat must be hauled out of the breakers before she pounds too much) and for managing the shore side of the enterprise including selling the fish. Up until 1936 the 'boy-ashore' worked a horse, for this walked round in a circle driving the capstan which hauled the lugger up the beach. After that year the motors came in. Aboard the boat there will be a modern fishing winch driven from the main engine, and in the living-quarters of the boat, called the 'fore-room', is generally a coal stove and cooking arrangements and a couple of bunks, for the boat often stays out for a few days in winter. The boat is launched over greased baulks of timber called troughs (rhymes with *goes*) and checked as she goes down with a *holding-anchor* – which a man carries and digs into the shingle to prevent the boat from 'taking charge'. Do not hang about downhill from a Lugger when she is being either let down or hauled up. It is dangerous. A fixed rope going off to a big anchor out at sea is used to haul the boat off through the breakers – a couple of turns being snatched round the bit of the trawl winch. The engine is going by the time she hits the breakers on launching and the propeller is put hard astern to haul her backwards through the breakers. When the boat is hauled up with her catch she lies over on one great full-bellied bilge or the other, and there are chocks for the purpose of keeping her there. Owing to her great height a ladder is needed to get aboard or lower the catch down.

There is a fish auction every morning except Sundays at a quarter past six. Most of the buyers are retailers from a range of about thirty miles. This means that if you live within that radius of Hastings you are likely to get that rare commodity – fresh fish. The fish are mostly expensive flat fish such as Dover sole, plaice, turbot and brill, the cheaper fish landed being skate, dabs and lemon sole, with whiting reserved nowadays for the cat. Soles are the most prized fish, and they are caught better by night in the summer and by day in the winter.

There are about twenty 'Luggers', or large decked trawlers, and many smaller boats. The traditional names for the smaller vessels are *Bogs* or three-quarter boats for smaller decked boats, and *Punts* for the open boats under four tons.

The modern Hastings Lugger is descended from the famous

Hastings Sailing Luggers of yore, and one of these has, thank God, been preserved for us to see. It is in the Fishermen's Chapel, on the Stade, which is the most interesting place in Hastings. The Lugger preserved here is the *Enterprise*, built at Hastings in 1909, fishing until 1954, and presented to the museum by her owner, Mr Harold Pepper. She is twenty-seven feet along the keel, eleven feet eight inches beam and four feet six draft. Her registered tonnage is 11.44 gross and the same nett. She was built for sail but later had an engine fitted. She was built for drifting, not trawling, but nevertheless trawled as well. Her best night's haul at drifting was twelve last of herrings – that is 160,000 fish or eighteen tons. She carried six men when drifting, three when trawling. She would start each season at Lowestoft in the autumn, follow the herring south until the 'Channel fishing' near home, fish at home for the worst months of the winter, and set off for Cornwall, with most of the other Hastings boats, in the spring for the 'Mackerel Voyage'. It is strange that boats that could be hauled up on the beach by a horse could be used for extensive voyages such as these, being away for months at a time with the crew living hugger-mugger aboard. But they were.

Enterprise was a lute stern. This is a kind of extended transom that makes a long overhang for the sea to get under and provide lift when she launches or comes to land. About 1880 the elliptical stern came into vogue, such as we see in many of the Hastings boats today. This is something like a cruiser-stern, but it reminds one in shape somewhat of the 'belly' of a mandolin. Originally the Luggers had three masts – all carrying dipping lugs and sometimes the main, in the middle, setting a topsail. When trawling came in the main was done away with to make room for the trawl winch, fore and mizzen were made much bigger, and a staysail was rigged on the forestay of the mizzen. The boats had long bowsprits and even longer bumkins – long poles sticking out aft for the mizzen to sheet to. The masts were in tabernacles for easy lowering. *Enterprise*, typically after trawling started, had a heavy iron capstan amidships where the main mast should have been. This was used for hauling the trawl, hauling the boat off the beach to her seaward anchor, and for any other hauling jobs that needed doing. Note, when you see her, the sweeps, or long oars, lashed to the side of the vessel. These were needed to get her away when there was an on-shore wind. Fine sea-boats though these south coast vessels were, one cannot but suppose that they would have been completely outsailed by the zulus, scafies, cobles and other piratical-looking rakish vessels of the north. Those tubby lines, enormously high freeboard, and terribly low-aspect sail plan, were never made to sail fast to windward whatever else they were made for.

The *Enterprise*, like nearly all the other Hastings Luggers, went to Dunkirk to ferry men off the beaches to the ships in 1940. She was one of the ones that got back.

The famous 'Net Shops' of Hastings were built that way to save space on the limited amount of ground available for the fishermen between the cliffs and the sea. They serve well for their purpose of storing nets and tackle and are very beautiful. They are known to have been there in Elizabethan days (or ones like them) and there are about forty of them now. Some were rebuilt after a disastrous fire of 1961 by money subscribed by the public, for the Hastings people are quite rightly proud of these extraordinary buildings.

Hastings fishermen are called by the irreverent 'Chopbacks', because a Hastings man, in a *fracas* at sea about 1760, split a Dutchman or Dunkirker right down the back with an axe, and since then they have had this name. Hastings fishermen have quite an extensive vocabulary of their own. A long list of their special words may be found in *The Fishing Luggers of Hastings* by James Hornell (1938).

To wander through the Old Town, when it is not too crowded with holidaymakers, is a delight. All Saints Street is simply fine, so is Main Street. There are many fine pubs – some quite unspoiled. At 94 All Saints Street is the headquarters of the Winkle Club. This is a fine benevolent institution founded by the fishermen in 1832. Each member must carry a winkle shell in his pocket, and if he is challenged by a fellow member with 'Up Winkle!' he must produce it or be fined. Sir Winston Churchill was made a member, and so have several other prominent if non-seafaring gentlemen.

There isn't much left of **Hastings Castle** (the *Hestea Ceastra* of the Bayeux Tapestry) but what there is is worth going to see for the splendid view from the hilltop, and there is good climbing for small boys among the surrounding sandstone cliffs. Then there are the Caves, which are both extensive and bizarre, much commercialised by the Corporation, and you have to go round them in parties under guides. The guides are amusing and skilled at making a lot out of very little, the caves are rambling, partly natural and partly man-made but there is not really much in them. They were blocked up by the owner of the land, Edward Milward, in 1811, to stop them being used by smugglers we are told, reopened by another landowner named Scott and, more especially, by his gardener, Joseph Golding – a market gardener and greengrocer, and in 1820

Golding started surreptitiously digging sand. Some of this was shipped off to the Low Countries for glass-making. A visitor found him at it and let the cat out of the bag (he had no right to) so Golding thereupon applied for a formal lease of the caves and opened them up to visitors (on 28th July, 1827) at sixpence a time just to look at them and a shilling if you wanted to *dance*! The indefatigable Mr Golding went on digging out the sandstone, enlarging the caves, making passages from one to another, there are strange crude figures cut out by him and we are told he used to keep his money behind the bust of the Duke of Wellington. The Ashdown Sandstone of which the caves are formed was laid down in the Lower Cretaceous period (over a hundred million years ago) when a great deltaic estuary covered southern England. The sands were laid down in fresh water, then overlaid with the chalk of the Lower Cretaceous, and subsequently denuded again by water action on the chalk. The fissures that Mr Golding so assiduously enlarged and joined together must have been made in some earthquake of long ago, for there is no evidence that they were cut by water. Whatever the guide tells you there is no evidence that these caves were used either by smugglers, or by Romans. The *Caverners' Jazz Band* makes the welkin ring down there on Tuesdays and on Fridays – it is surprising that the roof stands up to it.

Whether or not smugglers used these caves (and while there is no evidence to show that they did there is also no evidence to show that they did not) there were plenty of these gentlemen in Hastings. In October, 1734, a company of Foot had to be stationed here to help the hard-pressed Dragoons.

At first the smuggling was mostly raw wool *out*, for in order to encourage the English textile industry several monarchs from Edward III down forbade the export of raw wool. But as time went on it was other things *in* – things that could not be produced in this country but the import of which was heavily taxed by the government as a means of screwing money out of people, generally for stupid purposes. One owler gang in particular – the Hawkhurst Gang (that traditionally always has the adjective 'notorious' put in front of it) was very active around Hastings in the 1730s. In 1734 ten preventive men and some soldiers laid an ambush for this gang as it was making a run. The ambushers managed to let the scouts get past (always the ticklish moment in an ambush) then Carswell, the officer in charge, stepped out and shouted: 'What goods have you got?'

'None for you!' was the reply.

The soldiers fired and killed one man. There was a running fight, the Hawkhurst men got away with all the goods, and the soldiers were subsequently charged with manslaughter!

It was the Hawkhurst Gang which attacked the Customs House in Poole and sprung the impounded goods there.

One local smuggler, poor Ambrose Cannan, wanted by the authorities, skipped abroad for thirteen years of exile. Then, hoping that he would have been forgotten, came home bringing with him his wife and three children. He was not forgotten though, and was taken and hanged at Horsham. The 'crime' he had committed was done by his master when he was still a small boy, and there was a great public outcry at his committal.

The smugglers went under nicknames, as indeed do modern Hastings fishermen, but the latter don't have names as flamboyant as Nasty Face, Flushing Jack, Joseph Nobody and Curse-Mother-Jack.

The free trade was so profitable that big money was put into it. Squires, parsons and gentlemen generally were quite willing to put money into so profitable an industry. At the end of the seventeenth century a Captain Southgate, of the Preventive Service, wrote in his report: 'The vessels now in ye smugeling trade become so large and formable that we are not only repulsed, insulted, and beet by them, but are actuely in danger of being run down and sunke by them, who not onely thrattened to do so, but also atampted it.'

But when a tub of three and a half gallons of brandy could be bought for from 10/6d to 12/- in France – already roped for slinging to ponies if you wanted it – and was so overproof that it could be broken down with water to make six gallons, and would then sell in England for from £3 to £4, it will be seen that the game was worth the occasional exchange of hot shot.

But in 1817 the government formed the Coast Blockade, with ships relieved of having to fight Napoleon. The heat was on for the owlers. In 1821 a Coast Blockade man, George England, started searching a fishing boat that had just come ashore at Hastings Beach, skippered by a man named Joseph Swaine. There was a brawl and England shot and killed Swaine. England was tried and sentenced to be hanged but was given, from on high, a free pardon, but so much was public opinion on the side of the owlers that £99 – a huge sum in those days – was raised for Swaine's widow by public subscription.

Whether all the government's efforts would finally have suppressed the owlers is doubtful: times were desperately hard and here was a way for poor men to make a lot of money. The smugglers were not desperadoes or villains, as it is nowadays fashionable to make them out to be: they were honest fishermen who had always had to earn a living in the hardest and most dangerous of callings – the sort of men who would put their own lives at extreme risk to go and rescue total strangers from shipwreck with no thought of gain – in fact, just the sort of men who man our lifeboats to-day. They were only trying desperately to keep their wives and children fed. But what did eventually kill the trade, or at least reduce it – it is still not dead – was the growing prosperity of the seaside resorts. By the latter end of the eighteenth century Hastings was already developing in this way (in 1768 even, there had already been a plan to convert some stable buildings into an 'Assembly Room'). There was work ashore for women and girls in 'service', there were bathing machines to be built and manned, large crescents of 'gentlemen's houses' to be built, and, above all, a good market for fresh fish.

Trawling started at Hastings about 1800 – for, of course, it was the 'quality fish' such as Dover sole, brill, turbot and plaice that were most in demand – such as can best be scraped off the bottom of the sea with the trawl net – and so at least there was an alternative to smuggling. It lingered on well into the century though. Byron wrote from Hastings to a friend mentioning the importance of the free trade there and Charles Lamb, also from Hastings, wrote: 'I like a smuggler. He is the only honest thief. He robs nothing but the revenue – an abstraction I never greatly cared about.' But the Preventive Service increased in strength and effectiveness. It made four captures around Hastings in 1829 and eight in 1830 – in the latter year there was a spectacular fight on the Marine Parade on a Sunday morning in December. In July the next year a run was made by owlers armed with bludgeons near No. 38 Martello Tower (the towers were made full use of by the Preventive Service) and a reward of £200 was offered for information. In October of the same year two revenue men were badly wounded while trying to interfere with a run and a reward of £500 was offered, but to no avail. Then on Sunday night, 1st January, 1832, there was a great fight at the new town of St Leonards, at least three smugglers were killed, many on both sides injured, a reward of £500 for information without result. Three coastguards were killed in February of that year at No. 40 Tower. Then the government sent a detachment of Dragoons down, and later a unit of the Rifle Brigade, and this and other measures put an end to large-scale smuggling. The game became not worth the candle.

There is a lot to see and do in the New Town of Hastings, such as a most excellent museum (whatever you do don't miss the Durbar Room in it – amongst other memorable items the tusk of an elephant that *collided with a train*), what Sir Francis Drake would have made of the *Indoor Bowling Green* can only be guessed, and somewhere on the Hastings foreshore lies buried the wreck of the Dutch East Indiaman, *Amsterdam*, lost in 1749.

There was a twelfth-century priory where the old Ritz Cinema was. The site is currently being excavated by the local archaeological research group.

In 1824 a four-oared galley with a gentleman coxswain set out from Hastings for Brighton, the gentleman coxswain having made a wager of £50 that she could get there in eight hours. She got there in six and three quarters.

CHAPTER 9

St Leonards to Seaford

St Leonards was built all of a piece by a man named James Burton in the 1820s and 30s as a new resort for 'people of the best fashion': a sort of Jane Austen paradise. Burton was a builder who had already covered some two hundred and fifty acres of North London with bricks and mortar, and St Leonards was his creation entirely and very elegant it looked. Much of his building remains, marred every now and then by modern interpolations of peculiar crassness, and the place is really just a part of modern Hastings. A scholarly little book called *Burton's St Leonard's* by J. Manwaring Baines is on sale at Hastings Museum and elsewhere.

Bulverhythe may or may not be one of the most historically interesting places in Britain, for many people believe that Duke William landed there, to change the suffix of his name from Bastard to Conqueror (although the fact that he became the latter didn't make him any the less of the former). Other people put the landing at Pevensey, and we shall discuss the dire event when we get there.

There is a legend that Bulverhythe takes its name from the fact that William promised a follower (evidently not one of his favourites!) the amount of land that could be covered by a bull's hide. The wily fellow cut the hide in a spiral of one thin strip (the way we used to make *riem*, or raw-hide rope, in Africa – subsequently hanging the rope in loops over the branch of a tree, hanging a heavy rock on it, and twisting it and letting it spin all day every day for a week. It is interesting that the rigging of the ships of Homer's heroes was made like this – besides the *trek-riem* that pulled the great ox-wagons of the Boers). Anyway this wily chap surrounded a decent area of land with this *riem* and William gave it to him. A much more likely explanation is that the name came from one of the names of Odin.

Bulverhythe once had a harbour: it will be seen that the mouth of a small stream once came in here. A harbour is mentioned in writings of 1679. But the sea is encroaching here – the railway has to be expensively protected from it. The railway, being right along the foreshore, has made this rather a depressing place. If William

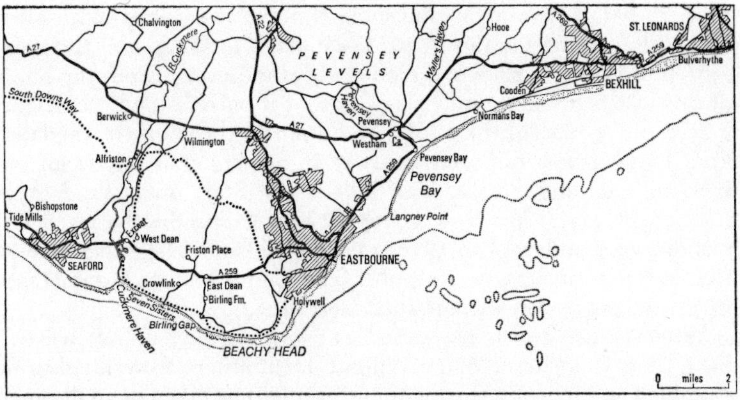

the Conqueror had landed here to-day he would probably have turned right round and sailed back to Normandy.

Bexhill is a quiet, unassuming, and very respectable small seaside resort, with an enormous building called the De La Warr Pavilion, designed by Erich Mendelsohn and Chermayeff, and built from 1933 to 1936. It is very typical of its period (although it seemed far-out then) and to my eyes very ugly. It is, however, most useful for concerts, theatre and the like and a very nice thing for a small resort to have. There is an old church at Bexhill with an eighth-century stone in it.

Cooden, now a suburb of Bexhill, has a vestigial fishing community, the members of which keep their boats – at the time of writing – along the shore towards Eastbourne, on the very narrow strip of shingle between the sea and the railway, where they have small windlasses driven by engines. There are two full-time fishermen in this unlikely and inhospitable spot. They set pots and also trammel nets, mostly on some rock ledges from a mile to a mile and a half from shore. The over-prevalence of small crabs, and the rocks in shoal water, make clearing the trammel nets a troublesome job. The landing place is precarious, it is liable to be shifted by either the sea or the River Board, and these men should be provided with a proper landing on a suitable place near their homes: or is Bexhill too respectable to care about common fishermen? The sea defences along this shore are formidable, and it is obvious that if they were neglected the sea would attack the railway and subsequently flood the Pevensey Levels.

Normans Bay, where most people think the Conqueror landed (but who is to say that all his nine hundred ships landed in the same place?) has caravans, a minuscule church, two gaunt old houses, one with a weird shop in it, old coastguard cottages, and the great outfall of Waller's Haven, which drains the Levels. From the name of this watercourse we may suppose that it once formed a harbour. There is also the loneliest railway station in the south of England, and inland a few hundred yards is an ancient pub beside an old moss-covered sluice gate. The pub is the Star, once the Star of Bethlehem, and it has deeds going back for six hundred years. It is – wonder of wonders – untarted, unspoiled, and altogether one of this writer's most favourite pubs. The Lamb Inn at **Hooe**, three miles inland, is also ancient and interesting.

Whether the Normans landed at Normans Bay or not we will have them land here. When William leapt ashore from his ship he stumbled and fell, and fearing that this might be taken as an ill-omen he clutched up some sand and cried: 'Look how eager I am to grasp the English earth!' He took the bold course of burning his ships, so that there could be no thought of retreat.

William got the Pope's approval for the conquest of England, arguing that Harold had made the kingdom over to him while his guest in Normandy (in fact Harold was his prisoner), and that under the Donation of Constantine all *islands* belonged to the Pope, to dispose of how he would. The Donation, incidentally, was completely discredited in 1440 by Lorenzo Valla but it was then a little too late. Anyway, Pope Alexander II generously gave the British Isles to William, and every landless adventurer in France who could raise a few men went and joined his standard. Various men came up with ships: William Fitz Osbert with sixty, Bishop Odo with fifty, the Bishop of Mans with thirty. William mustered his fleet in the mouth of the River Dive between the Seine and the Orme. He tried to sail, but a gale got up and the fleet was forced to run for St Valéry. The wind held foul, and if it had held foul long enough it would have prevented the conquest of England; for firstly William's army would have melted away, and secondly Harold would have had time to defeat Hadraader in Yorkshire and come south again and rest and reorganise his army. But the bones of St Valéry were paraded through the streets and the intercession of the saint requested, the wind changed, and William sailed with not quite 700 transports and 200 smaller vessels. He himself took the sea in *Mora*, a gift from his wife Matilda. Her great square sail was striped red and yellow, at her prow was 'a child in brass bearing a charged bow' and the *Gonfanon*, a long pennant blessed by the Pope, streamed from her masthead.

After William landed he lodged for a time in Pevensey Castle, but soon moved to Hastings, where he fortified the old castle there. The Battle of Hastings is hardly within our scope.

If we have the hardihood to keep slogging along the shingle, westward-ho, we come to **Pevensey Bay**, which is a paradise of little bungalows which claim the beach in front of them and have shingle 'gardens' out the back – desperately trying to be English-suburban in this shingle world. A boat, the *Lady Admiral*, works from one of these bungalows, and she has to have her own *pharos* to guide her home: electric lights slung high on a television aerial.

Out at sea we can see the *Royal Sovereign*, formerly a famous lightship, now an automatic beacon resting on the sea bed, and put there in 1971. It is radio-controlled from Newhaven and saves a lot of money.

The **Pevensey Levels** are a rehearsal for Romney Marsh, just as **Langney Point**, to the west of them, is a rehearsal for Dungeness. The shingle is accreting at Langney Point just as it is at Dungeness. The Levels are the seaward end of the Vale of Sussex, and consist of heavy Wealden Clay, just as Romney Marsh is the seaward extension of the Vale of Kent. These two parallel vales have the High Weald, or Forest Ridges, separating them, and are flanked by the North and South Downs each side. We can see the seaward end of the South Downs very clearly from Pevensey.

It was in Pevensey Bay that the big Dutch East Indiaman *Twee Cornelissen*, 750 tons, ninety-two days out from Batavia and bound for Amsterdam, brought up to wait for a pilot. A south-south-west gale blew up and the ship found herself embayed (of course, she should never have been there in the first place) and she dragged during the night, went ashore, eighteen men managed to get ashore in the long boat, leaving the captain, mate, and twelve men still aboard. At high tide great waves broke over the ship and drove the men into the rigging. At 10.30 the Eastbourne lifeboat ran down from the windward and rounded under the stern of the ship, between the ship and the shore, and managed to get thirteen men off, all in a state of collapse. One man was left lashed to the rigging, and finally coastguards were able to get off in a boat from the beach and cut him down but he was dead. Two days later the great ship had completely broken to pieces.

Pevensey is interesting as being the site of **Anderida**, or **Anderita** as the Ordnance Survey has it. This was a very large fort of the Saxon Shore, probably built by Carausius when he built the others in the second half of the third century (see under Dover). It is a great egg-shaped fortification, enclosing about ten acres, surrounded by a wall of immense strength. The Romans made a bed fifteen feet wide of clay stamped into oak stakes, and above this three feet of flints set in clay. Over this was a layer of heavy timber set in concrete. The wall was built on this platform twelve feet wide and twenty-eight feet high with blocks of greensand with a rubble core. Typically Roman bonding courses of red tiles at intervals go right through the thickness of the wall.

According to *The Saxon Shore* by J. Mothersole (Bodley Head) one of the commanders of the garrison here (after the downfall of Carausius – when the forts had returned to the rule of Rome, of course) was the Commander of the Abulcian Band. Tiles have been found here stamped CL BR, standing for *Classis Britannica*, or the British Fleet.

In the nineteenth century a well was discovered which had wolf skulls in it. Later an even older well was unearthed, and this had leather sandals, bark rope (the only bit of Roman rope in Britain), wood of the beech tree (indicating perhaps that the beech had arrived in England at this juncture: it was not indigenous. Although couldn't the Romans have brought some beech wood with them?), many identifiable seeds, and the bones of the domestic cat.

The Romans, having left this rubbish, went, and the English arrived and promptly set about the Celts, or Britons. Henry of Huntingdon, writing in the twelfth century, describes how a band of Britons took refuge in Anderida until 'worn down by long want of food, when they could no longer sustain the multitude of assailants, (the citizens) were all devoured by the sword, with the women and little ones, so that not an individual escaped'. This happened early on in the Saxon incursion.

The Normans, as we have seen, made use of Anderida as soon as they had landed, and they very soon built a strong Norman castle within. It is significant that they found the Roman walls still good enough to use for their outer bailey eight hundred years after they had been built, but also, eight hundred years after the Normans came, these walls were still good enough to be fortified against the Germans in 1940.

Odo, Bishop of Bayeux, who was so close to the Conqueror, held the fort against King Rufus in 1088, and Gilbert de Aquila, Earl of Pembroke, held it against King Stephen in 1147. No less than three of Gilbert's sons, incidentally, were drowned, together with the son of Henry I, in the wreck of the White Ship. The younger Simon de Montfort besieged it, unsuccessfully, in 1264 and 1265, and Richard II besieged it in his war against Bolingbroke, but the garrison, led by Lady Pelham, held out. So in its life as a Norman and medieval fortress it passed through exciting times.

Pevensey Castle was surveyed at the time of the Armada, but by then the sea had deserted it and it was considered to be of no value. A glance at the map will show that, before this recession of the sea, Pevensey Haven was really a haven – a harbour for ships that ran right up to the castle. The Romans built their great fort on the end of a sharp narrow peninsula, which had tidal swamps on three sides of it, and no doubt a deep water harbour right up to its walls. It was noted in the Elizabethan survey that the castle was armed with two demi-culverins. One of these is still there, near the entrance to the Inner Bailey. It is made of Sussex iron, and is

Plan of Pevensey Castle

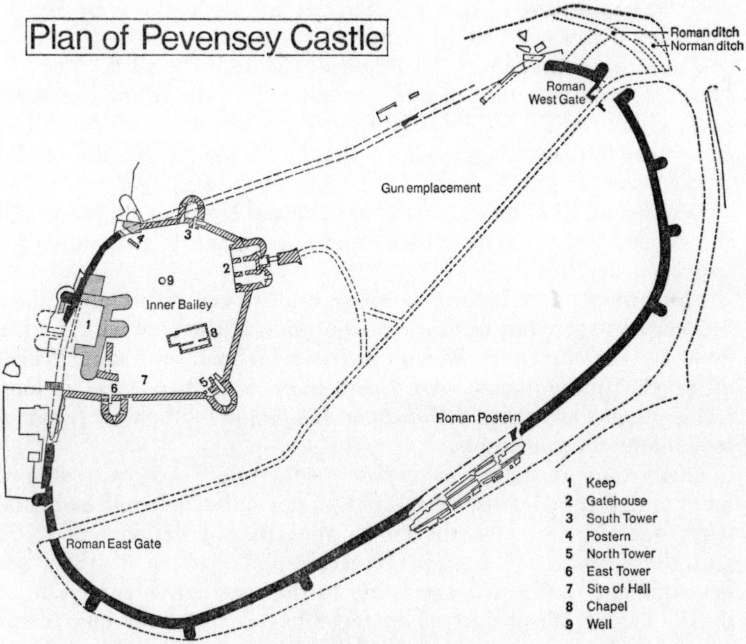

stamped with a crown, a Tudor rose, and the letters E.R. The inner bailey and the keep are cared for and locked up at night by the Department of the Environment, but the great Roman fort is open all the time and children have hung ropes from the trees on the south side and have fun swinging about like Tarzan of the Apes.

Domesday mentions that there was a mint at Pevensey, and there are indeed four coins struck here in the British Museum.

The inner bailey of the castle is partly mid-thirteenth century. It has three semi-circular towers. The keep has unusual apsidal buttresses.

In Henry VIII's time the original Merry Andrew lived here – Andrew Borde, a 'man of infinite jest', court physician, and author of the *Tales of the Wise Men of Gotham.* Gotham is just south of the Trent, opposite Nottingham.

Pevensey was a limb of the Cinque Ports. The Ports had the privilege of *drowning* their wrong-doers, and it is said that condemned men were thrown off Pevensey Bridge. The big drain that runs through Pevensey to the sea is called Pevensey Haven. Below the bridge it is called Salt Haven – above it Broad Haven. There is good coarse fishing in it – you can get tickets at the New Inn in Pevensey if you want to fish legally.

The curate in charge of Pevensey Church in 1826, Rev. St Quinton, told the story of one day going into the disused chancel of his church and finding spirits there – not ghostly ones, but a keg of brandy left by smugglers as a thank-offering for the use of this storage space.

Westham, hard by the castle, has a grand Norman church which should certainly not be missed, and the village is too pretty for words.

Eastbourne is a county borough and a very respectable place indeed, and sheltered from the uncouthness of the west wind by the great butt of the South Downs. It has a lifeboat, and a small fleet of beach fishing boats, and Eastbourne fishermen have a long tradition and are called *Whillicks* or *Whillickers* by their brethren: a local name for guillemots.

Eastbourne on the sea is very new – the Old Town being inland hard under the Downs, where it was not only sheltered from the wind but also from sea rovers. In 1801 its population was 1,668 and there were 243 houses. It received a charter in 1883. Its development has been largely due to the speculative enterprise of the Dukes of Devonshire. The town has facilities for enjoyment galore, such as a theatre that will hold two thousand people, two smaller theatres open in summer, a far-out silver-domed bandstand which seats 3,500 people, and a pier opened in 1870. Beyond the pier is the largest of all the Martello Towers. It is said to contain 50,000 bricks in each one of its courses. It mounted eleven twenty-four-pounders and could accommodate 350 men. Edison said of them: 'whilst cosily seated by the blazing fire within, could (had they also a steaming glass of smuggled whisky before them? We by no means assert such *was* the case) laugh to scorn the roaring tempest without'. Near it is the Lifeboat Museum, well worth going to see.

In Holywell Quarry, where is now a pumping station, chalk used to be loaded into Rye smacks for transport to that place for lime burning and other uses. Eastbourne had its seaborne trade, too – colliers used to beach at a point opposite St Aubyn's Road and unload their coal into carts to go to Mr Vine's yard. The 189-ton collier brig *Tally Ho*, built by May of Shoreham, was wrecked at Eastbourne near the Redoubt: on Boxing Day, 1886, her captain ran her ashore here in desperation after a south-wester had started her leaking. People ran out and lit fires to provide light, and they could hear pathetic cries of 'heave us a line!' but how can you heave a line across a gale? One sailor managed to swim ashore himself but died when he got there. Two others tried it and were drowned in the breakers. Eventually a line was got to the ship and three men were saved by it.

It is sad that, so far as I can find, there are none of the old Eastbourne Bath Chair Pushers left. There should be an annual race, with elderly gentlemen in straw hats being pushed along the prom by even more elderly gentlemen in bowler hats.

Beachy Head, a popular place for suicides, has a sublimity about it, particularly when seen from the sea. It is 536 feet high and therefore much higher than the more famous cliffs of Dover. In 1831 the Belle Toute Lightship was built on a rocky promontory west of the Head – to have built it on top would have been useless because in days of low cloud it would have been obscured in vapour. The East Indiaman *Dalhousie* was wrecked down below the Head on 24th October, 1853. The fate of her crew (which was a nasty one) inspired the Vicar of East Dean, the Reverend Darby, to cut a cave in the chalk down below for stranded mariners to get a foothold in.

On 30th June, 1690, was fought the Battle of Beachy Head, wherein the French defeated the combined Dutch and English fleets. Macaulay wrote: 'There has scarcely been so sad a day in London as that on which the news of the Battle of Beachey Head arrived. The shame was insupportable: the peril imminent.'

East Dean, the vicar of which dug the hole, has a church with a Saxon tower and a Norman nave. We are coming into a great country of small Saxon and early Norman churches now. The comparatively barren Downland country, cut off from the rest of England by miles of heavy clay forest, had none of those surges of prosperity such as enabled the great 'wool churches' of East Anglia to be built, and therefore the more humble but very beautiful early work remained. There was no great flowering in this area of later periods of architecture.

At **Friston Place** there is said to be a well with a donkey wheel over it but I have never seen it. The donkey walked round inside the wheel.

Birling Farm, of Major Davies Gilbert, is a fine example of a big fortress-like farmhouse in the flint country. The chalk downs here are littered with flint, and flint is everywhere. **Birling Gap** has coastguard cottages and a pub. In summer steps are rigged down the face of the cliff but are apt to fade away in the winter time. There is a curious device for lowering down and hauling up a boat to the sea far below.

An owler named 'Jevington' Jigg used to run cargoes into Birling Gap and a right sweat it must have been for his men to get them up the cliff. He used to stow the stuff at Crowlink Farm near Friston (the farm is still a very remote one, and belongs to the National Trust). Then, when the coast was clear, he would run the cargoes inland to **Jevington**, which had a sensible parson who would let him make use of the church for storage purposes. There is a memorial tablet in this church dated 169½ (something to do with the changing of the calendar), and there is a stone relief, probably Saxon, depicting Christ driving a staff into a serpent's head.

At **West Dean** King Alfred is supposed to have kept court, for Bishop Asser, the North Pembrokeshire man who was Alfred's chronicler, describes meeting the king at 'a town royal that was called Dene'. There is a great court here now (a private house), a splendid little Norman church, a parsonage house which is one of the oldest continuously inhabited houses in the country, made of stone and flint and with a narrow spiral staircase inside its immensely thick walls, deeply splayed lancet windows and great beams. This house is supposed to have been built by monks from Wilmington. West Dean is a little dream of a place, set among great trees and backed by forest. It all feels a shade mummified now – it is hard to imagine the mighty ale-drinkers and mead-swillers of Alfred's court here. The Forestry Commission has planted two thousand acres nearby with a mixture of beech and soft-wood, and some of the houses are occupied by forestry men.

It is very hard to imagine West Dean as a port, but it was. Ships came up the River Cuckmere, and thus the old Dene was on the edge of the estuary.

Cuckmere Haven is a beautiful place on a fine day, with the river running out in the shingle beach, the Seven Sisters towering up along the cliffs towards Beachy Head, the New Cut dug by the River Board and the old course of the river with its meanders coming through the flat valley, and steep chalk downs on both sides.

The winding river, now cut off from the rest of the watery world by the River Board's new works, is used by swans and the rowing crews of Eastbourne School. A Roman burial ground was found not far from the mouth of the river, and also a mammoth's tusk. It is strange to find that the Cuckmere is seldom if ever penetrated by vessels from the sea. At high water springs on a calm day it would be easy to sail in there and it would make a delightful anchorage. I have to admit I have never done so. There is a pub at the bridge which would be the limit of navigation. In medieval times it was a well-used river, and there is a gravestone in the church of Alfriston of John Lower, born 1725, and the epitaph: 'Here lies he who last navigated the dying Cuckmere between Alfriston and the Sea.' The Cuckmere was much used by owlers, as one would expect. There is a record of one very big run of brandy in half-anchors brazenly landed at high noon in June, 1829. Coastguards were established here in 1856. Already in 1824 a voluntary lifeboat had been established here and there were several fishing boats working from the beach. Now there is nothing.

One of the famous 'Flying P's' of Hamburg, the most sophisticated sailing ships ever devised, the *Polynesia*, 985 tons, built in 1874, out of Iquique in Chile sailing home with £30,000 worth of nitrate, went ashore three hundred yards east of Birling Gap in April, 1890. She was lightened into other vessels, tugs got her off the beach but she leaked so badly that they had to beach her again in Cuckmere Haven. Lying in that lonely spot she must have looked a marvellous and incongruous sight. She had to be broken up and was sold for £125.

Hard by the first bridge on the Cuckmere, on the east shore, is a farmhouse with the weird name of Exceat (pronounced *exeet*). In the twelfth century this was a bigger place than West Dean was, and the two places together paid more taxes than the town of Lewes. It had a church, the site of which is now marked with a single stone, and it was, no doubt, as West Dean was, a port. The Black Death of the fourteenth century hit it hard and the French came and finished it off. By 1400 there were only two houses – now there is one.

Following up Cuckmere, in the wake of the medieval shipmen, we come to the village of **Alfriston** (once 'Alfred's Tun', or estate) to port, and here is a magnificent pub, the Star, fifteenth century, and at one time law-breakers could claim sanctuary in it. Whether this fact renders the present landlord immune from the licensing laws has yet to be ascertained. It was originally a hostel for mendicant friars and such, and was no doubt called the Star of Bethlehem. Here also is the first house ever bought by the National Trust (they paid a tenner for it), the Clergy House, a beautiful little timber-framed building and open to the public, there is a Saxon cemetery north-west of the village, in which were found pagan mixed inhumation burials, iron knives, spear heads, shield bosses, conical drinking horns of glass, fifth-century pottery, Roman beads, and a fine brooch. On the downs just west of the village is a long barrow, and near that a round one. The old Market House in Alfriston is now a hotel, has a warren of passages, secret recesses, and was a haunt of smugglers. But the whole village is a museum.

Wilmington, a mile and a half from the river farther up, must have had its staithe on the river for ships to come alongside for it was an important place. There was a priory here, a part of the buildings of which still remain and have been turned into an agricultural museum by the Sussex Archaeological Society. The buildings are beautiful and have great atmosphere. There is a little guide book within and the curator is most helpful and informative. The ox-yokes and other draught-ox equipment are very interesting. Sussex held on to the draught-ox longer than most parts of England. The reason may have been the heavy clays of the Weald, where the ox perhaps was happier than the horse, although the other place where oxen were working within living memory was the Cotswolds, where the land was light.

The Long Man of Wilmington will by now have made himself evident. This gentleman is of uncertain age and ancestry, but many savants put him in the Bronze Age. He is 230 feet high. Sir William Burrell says that the two staffs he is holding were originally a rake and a hoe and that he was a fertility symbol. Others have conjectured that he is Sol the Sun God, pushing apart the gates of darkness. He was cut with great skill, for if seen from a point in the sky he would appear very long and narrow, but seen from the plain in front of him he looks the right shape. Kipling wrote:

> I will go out against the sun
> Where the rolléd scarp retires,
> And the Long Man of Wilmington
> Looks naked towards the Shires.

This whole piece of the Downs around here, around Windover Hill, is peppered with Bronze Age and Neolithic remains.

Back near the river is **Drusilla's Zoo**, a splendid place for the young, founded by Mr Ann, who runs it as he ran it fifty years ago. There is a small collection of rare breeds of farm animals – some Old British White Cattle and some Old Sussex, many smaller breeds of animals including whole villages inhabited by guinea pigs with proper houses (like our houses only smaller), and old farm machinery. There is a restaurant.

Seaford is more interesting than it sounds or looks. Near Fitzgerald Avenue, south-east of the town, a Roman burial ground was excavated in 1934 and found to contain graves of from AD 100 to 300, and there is an Iron Age fort on the promontory a mile south-east of the town. Seaford was a Cinque Port limb of Hastings. The mouth of the River Ouse used to be at Seaford instead of at Newhaven where it now is and Seaford, once a not inconsiderable seaport, suffered from the curse which seemed to have fallen on all the Cinque Ports and their limbs: the creeping death caused by silting up of harbours and shifting of river mouths. Dover is the only Cinque Port that remains a port of any consequence, and besides the original five there were thirty-seven limbs and members.

Seaford anyway is an ancient town and may well have been the Celtic or Ancient British Morcryd (Welsh *mor* – sea and *rhyd* – ford) later the Saxon Mercredesburn. If this is so then it was the site of a great battle between the Saxons and the Welsh in AD 485. Seaford was nearly depopulated by the Black Death, and raided by the French many times. In 1545 a big French fleet led by Admiral Claude d'Annebault landed but were repulsed with heavy losses by the local men led by Sir Nicholas Pelham. This gave rise to what must be the most villainous couplet in the English language:

> What time the French sought to have sackt Sea-ford
> This Pelham did repel 'em backaboord.

There is little of historical interest to see in the town to-day. The church is interesting, with a fifteenth-century tower built inside the Norman nave walls like a morris tube inside a rifle barrel, and there is a house called *The Folly* built over a fine Early English vaulted room. There are some rather stranded-looking hotels on the seafront backed by a kind of no-man's-land of waste ground.

Bishopstone, hard by, has a superb Saxon church. The tiny village has the very *wealthy* look about it of all these small and pretty Sussex villages, but at least what is old and good is being preserved, and not just allowed to fall down and be replaced with rubbish. In 1972 the Brighton and Hove Archaeological Society began excavating on Rookery Hill here, and found traces of occupation from Early Iron Age to Saxon.

One of the most interesting non-existent places I know is **Tide Mills**. This is some flint wall foundations, very hard to read, and a complex system of tide-filled lakes and channels near the coast between Seaford and Newhaven. These pathetic remains are all that is left of what was, in its time, perhaps the greatest flour mill in the world.

The first elements of this mill were built by the Pelhams of Lawton, in 1761, but the mill was gradually developed and enlarged by a subsequent miller named William Catt (whose grave is in Bishopstone churchyard), and when he had finished it it had three huge water wheels – one of them said to have been the biggest water wheel in the world. There was also an enormous windmill towering over it all. This was to provide power when the tide was slack for driving the hoists that loaded and unloaded the ships that came in with corn, and went away with flour and meal.

Of course, a tidal mill can only work when the tide is running, and in the case of this one this was sixteen hours out of the twenty-four. The mill building had five stories and was vast. It was the summit of technological invention before the steam age set in.

In the Napoleonic wars Wellington's armies in the Peninsula were largely supplied with flour from this mill. Wheat was brought down the Ouse from up in the country in barges, ground at the mill, and loaded into ships that came into the considerable harbour that had been built there. In Catt's time (he died in 1853) the mill was producing 1,600 sacks a week. There was a village of thirteen houses for the workers to live in, and in living memory there were 105 people living there. The rent tor a cottage was 2/6d a week.

The mill and village were much painted by artists, and indeed the vast very good-looking mill buildings, the schooners and ketches lying under the lofty gantries, the windmill towering over all, made a superb subject. The mill itself was a masterpiece of mechanical ingenuity, and Catt was invited to tour various European countries to tell millers how to build better mills. It was in its time the most famous flour mill in the world.

In 1875 a great storm flooded the mill and did great damage to it. Catt was dead by then, steam was competing hard against wind and water, and the mill never really recovered. In 1880 the windmill was blown down in a storm. The tide mill went on working until 1884 and then went out of production. In 1901 the great mill building was pulled down, but the 'Mill Village' remained, and went on being a good home for many people. The people who remember living there all still talk of it with great affection and nostalgia. Then in 1939 an almost unbelievable thing happened. Along came the army, its regular officers presumably rendered hysterical because there was a war on, and gave the inhabitants of Mill Village *one hour* to vacate their houses and get all their valuables out. Exactly one hour later, long before the people had been able to salvage more than the bare necessities of their existence, the whole village was blown to pieces. The military reason for this crass action was, of course, that the army commander in the locality had decided to occupy the heights around the flat coastal plain of the Ouse mouth, and use the open plain as a killing ground should the enemy attempt a landing. The village if left standing might have provided cover for the enemy. There was not even a threat of invasion at the time, and the whole thing was wanton, stupid, and quite unnecessary. The inhabitants of the village, who were living so happily there, were rendered homeless and desolate.

Among the other achievements of the remarkable Mr Catt was the creation of the William Pear. This, named after him, is one of the best dessert pears in existence. The first William Pear tree ever grew against the wall of the big mill house, and is depicted in many contemporary paintings. The Army did for it what they did for the village, of course, but its progeny grow all over the world, where pears are possible.

CHAPTER 10

Newhaven to Brighton

IT is thought that there was some sort of a haven at **Newhaven** during Roman times, but it was not until the great storm of 1578 altered the course of the Ouse so that it ran into the sea at **Meeching** and deserted Seaford that Meeching, soon called Newhaven, became a port of any substance. In 1664 John Russell was given a licence to improve the river navigation up to Lewes, and to build piers to protect the harbour, and also forts, and a slaughterhouse.

A subsequent chronology of the development of the harbour would be thus:

1689	Protests that the harbour was choking up.
1730s	Ships of fifty tons dare not enter the choked river.
1731	An Act of Parliament for the repairing of the harbour.
1764	A fort was built on Castle Hill.
1803	A lifeboat installed: the third in England.
1823	Piers built.
1838	East Pier extended a further 130 feet.
1847	A second Harbour Improvement Act.
1860s	The Swing Bridge built.
1864	Battery established on the headland.
1880	Breakwater begun. It was to be 3000 feet long and contain 175,000 tons of concrete.
1891	Breakwater completed.
1914–18	Base for armed trawlers.
1926	Southern Railway took over old Harbour Company.
1939–45	Base for hospital ships.
1964	Car ferry started, and roll-on-roll-off for lorries.
1965	Cresta Marina started.
1973	New bridge begun to replace that of 1930s.

The present traffic of the port, which is expanding and developing fast like most other little ports, is extremely varied. In 1972 there were 158,520 tons of exports and 844,409 tons of imports, all of the most diverse nature. But of the imports were 383,803 tons of marine ballast: in other words sand dredged from the bottom of the sea. This marine ballast dredging is one of the growth-industries of the country. The demand for sand for concrete-mixing seems insatiable,

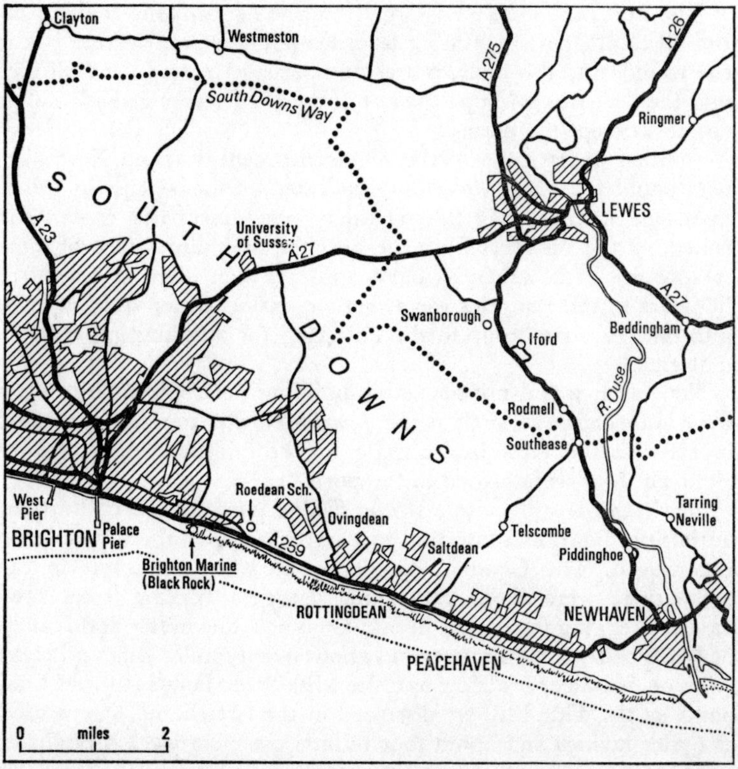

terrestrial supplies are drying up, and so the bottom of the sea must yield its sand. Timber, salt, fertiliser, and pumice from Italy are other bulk imports (the pumice, being light, goes to make breeze-blocks, taking the place of the cinder ash that used to be used for these articles), but the roll-on-roll-off lorries bring in an astonishing variety of commodities.

In the 1880s Newhaven had the Bull Line of sailing ships, a fine fleet of little vessels, most of them built in the port. Among them were the brig *Caledonia* (301 tons), the snow *Commerce* (260), the schooner *Emily Smeed* (299), the brigantine *Fannie C* (316). The *Merchant* (282 tons) and the *Pennine* (296) joined the fleet in the 1880s. The *Merchant* sailed into Constanza in 1877 when the Russo-Turkish War was on and barely escaped being captured by the Russians. Another snow, the *Pennine*, was lost in Yarmouth Roads in 1892 with one survivor.

The Bull Line ships were largely engaged in bringing coal in from the north of England, timber from Scandinavia, and taking oak in the round out, also flour, butter and corn. In 1907 John Bull died and the fleet was sold up: the last of the big fleets of English sailing coasters except the barges.

Another great trade of the nineteenth century from Newhaven was 'boulders'. These were flints, collected off the beaches by fishermen and others. A big fleet of thirty-foot smacks was engaged in collecting the boulders from the beaches, and ships, some of them steam-ships of as much as 8,000 tons burthen, used to carry the boulders to the Potteries (or at least to Runcorn for transhipment into narrow boats to go to the Potteries) for grinding into pottery material.

Newhaven was a not-negligible building port. Quite large ships were launched here, such as the *Jamaica Planter*, 400 tons, launched in 1784 for the West Indies trade. In the mid-nineteenth century eighteen ships were owned in the port.

Newhaven is still quite a strong fishing port, and if the harbour authorities had any sense this part of their responsibility would be encouraged. The Channel Tunnel won't affect *that*. But in the 1880s there were about 120 sailing dredgers working from Newhaven, dredging for oysters in mid-Channel. The oyster and scallop beds are half-way to France, and about twenty miles long and eight miles across. Sleeper's Hole and the Mill Creek Ponds (the old tidal ponds of the Tide Mill we discussed in the last chapter) were used as oyster layings and about four million oysters a week brought in from the sea and laid down on the mud here to fatten. Whether the beds were dredged out, or for whatever reason, in 1873 most of the fleet sailed away to fish from Weymouth, where there were more oysters, but by then ships of the Bull Line were importing seed oysters from Portugal.

Another great fishery was scallops. Large powerful smacks (called on the east coast *slessingers* because they used to dredge off Scheveningen and that was the nearest the east coast men could get to pronouncing that formidable name) used to range all over the Channel and the southern North Sea. One of them, the *Echo*, was a big schooner. This trade was suddenly killed dead by a poison scare. Several big Brixham sailing trawlers fished from here for many years. Newhaven, too, was a big herring port, and the migratory herring fleet used to come in so that there was not room to accommodate another vessel. This, of course, is now finished, the herrings having been exterminated by mid-water trawling.

But there is still a little fleet operating from here, in 1973 nineteen

Above, Netley Abbey, built by Cistercian monks from Beaulieu. *Below,* Langstone. Its great tidal 'harbour' was once famous for oysters.

Above, the Custom House in Poole, built in 1813. *Below,* Freshwater Bay, Isle of Wight.

medium trawlers, five full-time 'punts' mostly trammel fishing, and about twenty 'hooking boats' – in other words boats which take fishing parties out at so much a day.

Newhaven Church is very early Norman and very fine. Note the carvings on the corbels under the tower roof outside. There is a tablet to seventy-five men who were drowned in H.M.S. *Brazen* when, in 1800, that sloop went ashore at the foot of the cliffs at Newhaven in a south-west gale with heavy rain. 'Machines' lowered men down from the cliff-top to try to rescue her crew, but to no avail. This disaster precipitated the provision of the lifeboat here.

At No. 48 Meeching Rise stands a totem pole. In the elegant little public library are three fine ship paintings – the one of the *Sussex Maid*, a real beauty. In Newhaven lived the remarkable Tom Tipper, brewer extraordinary, bon viveur, winner of extravagant bets, and crony of the Prince Regent. His epitaph, in the church, runs thus:

> Reader, with kind regards this Grave survey,
> Nor heedless pass where *Tipper*'s ashes lay;
> Honest he was, ingenious, blunt and kind;
> And dared to do what few do, speak his mind.
> Philosophy and History well he knew,
> Was versed in Physick and in Surgery too,
> The best old Stingo he both brewed and sold;
> Nor did one knavish act to get his Gold.
> He played through Life a varied comic part,
> And knew immortal Hudibras by heart –
> Reader, in real truth such was the man,
> Be better, wiser, laugh more if you can.

Down the river, in what were old oyster layings, Cresta Marina supplies everything – but *everything* – for the modern yachtsman. About five hundred cruisers of one kind or another, mostly plastic, are moored here. There is a floating oiling jetty and a private radio station.

On the strange little island just above the bridge is the yard of R. Lowe and Sons, where they still build fine wooden boats, including many Sussex Beach Yawls in the traditional manner. The Lowes use much elm for planking, for this is the traditional wood for strakes along this coast, but the incidence of Dutch Elm disease looks like removing this source of timber. It would be a tragedy if this killed this excellent enterprise. Maybe they will have to go over to larch, which has been good enough for the Scots and north of England builders for a good many hundred years, although it is not as good as elm. The old slipway down which sailing vessels of old were launched, and which had been lost under the mud, has recently been brought to light again, and is being used for its proper purpose again. The Lowes are the last builders of wooden boats at Newhaven, although there are several yards turning out plastic boats.

The Newhaven lifeboat was installed in 1803, twenty-one years before the founding of the Royal National Lifeboat Institution. In November, 1881, she launched to the brig *Harriet* of Newhaven in a gale and was overturned by a great wave but no lives were lost. In 1904 the first engined lifeboat was sent here for trials. In December, 1909, Joseph Richards, a member of the crew, died from exposure after service. In 1924 Coxswain Richard Payne got a bronze medal for saving the crew of the tug *Richmere*, and in 1930 he got a silver medal for rescuing the crew of the Danish schooner *Mogens Zoch* which had been wrecked at Cuckmere. In 1943 Bill Clark, one of the crew, was washed overboard and drowned on a service.

It is sad that, in the welcome expansion of Newhaven as a port for merchant shipping, the needs of the fishermen are being forgotten. There is a move to drive them out altogether and make them migrate to the new 'Marina' at Brighton. The authorities might do well to remember – lifeboats won't go to sea on their own. Yet.

If we cruise up the Ouse towards Lewes we come first to **Piddinghoe**, where is a staging used for private moorings or the Newhaven Deep Sea Anglers Association and what a nice place it would be to keep a boat and what a nice collection of craft they are too – real boats of wood that look like boats and not floating motor cars. There is a good pub here and a fine church with a winch organ inside it.

As we cruise on up this river we can well imagine what is in fact the case – that it was once a wide estuary, or arm of the sea, going right up to the gate in the Downs at Lewes.

Tarring Neville (to starboard) and Southease, Rodmell, Iford and **Swanborough** to port are splendid little villages all with ancient churches. **Southease** church has faded murals which have an air of simple sturdy faith and great antiquity. The British Museum holds the charter of this place, rewritten in gold on vellum about 1110, giving this church to the Abbey of Hyde, Winchester, by King Eadgar. The tower is round. Of course, this was because the builders couldn't get much freestone – only flint, and you cannot build corners satisfactorily of the latter material. It was written up in Southease Church in 1623:

Every reaper must have allowed him, at the cost of the lord or his farmer, one drinkinge in the morning of bread and cheese, and a dinner at noone consisting of rostemeate and other good victualls, meet for men and women in harvest time, and two drinkinges in the afternoone, one in the middest of their afternoone's work and the other at the ende of their day's work as neede shall require.

But that, of course, was before the Industrial Revolution came to 'put an end to poverty and hunger in the land'.

At **Rodmell** the school, church, and a great farmyard are all mixed up, as such things should be. The great manor house which was near this complex is no more, but its orchards are, and there are mulberry trees, and the cellars of ice houses. Anne Boleyn used to stay here, and it is thought that Elizabeth I may have done, while a child.

Iford has a gem of a little early Norman church, not too mucked about either, near an enormous farmhouse with a fine late barn of flint with frequent brick courses.

Swanborough Manor (but we are miles from the river here – to port over the marshes) has a hall of 1200, altered in the fifteenth century with the addition of a ceiling and an upper floor, and part of a fifteenth-century screen survives.

There is a swing-bridge over the Ouse near Southease, by the way, which is closed to land traffic by the Ouse River Authority, which owns it. There is a tiny wharf here, a slip and windlass, and there are all sorts of signs up saying you mustn't do this and you mustn't do that. If you can get under the bridge, and don't have to ask the Authority to open it for you, note that the tide is very strong. The safest way, if you have the tide with you and have power, is to turn round and drop astern slowly, giving a kick ahead occasionally to keep her straight against the sluicing tide.

And so we come to **Lewes**. The river comes alongside the road just before it. The very steep chalk downs to starboard and the encroaching spur of downs to the west, up which Lewes straggles, make a narrow gap through the steep downs through which river, rail and road are bound to go, and which must have been very defensible in days gone by. Also Lewes was a port, and could easily be one again. Nothing is immutable, including the ascendancy of road transport. Look what happened to the canals.

Sea-going spritsail barges used to come up here in living memory, there is a fine poster owned by Harvey's Brewery of the brewery, in all its glory, with a number of spritties lying in the river before it, having sailed in with malt, and loading barrels of beer for away.

This brewery is still working, thank God, and independent, and producing the most excellent ale.

Lewes was a considerable ship-building town – and not only of small ships either. For example, the *Lewes* was built here in 1753 for the Barbados sugar trade. The yard of Richman and Godlee was building ships up to 1866, when the *Wallands* was launched. The brig *Harriett*, 182 tons, was built *above* the bridge and launched without her gunwales so she should have briggage (i.e. would be able to go under the bridge). The gunwales were added below the bridge. She carried coal to Newhaven for forty years, and was wrecked off the Yorkshire coast on 18th November, 1893. River barges traded far inland from Lewes: in 1790 an Act was passed to open the navigation to **Lindfield**, and this was done by 1812.

As we come to the outskirts of the town we find a slipway, several boats hauled up on a bank or tied to stagings in the water, and the place where eight people were killed on Christmas Eve in 1830 when a great avalanche of snow overwhelmed some houses, and also the Snowdrop Inn.

The first inhabited place at Lewes was probably Mount Caburn, two miles south-east of the present town. In 200 BC this was a large open village, in 100 BC it was a fortified camp and probably a market town, too, for many foreign coins have been found there. The inhabitants had crucibles for bronze-smelting, iron tools, swords, daggers and razors and even safety pins.

In Saxon times Lewes was important, at times the court of the King of Sussex, and it had two mints. The name comes from *hlaew*, Old English for hill. The Normans made it important, too, the Conqueror gave it to William de Warrenne and his wife Gundrada (the latter apparently out of the running now for being the Conqueror's daughter), and the de Warrennes, who were created Earls of Surrey, built a strong castle and a Cluniac priory.

In 1264 Henry III made the Priory his headquarters when at war with the barons led by Simon de Montford. De Montford camped at Fletching on 13th May, marched towards Lewes next day, and the armies clashed on the slopes of the Downs below Mount Harry. The king was defeated and forced to sign a document called the *Mise of Lewes*, held by some historians to have been the beginning of parliamentary government. The king's brother, who called himself 'King of the Romans', fled from the battle and was found hiding in a flour bin and covered in flour.

Thomas Cromwell completely destroyed the enormous priory at the Dissolution, and when the London and Brighton Railway was being built in 1845 a huge cutting was made right through the priory ruins and the coffins of William de Warrenne and his countess brought to light. They are now at Southover Church.

Tom Paine lived at Bull House in Lewes, where he was an excise officer. He was chosen by his fellow officers to petition parliament for more pay, and wrote his first pamphlet, *The Case of the Officers of the Excise*, in doing so. For this he got the sack. He was a respected man in Lewes, though, and served on the council, then called 'The Council of Twelve'. He went to America, where he was one of the leaders of the War of Independence, then to France, where he was a prophet of the French Revolution. He wrote to George Washington: 'A share in two revolutions is living to some purpose.' His writing, notably the *Rights of Man* and the *Age of Reason*, did much to shape the modern world. He was one of the most influential men of the eighteenth century.

There was a heavy crop of martyrs in Lewes during the Marian persecutions, and there are great celebrations in the town every 5th November, when the Pope is burned in effigy instead of Guy Fawkes and blazing tar barrels are, traditionally, rolled down into the river by the members of the several bonfire societies.

As for Lewes to-day it is a beautiful little town, although racked with traffic. All the by-passes in the world don't seem to cure it. There is Anne of Cleves' House, built by Anne from the stone of the priory that her husband had just caused to be pulled down. There is a folk museum in it. There is the Castle, unique (or almost) in having two artificial mounds or mottes. It also has very early masonry – built when most fort-building was in earth or wood, although the towers in the shell keep are thirteenth century and the great barbican, still standing, is fourteenth. The Sussex Archaeological Society has taken over and repaired the castle, and runs a fine small museum in an ancient house over the road. There is a great deal of local interest in it, such as the fine Sussex fire-back with 'Richard Leonard, at Brede Fournis, 1636' cast on it. Lewes was one of the ports of export for the iron industry, and many cannon were smuggled out of the country from here against the orders of the government, which did not particularly want English cannon to be fired at English ships.

The Sussex Weald was the most important iron producing area of the Roman Empire, and by Tudor times this area was the Black Country of the British Isles. In 1543 Ralph Hogg and Peter Baude of Buxted produced the first iron cannon cast in one piece. Baude and Peter van Cullen also made the first hollow shell to be filled with gunpowder and fired at an enemy, a precursor of even more unpleasant things to come. The Armada was defeated by Wealden guns. The iron was smelted with local oak, and the forests were very much depleted. In 1740 ten furnaces in the Weald were producing 1,400 tons of iron a year. Fortunately, the art of smelting with coke was developed in the eighteenth century and the murder of fine trees halted, and the iron industry moved to the coal-rich north and midlands. By 1788 there were only two furnaces left in Sussex. The last of these, at Ashburnham, was extinguished soon after 1810.

Lewes was an iron town later than most places in Sussex owing to the enterprise of John Every, an unemployed iron worker who walked into the town in 1832 and set up a furnace in an old sugar hogshead lined with clay and bound with iron, with a blast created by a fan worked by a horse walking round in a circle. Much of the fine ornamental ironwork in Brighton was cast by Every, who developed his foundry until it was a big place. When the foundry was burnt down he built it up again, on the banks of the Ouse, and called it *The Phoenix Iron Works*. There were four generations of Everys in the business before the last one gave up, and the foundry went to the East Sussex Engineering Company.

Kipling wrote:

> Out of the Weald, the secret Weald
> Men sent in ancient years
> The horseshoes used at Flodden Field
> The arrows of Poitiers.

Back at the coast, **Peacehaven** is the place most people love to hate. I try my best, but really I cannot find anything so terrible about a township knocked up by ex-soldiers after 1918, with their pathetic little gratuities, in order to have somewhere to live away from noise and violence, of which they had presumably had enough. They bought this piece of land on the top of vertical chalk cliffs and built bungalows on it – hundreds and hundreds of them. It is the greatest flowering of bungalow architecture in England. The bungalows go from near the dangerous edge of the cliffs to where they kind of peter out in flat fields inland, along the fascinating muddy ends of unmade roads. The whole place is redolent of the 1920s and thirties. Look at the French cartoons hung up in the Castle Hotel bar. Look at the monument on the cliff-top which serves three purposes, of commemorating George V, of pointing the direction and telling the mileage of various far-away places in his empire, and of marking the Meridian of Greenwich, which passes through this very spot. There *is* a way down to the beach, and the beach is mostly bare chalk or rock, covered at high tide.

No place for making sand castles and not a very safe place for bathing either. But one of the greatest folk singers in our country, Bob Copper, lives at Peacehaven, so it must have something good about it. He sings occasionally at the Central Club, but not often enough, for he sings very well. He wrote the most excellent book: *A Song for every Season.*

Peacehaven thrusts its arms inland towards **Telscombe** which is an exquisite little hamlet in a fold of the Downs, quite beautiful, the medieval farms and dwellings a most piquant contrast to nearby Peacehaven, with its most typical architecture of our time. The present inhabitants of the hamlet seem to have hauled up their drawbridge and lowered their portcullis against the encroaching twentieth century – and who can blame them? But there is no doubt which place looks the more *democratic* (although Telscombe *does* belong to Brighton Corporation).

Now we are coming to the suburbs of the Brighton metropolis, with **Saltdean** and then **Rottingdean**. The latter tries hard to look like an English village it once was, but just *too* much money has been poured into it. The fine church, built by William de Warrenne soon after the Conquest, was copied exactly in the Forest Lawn Cemetry in Los Angeles, rendered so world-famous by Evelyn Waugh's book *The Loved Ones*. They wanted to pull the whole church down and cart it away stone by stone but the parishioners objected. The smock mill is eighteenth century. Rudyard Kipling lived in The Elms and wrote *The Recessional*, *Kim*, *The Just-So Stories*, some of the *Stalky* stories and *Sussex* there. He came in 1896 and left – driven away by sightseers – in 1902, and he moved to Bateman House at Burwash: a house built by one of the Sussex iron founders. Sir Edward Burne Jones, Kipling's uncle, lived at North End House. Angela Thirkell describes this in *Three Houses*. Enid Bagnold (Lady Roderick Jones) still, so far as I know, lives there. There is a doll museum in The Grange and a public library downstairs. The waterfront consists of a gap in the high chalk cliffs – it would be a horrible place to have to run for in bad weather. The French managed to make it, though, in 1377, when they burnt the church with most of the people in it.

There was a small community of longshoremen here in pre-Kipling days. They set forth in a four-oared galley on 15th February, 1859, to board the barque *Biscaya*, of Bilbao, which had been damaged in a collision and abandoned by her crew. They managed to salvage her and get her into port, thus reaping a rich reward. These oared galleys were generally used for the one job, though – and that was to get quickly over to France and come back with some contraband. A fast oared boat could *always* get away from a sailing ship (except in a gale) by rowing dead to windward.

One feels a desperate attempt at Rottingdean to hang on to what little beach there still is under the nearly vertical chalk cliffs. Massive concrete groins stretch out into the sea as though trying to clutch what shingle they can from a short supply. If you see large concrete blocks, apparently pointless, on the beach at low tide between Rottingdean and Brighton – they are all that remains of an eccentric electric railway built by a man named Magnus Volk, the son of a German clockmaker. This was his second electric railway, built in 1896, and dismantled in 1900, when the Corporation decided to build those massive groins. The first was built in 1883 – the first electric railway in the world no less – on Brighton beach. And it is still going strong.

Roedean School, for the politest of polite young ladies, was founded in 1883 by the Misses Lawrence, but the present buildings are 'free Jacobean' of 1898–9. **Ovingdean** has a partly Saxon church.

Now we come to **Black Rock**, and by the time this book is published we should be able to sail into a new harbour there. This is a project of enormous scale and ambition: a vast artificial harbour built out into the open sea, to enclose 120 acres, and accommodate 3,000 yachts. The estimate at the time of writing of this enterprise is just the forty million pounds, but if the estimate has to alter it is never in a downward direction. The whole thing was the idea of Mr Henry Cohen, a local garage owner who couldn't find anywhere to keep his motor boat, but now Westmoreland Properties and EMI Limited are also taking a hand. Taylor Woodrow are building the piers, using a new and obviously highly effective technique. A portal crane, weighing itself over a thousand tons, carries 600-ton concrete caissons, which have been cast ashore and brought within reach of the crane by transfer car, and it lowers them, each one interlocking with the one before, down to the seabed, which has been previously prepared by divers who have laid a concrete foundation there. The caissons are then filled with sand and later a superstructure will be built on them. The West Pier, obviously the critical one because it takes the force of the south-west gales, will be about half a mile long, more or less straight out to sea, and the East Pier will curve round inside it.

The water area of the harbour will be split in two by a wide concrete spine, parallel with the shore. Outside of this the harbour will be tidal; inside it a level will be maintained at all times and the gate will only be opened at high tide. On the concrete spine blocks

Above, the River Avon at Christchurch, before it opens out into the beautiful natural harbour. *Below,* Lymington Harbour, in Hampshire, as it was before it became as popular as it is today.

Above, Old Harry Rocks, north of Swanage, of the same chalk ridge as the Needles are made of. *Below,* St Oswald's Bay in Dorset, where the chalk breaks out to the sea again.

of flats and other superstructure will be built. The harbour will be the centre of a vast complex of things to amuse people. It will probably be the most expensive object purely for the amusement of mankind ever built in Britain. There will be an erection known as a Marinadrome, in which winter will be turned into summer, there will be two five-star hotels, also *boatels* (the marine equivalent of *motels*), and its promoters describe it as Venice Under the Cliffs. I feel it will differ from Venice in several important respects, but a country cannot have too many *harbours*, and if ever – in the non-foreseeable future – it is no longer needed for yachts it will make a splendid working harbour, and will probably last a very long time. Amongst other delights we will be able to learn to sail in it in a computerised dummy boat that never goes on the nasty water at all.

Brighton is now simply a part of London that has become detached from it and drifted to the sea. There was a considerable fishing village here, even before the piece of London got shifted, and local tradition has it that there is a village of six hundred houses under the sea for the sea has encroached here. Certainly in the great gale of 1705 all the houses on the alluvial flats below the cliffs were washed away.

That Brighthelmstone, as it was then called, was more than the 'tiny village' of popular imagination before it became a resort is shown by the fact that it certainly had a brewery, for in 1554 the brewer, Derek Carver, was arrested while at prayer, accused of the sin of being a Protestant, imprisoned for seven months, and then burnt at the stake. And far from being a 'tiny fishing village' it was quite a big fishing town. In 1580 we know that Brighthelmstone had eighty deep-sea fishing vessels, four hundred fishermen and ten thousand nets. Then as now there was no harbour and the fishermen hauled their boats up the beach. We don't know where the landing place of those days was, but we know they used to go as far as Great Yarmouth for the herring voyage.

But big changes were in store for the fishing village. As early as 1660 a doctor in far-away Scarborough, Dr Witte, wrote a book commending the drinking of sea water for the cure of all ills. In 1702 two London doctors, Floyer and Baynard, claimed that this liquid, fortunately in such abundant supply, would cure cancer and consumption, rupture and madness, and further they hinted at other qualities and powers in the following haunting piece of verse:

Cold bathing has this good alone
It makes old John to hug old Joan.
And does fresh kindness yet entail
On wife tasteless, old and stale.

But it was a Lewes practitioner, Dr Richard Russell, who really began to cash in on this readiness of the hypochondriac rich to drink anything provided it tasted horrible enough, and he began to send his patients to Brighthelmstone to drink the sea water, and furthermore to immerse their bodies therein. This, of course, was before England started discharging millions of tons of raw sewage into the open sea every year. The good doctor built himself a house at Brighthelmstone, to be nearer the healing flood, and this house eventually became the Royal Albion Hotel.

And then, in 1783, came the Prince of Wales, later to become Prince Regent. He was then twenty-one, and he stayed with his naughty old uncle, the Duke of Cumberland, who had a house on the Old Steine, and who introduced the young prince to all sorts of pleasures that he had never known in his father's puritanical court. By 1811 George III had already taken complete leave of his senses, and 'Prinny' became Prince Regent and was really able to indulge his gay fancies at Brighton, as it had then come to be called, the place of his delight.

First he commissioned Henry Holland to design for him a Marine Pavilion, then he roped John Nash in, about 1815, to start the building of the Royal Pavilion, which is surely one of the most extraordinary buildings in the world. Whether or not we admire the taste that wished to live in such a fantasia (which anticipated Walt Disney by a hundred years) we cannot but enjoy going and *looking* at it. It has been restored by the Corporation to its full glory and it really is a knock-out. The kitchen is very interesting, and so are the specimen royal menus, particularly when we compare these with the menus of local farm labourers described by William Cobbett, who travelled the area at about that time (and indeed described the Pavilion – comparing it to so many inverted onions) – the people who actually produced the food.

Byron wrote:

> Shut up the King – No the Pavilion,
> Lest it will cost us all another million!

There is much 'artificial stone' in the Pavilion, made (or at least marketed) by the ingenious Eleanor Coade, who invented it. It was a mixture of china clay, felspar, potash and litanium oxide fired at 1,000 degrees centigrade.

Brighton, under the sway of the Prince Regent, became the haunt of half the rakes, bucks, gamblers and pleasure-seekers in the kingdom. It was said that between 1788 and 1823 Brighton was the gayest and most fashionable place in Europe. A disgruntled Welsh journalist, with the *nom-de-plume* of Anthony Pasquin, wrote in the New Brighton Guide of 1796:

Brighton is one of those numerous watering places which beskirt this polluted island and operate as apologies for idleness, sensuality and nearly all the ramifications of social imposture: where the barren seek a stimulus for fecundity; the voluptuary to wash the cobwebs from the interstices of his flaccid anatomy.

. . .The coast is like the greater part of its visitors, bold, saucy, intrusive and dangerous. The bathing machines, even for the ladies, have no awning or covering as at Weymouth, Margate and Scarborough, consequently, they are all severely inspected by the aid of telescopes, not only as they confusedly ascend from the sea, but as they kick and sprawl and flounder about its muddy margin, like so many naiads in flannel smocks.

The Chain Pier, a wonder of its age, was built in 1823, designed by a naval officer, Captain Samuel Brown. It was 350 feet long, supported by chains slung on oak piles driven into the sea. It was destroyed by a gale in December, 1869. The West Pier was opened in 1866 and the Palace Pier in 1901. The Lanes, now all antique dealers (Brighton has become a world centre of the antique trade), are all that remains of the pre-Prince Regent Brighthelmstone, and their layout has probably not changed much since the town (I refuse to call it a village) was rebuilt after the French had burned it down in 1514.

The Brighton Aquarium is justly famous, and the Dolphinarium, in which six sapient animals, so much more human than humans, perform their amazing antics with every appearance of enjoyment (but maybe they would enjoy more being let out to range the wide Atlantic) is a marvel. The Booth Bird Museum, in Dyke Road, is a must for all stuffed-bird lovers.

There are still streets and streets of fine Regency houses in Brighton: was it not the High Temple of that period? The place has a very civilised and urbane air which seems to survive well the pressures of modern pop culture and bingo. Brighton appeals to people who love above all cities. 'Show business' personalities, rich property developers, criminals on the run from London, businessmen accompanied by their secretaries and traditionally signing in at the hotel 'Mr and Mrs Smith', brash young men in sports cars anxious to impress their young ladies with their *savoir faire*, all these love Brighton.

The area to the north of the railway station, though, is exactly like one of the slummier parts of London, indeed you feel when you are there that you are in that great city. The map of this area was used as an example of senseless non-planning, compared with a map of medieval Chichester, by Eric Gill in his autobiography, and given as the reason why Gill embraced Roman Catholicism. But the great Regency terraces are as good as anything in the country.

The new University of Sussex, along the road to Lewes, was designed by Sir Basil Spence, started in 1961, and is expanding at a terrific rate.

Brighton never had a harbour as we have seen, so, of course, in sailing ship days was an open-beach port, as Hastings was, and many other harbourless seaside resorts. But in October, 1807, three collier brigs were lost in one gale, trying to claw themselves off the beach after a shift of wind, and by 1830 insurance rates had become so high for this trade that it was no longer profitable. Maybe with the completion of the new 'yacht harbour' Brighton will become a commercial port. It badly needs something else besides sheer pleasure-seeking to provide variety and interest for resident and visitor alike.

Whatever you do, go and look at the font of St Nicholas's Church.

CHAPTER II

Hove to Arundel

AT Domesday time **Hove** was populated by fourteen villeins, eight bondmen, had land for six ploughs, and six salt pans. Now it is much larger and I can never see where Brighton ends and Hove begins. Modern Hove was the creation of Amon Wilds and Charles Augustus Busby, who published designs for a new town in 1823 to be called Brunswick Town. The town that they planned is still there and architecturally most significant.

Portslade by Sea is nowhere near the sea and is like a chunk of the industrial midlands, cut off from Shoreham Harbour by the railway.

Shoreham is an old and very interesting place, the port at the mouth of the Adur River. The Romans had a port there – Portus Adurni, of which some savants say it is now at the bottom of the sea, others that it was right up the river at Bramber. I think it was at Old Shoreham. But wherever it was we know that the Romans had a road from it to Croydon. People lived there long before the Romans came. The name of the river, Adur, is Welsh, from *Dwr* – water. The foundations of a Roman villa and Roman interments were dug up in 1828 at Lancing, and also many coins, from Claudius to Gallienus, were discovered.

In 477, after the Romans had had the sense to go back to their own country, the Saxon Ella and his three sons Cymen, Wenceling or Wlencing, and Cissa, with their merry men, landed at Kynor, West Wittering, and fought a great battle with the Welsh on Slonk Hill, which is just behind Shoreham. Slonk means slaughter, and is still used in parts of Sussex to mean the slaughter of animals. A new housing estate of great banality spreads out over the battlefield.

Old Shoreham became the main Saxon settlement, and the fine church there has many Saxon elements in it: the nave is a good example of the architecture of this period. It is an astonishing building. The waters of the harbour once washed right up to its walls, as witness earth retaining walls of the old time to restrain them from going any farther.

After the Normans arrived the whole area was given over to one

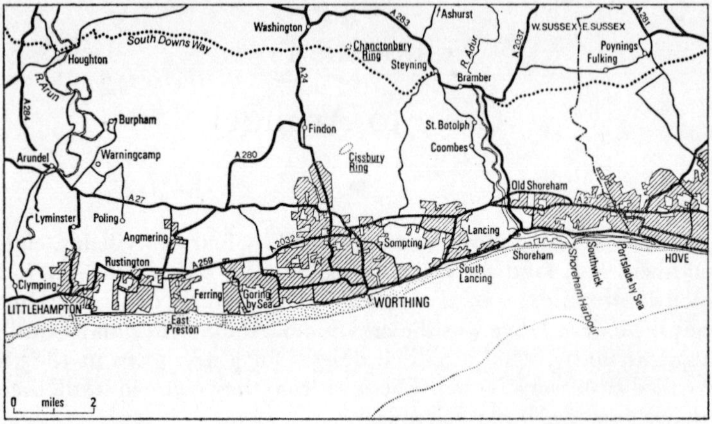

of the Conqueror's robber barons, William de Braose, the man who went far towards settling what no doubt was called 'the Welsh problem' by slaughtering the flower of the young men of Gwent in the banqueting hall of Abergavenny Castle, to which they had come as his guests – were therefore disarmed and no doubt drunk. Their compatriots partially avenged them by attacking and burning Abergavenny Castle but unfortunately only managed to wound de Braose. A later de Braose fell from favour with King John and had to flee to France as an outlaw, where he eked out the rest of his miserable life by begging while his wife, Maud de Valerie, was starved to death by the king in one of his dungeons at Windsor. Before all this happened, though, Richard I and his brother John sailed from Shoreham for Dieppe, returned to the same port from a crusade aboard a ship called *Trench-le-Mer* commanded by a Shoreham man whose name was Alan Trenchmere. John landed here on 25th May, 1199, to seize the crown, shortly after leaving with de Braose (not yet fallen from grace) for France to attack his half-brother Prince Arthur.

It has always seemed strange to me that Shoreham was not selected as one of the Cinque Ports, because it always had a much better harbour than some of the others. But it was always of naval significance. At the Siege of Calais in 1346 twenty-six ships sailed from Shoreham, with 329 men, which was a bigger force than London, Bristol, Southampton or Dover. In the fourteenth century there was lively piratical activity from here: a typical prize that got recorded had in her belly thirty-five bales of woad, six bales of alum, four cases of soap, three tons of flax and fourteen reams of paper: total value: £140.

We are told that in 1625 Shoreham was a big privateering port. By then there was much shipbuilding, as one would expect in a fine natural harbour down-stream from the great oak forests of Sussex. It is interesting that in 1619 one Robert Tranckmore – obviously a descendant of the master of the *Trench-le-Mer*, which brought the Lion Heart back from the Crusades – agreed to build ships for the East India Company, and he built five of 300 tons, four of 200, one of 180, one of 150 and one of 140. In 1628 there were contracts for a pinnace for the government (with ten guns on two decks) and then a long string of fourth, fifth and sixth raters. At least thirty warships were built here. Defoe said that shipbuilding was the chief trade of Shoreham.

In 1874 161 ships, barques and brigantines were owned in Shoreham, and of these eighty-eight were Shoreham-built. And in 1909 not *one* Shoreham-owned ship was still sailing the oceans! The chief nineteenth-century builders were James Britton Balley at the Old Ship Yard from 1838 to 1863, John May and T. Thwaites building at Kingston from 1838 to 1871, Dyer and Son at the Old Yard from 1875 to 1878, and Shuttleworth built at Southwick. Dyer launched the *Osman Pacha* in 1878: the last square-rigger to be built at Shoreham. She went missing in the Indian Ocean in 1892: her captain was notorious as a driver, and perhaps he drove her a little too hard. May and Thwaites built the famous brig *George* in 1839. She reigned until 1922 when she was wrecked off Hornsea in Lincolnshire.

Edward Lucas of Southwick built up a fleet of six sailing ships at Shoreham. In 1852 he handed the fleet over to his son-in-law Robert Penney from Poole, who increased the fleet and by 1870 was building iron sailing ships, and in the late seventies was introducing steam into the fleet. But to the last, Shoreham sail competed well with steam: only when crews for the sailing ships became impossible to obtain did canvas yield to steam. The Penney Line was trading until World War II, and the company is still in business as ship brokers and wharfingers, under the name of R. H. Penney and Sons, Ltd. The story of Shoreham shipping, and it is a fascinating one, is fully told in that fine book: *South Eastern Sail*, Bouquet.

A most peculiar revival of Shoreham shipbuilding occurred in the First World War, when concrete barges of 1,000 tons each were built there, and in 1917 two enormous 'mystery ships' were built by the Royal Engineers. These, which we shall discuss more fully when we come to the Isle of Wight, were intended to be mid-

Channel forts supporting an anti-submarine net, but the war was over before they could be used. One was broken up, and its shattered remains can still be found on the west side of the Adur, among huge rubbish dumps in which antique-bottle enthusiasts scratch about for their strange quarry; the other was towed away, on Sunday, 12th September, 1920, and sunk in its present position to guard the Spithead Channel. It is now called the Nab Tower.

The history of the harbour at Shoreham is made up of the old story of the fight against the eastward drift of shingle along this coast. In Roman and Saxon and medieval times there is no doubt but that the Adur Valley from Bramber to the sea was flooded at high water, and we know that Bramber itself was a port. But slowly the shingle drove eastward from the Lancing side, forcing the river to debouch ever farther towards the east until by 1759 it came out into the sea at Aldrington. It has been calculated that the mouth of the river moved eastward at a rate of about 118 feet per annum. The result of this was progressive silting-up of the old harbour, because the river found it harder and harder to carry its burden of sediments to the sea.

In 1760 no less than fifty-one 'commissioners' were appointed to 'cut a new cut through the sea-beach opposite Kingston and to make and maintain a new entrance'. In spite of their large number these august gentlemen proved quite ineffective. Perhaps if each one had taken to a spade, and not the rostrum, the result would have been different. But the harbour continued to silt up despite all the words poured out by the worthy commissioners. An Act of Parliament of 1816 caused some actual work to be done, though, and by 1821 the Kingston entrance was reopened and ships could get through it again. After this there was mounting activity. There was even a scheme to dig a canal to London by joining the Adur and the Arun, but this was never completed. But in 1826 the Middle Pier was built out into the harbour from the North Bank. This was done to keep the two ebbs that met there from meeting and thus to force them to go on out to sea and there deposit their silt. The elegant little lighthouse that still stands near the harbour entrance was built in 1846. The Southwick Canal, or Long Dock, from Southwick up to Aldrington Basin was opened on 20th February, 1855, and it was this event that was the making of Shoreham Harbour as we see it to-day. This was made by locking the ancient route of the river. Along this Long Dock the London, Brighton and South Coast Railway built their big wharf, and an existing trade in fruit and eggs from Havre, Honfleur, Caen, etc., and also cheese, cattle, wine and salt, grew to big proportions, and even now a great deal of wine is imported.

In 1933 the Prince George Lock, 240 feet long, was opened to admit big colliers to the power station, in 1957 more big improvements were made, and the Prince Philip Lock built which admits ships of up to 374 feet by 57 foot beam, and of up to 4,500 tons.

The four colliers belonging to the Central Electricity Generating Board which come into Shoreham are 340 feet long and 44 feet beam. It takes them three tides (about thirty-six hours) to get from the Tyne to Shoreham, and each ship can be discharged of her 3,400 tons of coal in about nine and a half hours, or one tide. But such is the appetite of the power station that more ships have to be called in from outside to help the Shoreham fleet. *Brighton B* Power Station also uses 280,000 gallons of sea water per minute. This is generally redischarged into the sea, but if the Harbourmaster wishes to raise the level of water in the dock, after locking has depleted it, the cooling water is pumped into the Dock instead. *Brighton B* is the largest coal-burning power station on the south coast. A tunnel, ninety feet below the bed of the harbour, carries cables to the mainland from what is almost an island, and it is interesting that when the shafts were driven down to make this tunnel they had to go through a layer of lignite, or low-grade coal, called *stromboli*, which we shall meet again farther west. This stuff (a sort of coaly-shale) derives its name from the island off Italy, because it is inflammable and Stromboli has an active volcano! It was once used as a medicine by the ingenious Dr Russell who, we have seen, did much to found Brighton as a health resort.

Shoreham, unencumbered by the great passenger traffic of the ports farther east, has been able to develop vigorously as a cargo port. In 1972 the total traffic exceeded three and a quarter million tonnes, and 3,037 ships came into the port. Oil made up 700,000 tonnes of this, there were a million tonnes of sea-dredged sand for concrete-making, and 48,000 tonnes of *pumice* – from the very island of Stromboli from which the lignite derived its name. This porous rock, being very light, is used for making light-weight breeze-blocks, in default of the coke-clinker that is no longer forthcoming. That huge carcase of a building being pulled down near the two power stations is the old gas-works which once produced the coke-clinker. And all the old traffics that the port used to handle in days gone by, such as fruit, vegetables, wines and spirits, all still come in in quantity, and most of this country's import of sherry.

Except for the coal, wine and oil, most of the bulk cargoes are landed in the tidal part of the port, in the Western Arm. The ships dry out and lie apparently higgledy-piggledy against a variety of wharfs. There is plenty of room amid all this commercial activity for small boats, and the club houses of the Sussex Yacht Club (founded 1892) and the Sussex Motor Yacht Club are there. Personally I find Shoreham a very sympathetic place, and far prefer it to many a posher seaside resort. The locked Eastern Arm, sometimes called the Southwick Canal, seems, except for colliers and tankers, underused, for there is miles of it. You can charter a dinghy from Mr Hurlock, at Fishergate, and row yourself up and down it. Mr Hurlock is the last of at least three generations of boat builders. One feels that there must once have been a big population of shipbuilders, boatmen, watermen, fishermen and hovellers at Shoreham in sailing ship days, and they are gone with very little trace. Mr Hurlock is a lone survivor on his part of the waterfront.

A strange long footbridge (opened 3rd February, 1921) leads over to **Shoreham Beach**, where spread bungalows and other 'development'. There were bungalows there before the Second World War but the Army blew 'em all up to make a killing ground. The council paid for them to be built again when the war was over, and now there is an ambitious housing development going on. At the west end of the West Arm of the harbour is a fascinating mud flat, just covered at high water, where is a floating village of people living in house boats of every size and shape, and long may they remain undisturbed by people who want the last man on Earth to move into a council house identical with those of all the others. The individuality can flower in such strange situations as in a converted M.T.B. on the Shoreham mud flats. The old sailing barge *Primrose* lies here, one of Farmer Wrinch's fleet of stacky barges from Shotley, in Suffolk. It is important that such links with a simpler and more robust past should be preserved. For a Suffolk man to stumble upon such a little ship, unexpectedly, in what is to him a foreign land, brings a shock of delight. The present writer knew her skipper.

The town of **New Shoreham**, which was new in Norman times, still has unity and shape, and the feel of an old sailing ship port about it. The church of St Nicholas de Haura (meaning 'of the harbour') is quite splendid, great Norman central tower and transept, a choir of the most vigorous Norman–Early English Transitional replacing the Norman apse. Really a most exciting building. We have mentioned the partly-Saxon church of Old Shoreham at the beginning of our dissertations on Shoreham. There is a most excellent guide to both of these exceptionally interesting buildings within them. The Marlipins is a medieval building, possibly once a customs house, which houses now a museum. The pub next door to it (a very fine unspoilt pub by the way) has within it a splendid recruiting poster, calling upon 'The Royal Tars of Old England' to report to Lieutenant W. I. Stephen, at his 'Rendeyvous, Shoreham, where they will be allowed to enter any SHIP OF WAR . . . Let us, who are Englishmen, protect and defend our good King and Country against the Attempts of all Republicans and Levellers, and against the designs of our Natural Enemies, who intend this year to invade Old England, our happy Country, to murder our gracious King as they have done *their own*, to make WHORES of our Wives and Daughters, to rob us of our Property, and teach us nothing but *the damned Art of murdering one another*! REPAIR! All who have good Hearts, who love their King, their Country, and Religion, who hate the FRENCH, and damn the POPE – to Lieutenant Stephen.'

One bizarre episode in the history of Shoreham was the royal escape. On 13th October, 1651, six weeks after his defeat at the Battle of Worcester, the man who later became Charles II, having failed to find a ship to take him to France from Lyme Regis, came, in disguise, to Brighthelmstone in the company of his friend Lord Wilmot and put up at the George Inn. The whole country was out looking for him and there was a price of £1,000 on his head. The two fugitives met up with a man named Nicholas Tettersell, master and owner of the collier brig *Surprise*, and told him they were two gentlemen wishing to escape from England because they were wanted for having fought a duel. Captain Tettersell recognised the king, and demanded more money for the job and also made them insure his ship for £200. Eventually a bargain was struck for £60 for the passage, the prince hardly being in a position to argue. The *Surprise* was aground on the mud at Shoreham, as many a good ship has been before and since, and so the escapers had to wait hidden aboard with what patience they could muster until the tide came and floated them off. The passage was made and the king put ashore by small boat at Fécamp in Normandy.

After the Restoration Tettersell sailed up the Thames in the *Surprise*, having renamed her *The Royal Escape*, flying the Royal Standard and much other bunting. He made himself known to the king, who rewarded him by giving him a commission in the Royal Navy and taking his little ship on the strength. He was dismissed the service in 1667 for some reason unknown, and returned to the small town of Brighthelmstone, where he was made High Constable and was, from all accounts, a blessed nuisance to his fellow townsmen until his death. He is buried in Brighton Parish Church of St

Nicholas under an epitaph so fatuously and extravagantly adulatory that it can only be supposed he made it up himself.

A pleasant side issue of all this is that the mate of the *Surprise* at the time of the escape, Thomas Craven, in spite of his name and unlike his master craving nothing for himself, did only crave that the king release many poor Quakers and other Dissenters, including one John Bunyan, from durance. The new king, being a reasonable chap and not a fanatic, agreed, and many poor people were let free from unnecessary imprisonment.

Another bizarre story connected with Shoreham was that on 7th March, 1889, a French oyster smack, out of le Havre but bound for Shoreham with a load of oysters, sighted an enormous sailing ship suddenly towering towards her out of the mist. This proved to be the *Vandalia*, of St John, New Brunswick. Her bows were seriously damaged and she had nobody on board: the only living thing the smacksmen found was a dog. The Frenchmen were unable to salvage her, and she sailed herself ashore near the West Pier at Shoreham, broke up, and 1,200 barrels of oil were washed out of her. It was later discovered that she had collided with the *Duke of Buccleuch*, a steamer of Barrow, and the fifty-three men of her crew were never seen again.

As for fisheries, Shoreham is strangely without much of a fishing fleet. Considering what a good harbour it is (although, of course, it *is* tidal – boats can only get in and out a few hours each side of low water) and what a huge market there is in nearby Brighton, it is a wonder that there is not a stronger fleet. In the 1850s upwards of a hundred smacks fished from the port, most of them dredging for oysters and scallops in the mid-Channel beds. During one year 20,000 *tons* of oysters were sent from Shoreham by rail. We are left to wonder what effect this had on the growth of population in the inland areas where they were consumed. But steam dredgers came along at the turn of the century, knocked the sailormen out, and in turn destroyed the beds and the industry by over-fishing. An interesting sidelight on the oyster fishery was the fact that the smack *John and Mary* was caught by the customs with no less than seventy-three tubs of brandy hidden under her oysters.

Steam packets started sailing from Shoreham to Dieppe, le Havre and Jersey, but these all had to go to Newhaven and Littlehampton in the First World War and never returned. This war did Shoreham immense harm as a port. And, of course, such a tidal port as Shoreham is would not make a good passenger port unless intensive dredging were undertaken so ships could come and go at low water.

If we cruise on up the Adur, under the Norfolk Bridge and the

Railway Bridge, we see ahead of us the old Toll Bridge, a thing of considerable beauty and now not used for motor traffic. Until we get quite close to it we may imagine that no vessel can get underneath it, so closely placed are its piers, but fear not, one can. To starboard on the mud near it are some old Adur River Barges, used not so very long ago for carrying cement down from the Bramber Cement Works. One of them repays inspection, for she has horizontal frames and vertical strakes – a very unusual form of construction.

Up-stream **Bramber** looms up to port, and here is a castle built by the reprehensible William de Braose, who, and whose family, we are told, terrorised the whole countryside, the people of which could get no redress from their tyranny. In the Civil War the castle was taken by the Parliamentary troops and dismantled (a good fate for it) but it is still worth looking at. Down in the village is a fifteenth-century house called St Mary's, which once belonged to the Knights Templar. It is opened in the summer, and is a fine example of timber-framing.

St Nicholas Church at Bramber was built as a chapel for secular priests. Edward the Confessor had given the parish of Bramber to the monks of Fécamp, one of the acts of stupidity of this too-pious man which led up to the Norman conquest: one of the several examples of the English kings giving an inch and then having taken a mile. After the Conquest de Braose built a rival college of Benedictines near his new castle, it is said in order to break the monopoly of Fécamp. This church we are looking at was its church. At that time, it must be remembered, Adur was a wide estuary, and ships could come right up under the walls of the castle. Camden, writing in Elizabeth I's time, said that 'in former times' the river was wont to carry ships in full sail up as far as Bramber, so that we may assume that when he wrote it did not. There is very little left now to show that Bramber was once a port.

Among other delights of Bramber, which in summer is infested with tourists and absolutely *persecuted* by the A 283, is the world's only *Smokiana.* This is a museum containing 22,000 exhibits connected with that disgusting habit, puffing the gaseous wastes of ignited tobacco.

Steyning, a mile farther up, is a fascinating little town. This again, with Bramber, provided one of the *causæ belli* for William of Normandy's invasion, for it was also given by the Confessor to the Abbey of Fécamp, and when Harold took it away it provided William with a holy excuse. The Church of St Andrew here is one of the choicest Norman churches in the county. But we could have had the Normans' architecture without the Normans. In the Saxon church which preceded the Norman one St Cuthman and King Ethelwulf were buried, the latter in 858 but his remains were later removed to Winchester. He was the father of Alfred who burnt the cakes. As for the saint – Steyning was once called Cuthman's Port.

The river was once navigable for many miles upstream, and we can still proceed a long way in a small boat. If you are puzzled by those strange ornamental towers to port, that rise up near the road to Ashurst – they are the silage towers of Wappingham Farm – the only ornamental silage towers known to this writer. Further, the man who had them built is the descendant of a man who went to Canada to build the Canadian Pacific Railway and an Indian chief's daughter that this engineer married, in the way of business some people have murmured, for the marriage did give him a right of way through his father-in-law's territory. Better than shooting, anyway.

Coming back down-stream is **St Botolph**, a tiny church on the west bank, which used to be the chapel of the monk whose charitable duty it was to care for a bridge over this part of the river. Floods of 1530 impoverished the little foundation and now no trace of a bridge remains. This bridge is supposed to have been originally built by the Romans as part of their Tin Road, along which tin was brought from Cornwall for shipment from Pevensey for Gaul. The church used to be called St Peter de Vetere Ponte, or St Peter of the Old Bridge. The bridge must either have been more in the nature of a causeway than a bridge, with a gap in the middle to allow ships to pass, bridged either by a floating or swinging section, or else a ferry. There are still Saxon elements in this strange lonely little church.

Coombes, just downstream and also on the west bank, has some perfectly amazing wall paintings of perhaps very early twelfth century.

Farther downstream we see (as we have seen for a long time) the vast chapel of **Lancing** College rearing up on the hill to starboard. We can hardly go into all this now, and there is plenty of literature in the chapel (which is open) to enlighten the uninitiated. The college was one of the Woodard Schools, progressive in 1868 no doubt but it does not seem to have changed much. Evelyn Waugh describes life there very thoroughly in his autobiography. Lancing is obviously good for boys who like plenty of organised religion and plenty of organised sport.

In the tidal water of the river here there is good angling for bass, plaice, eel, etc., and farther down, near saltier water, you may catch a ling or two also.

Lancing may have been named for Wlencing, who as we saw

landed at West Wittering in 477 with his father and two brothers, one of the first of the English. In the village is a church built in 1120, but substantially rebuilt between 1280 and 1300.

There is a very early airport just south of Lancing College. As early as 1910, when after all not so many flying machines were roaring about over our heads, a little machine called *The Mayfly*, belonging to H. Pifford, a Lancing Old Boy, used to hop about here, and on 6th March, 1911, O. C. Mornison flew from Hove to this field in seven minutes. In Old Shoreham Church, by the way, are graves of airmen killed while flying from this field in the Second World War.

Sompting has one of the finest pieces of Saxon building left in England in its church tower. The helm roof of the pure Saxon tower is unique in England, and there is carved Saxon stone inside the church. In 1154 the church was granted to the Knights Templar, and they pulled down the church except for this Saxon tower and built their own chapel on the south side of it. When they were suppressed the church went to the Knights of St John and they built a chapel in the fourteenth century, but this is now a ruin.

And so we come to the sunny town of **Worthing**, in the station waiting-room of which Ernest was found in a handbag in Wilde's *The Importance of Being Ernest*. It was Princess Amelia, the Prince Regent's younger sister, who boosted Worthing by her patronage as her brother did Brighton, but in altogether a less boisterous fashion. The place was a tiny fishing village (a part of **Broadwater**) before the end of the eighteenth century. But it is strange how ancient fishing communities manage to survive although surrounded and engulfed by quite alien commuter paradises, and such has happened at Worthing. There are still eight or nine full-time fishermen fishing from the open beach in tiny open boats, shooting trammel nets mostly about three miles from shore. They catch the usual flat fish and whiting, some cod nowadays in winter, and some put out pots for lobsters in summer. They sell their fish retail from stalls along the front, near their boats. The shingle beach gives way to flat sand at low water at Worthing, and in settled weather the fishermen are inclined to anchor their boats off instead of bothering to pull them up, and wade out to them in thigh boots. There was once a fleet of big luggers here but they have all disappeared. The fishermen are much hampered by the weather, for this coast is quite exposed, and it is often too rough to launch their little boats. They don't bother with angling parties – too much Board of Trade rigmarole.

There is a good museum in Worthing, with plenty of stuff from the ancient sites on the Downs inland. At **Cissbury Ring**, about four miles inland, there is an Early Iron Age fort, about 250 BC, and also filled-in flint mines of about 2000 BC (Neolithic). Cissbury was refortified in late Roman times against the Saxon pirates. At **Harrow Hill**, about three miles west of **Findon**, there is a small hill fort of about 500 BC and a group of flint mines. This area around Findon has been called 'The Sheffield of the Flint Industry', and even now some of the Downland about there is sprinkled with flint-chippings. These mines were formed by the sinking of vertical shafts down through the chalk, the chalk being picked out with red deer antlers, to the layer of big flints some distance down. Lateral tunnels were then driven out into this, but leaving pillars of flint to support the roof. Ultimately the tunnels were holed through from shaft to shaft, thus providing ventilation. The flints, hauled to the surface, were shaped into implements and exported to people all over Britain. A fine example of these mines, re-excavated and glassed in from the weather, can be seen near Brandon in Suffolk, where is another 'Sheffield'.

A more modern industry of Worthing is the glasshouse industry, for here has grown up a kind of Lea-Valley-by-the-Sea. There is an important mushroom research station near **Rustington**. **Ferring** has a fossilised old village within its modern residential area like a pearl in an oyster, and has musical instruments of its old church band in a glass case in its old church. The people should take them out and play them. **Angmering** still looks like a village and has a fine church and a Roman villa: a place of almost the scale of Fishbourne. As for the coast along this stretch, there are large and sombre wealthy residential areas with notices telling you to keep out, although why you should want to go there I cannot think.

Littlehampton is a fine little port, which still accommodates on average a ship a day, and imports a lot of the ubiquitous sea-ballast (sand dredged from the bottom of the sea for concrete mixing), besides timber, stone, and pumice from Italy. It is an efficient little port with moderate charges, good labour relations, and its trade is increasing: not decreasing as is the trade of the super-ports such as Liverpool and London. There are two small 'marinas', it is a good place to keep a yacht, and over five hundred of them are moored there or stored there during the winter time.

The harbour used to have the usual south coast trouble: it was always silting up. The river Arun broke out into the sea until the latter part of the fifteenth century at Lancing, ten miles to the east of where it is now. It had been pushed eastward by the eastward drift until it joined the mouth of the Adur. But the Adur pushed eastward on to Hove, and the Arun drew back progressively westward, finding new outlets at Worthing, Goring and Ferring, and, about 1500, it broke out at Littlehampton. Palmer's map of 1587 shows it approximately where it is now.

But new cuts had to be made through the shingle in 1600, 1628, 1657, and in 1715 the Mayor, Aldermen, Burgesses and inhabitants of Arundel (Littlehampton was in those days just the out-port of Arundel) petitioned Parliament for an Act enabling them to charge harbour dues, and thus raise money to improve their harbour. In 1732 the Littlehampton Harbour Act was passed, which authorised the building of piers and the cutting of a channel. In 1736 the harbour was opened with seven feet at medium tides and nine on the top of springs.

In 1739 a fort with seven guns was commissioned, to keep off privateers.

When the port was known simply as the Port of Arundel, and Littlehampton was merely the mouth of the river where the ships came in, not many records of shipping were made; but we know that in 1572 four ships were registered in the Port, one of them of a hundred tons, and that in 1643 dues were charged on: playing cards, cod fish, glass, wrought iron, oysters, mill stones, and French and Spanish wine. In 1675 Ogilvy, in his *Britannia Depicta*, wrote of Arundel having a fine wooden bridge, ships of a hundred tons coming up to it, and that several ships of war had been built there.

The Arun shared in the canal mania of the late eighteenth and early nineteenth centuries, and if the railways had not come along and pipped it it might have become an important artery. In May, 1785, came the Arun Navigation Act to improve the river above Houghton Bridge. But long before this men had been concerned about improving the river for navigation. As early as 1544 Henry Fitzalan came to the Earldom of Arundel, and set about improving the river navigation and preventing flooding. He set in motion what was a very big undertaking for his day. The river was made navigable as far inland as Pallingham, for the transport of timber outward to the sea.

There were twenty-nine weirs on the river between Houghton and Pallingham, which must have been a terrible hindrance to navigation. At that early date the pound lock had not been introduced into England (although Leonardo da Vinci had designed it on paper and maybe the Chinese had used it for a few thousand years), so these weirs would have been 'flash weirs'. A flash weir was a single water gate which impounded the water in the stretch above it so that this would be deep enough to float a barge. When a barge wanted to get down through the gate, the gate was simply allowed to open and the barge shot through like a canoe shooting a rapid. The gate then had to be hauled shut again against the weight of the water. When a barge wanted to go *up* through the gate, the gate was opened and the barge simply hauled up against the wall of water by the brute force of horses or windlasses. Whenever the gate was opened, of course, much water was lost from the pound above, and barges would have to wait until the level built up again. In times of drought this might take many days. Which partly explains why river bargemen were, on the whole, a hard drinking lot. It is also a measure of the extreme importance of water transport, in a land with virtually no good roads, that people went to all this trouble at all.

But the pound lock came, and enabled barges and boats to go up or down regardless, without wasting water, and in 1794 the Earl of Egrement spent £13,300 on making the West Rother, a tributary of the Arun, navigable to Petworth so as to carry coal in and lime, cordwood, timber, and 'Petworth Marble' out. Then in 1815 came a bill for the making of a very ambitious waterway indeed. W. G. Gates, in his *Illustrated History of Portsmouth* of 1900, wrote: 'Some sanguine spirits prophesied that half the trade of London' would pass along the canal about to be made, for it was to join London with Portsmouth and the English Channel. And it did too, but it was not a commercial success. A canal was dug from the River Arun at Ford to Chichester Harbour, and then there was a marked channel through the mud flats to Portsea Island and a canal thereon to Portsmouth. A canal was then dug all the way from the Arun to the River Wey, and that was made navigable to the Thames and thence to London. The hope was that ships bound for London would discharge their cargoes into barges at Portsmouth, thus saving themselves the tedious voyage around the Forelands of Kent, and the hazards of the Goodwins, and that the barges should deliver the cargoes to the capital and come back with goods for outward-bound ships.

Enormous enthusiasm was generated – people stampeded trying to buy shares. In a few days £20,000 had been raised in the city of Portsmouth alone. In 1817 came the Portsmouth and Arundel Canal Act and by then £101,250 had been subscribed to the company. On 20th August, 1818, John Williams, one of the promoters, cut the first sod at Portsmouth, and promptly retired to the Ship and Anchor Inn for a rest and a well-earned dram. By 9th September, 1822, the Portsea Canal was opened, and it had a big well out of which water had to be pumped to keep up a level.

In June, 1823, a barge got through – from Portsmouth to London! It took the first barge to come the other way three days to get from London to Chichester, and she reached Portsmouth four days after leaving the capital. From Portsmouth to London by waterway was 116 miles. The voyage round by sea was 216 miles.

But alas, in spite of the shorter distance, independence of the weather, and all the other advantages, it still cost never less than twenty-two and sixpence a ton by canal, compared with from ten shillings to sixteen shillings by the sea route. These figures were enough to show that the canal was doomed. The canal could never compete with the sea, and there was, furthermore, not enough traffic to be picked up along the way in the hinterland through which the waterway passed to make it pay. The waterway struggled on until 1894, simply because it was so much trouble to close it, and for years one old character used to ply along it with a narrow boat hauled by an old horse, simply picking up what traffic he could to give him a living. But in 1894 the Canal Company was wound up. Goldsmith Avenue, in Portsmouth, runs along the old bed of the Portsea Canal, and traces of the Ford Branch can be seen in the countryside west of Ford. And now we see the Wey and Arun Canal Society busily engaged in trying to open it all up again, and very good luck to them, too.

But, after these diversions up-stream, back to Littlehampton again. The Arun View Hotel, which is a fine place to stay incidentally, has written up on the wall outside: 'HEADQUARTERS OF THE LITTLEHAMPTON TOPE CLUB' and, as if this were not enough glory, *also* 'HEADQUARTERS OF THE TOPE CLUB OF LITTLEHAMPTON'. Actually, however, the headquarters of these two august bodies have moved down to the Britannia, nearer the sea. Littlehampton has fine sands, and is a fine little resort. There is an inflatable inshore rescue craft there.

As for **Arundel**, which we have already discussed as a port, for it was indissolubly tied up with Littlehampton, everyone with a boat which will go under the Ford railway bridge will wish to go there. There is eleven feet of briggage under this bridge at high water springs and twenty-one feet at L.W.S., but then there is only about three feet of water. With a small boat you can get on to Houghton, and with great care even to Pulborough. Boats can be hired at Arundel for the voyage, and there is a regular motor boat service for passengers, in the summer, between Littlehampton and Arundel, and there are day trips beyond Arundel. And for God's sake don't miss **Burpham**, a beautiful little place. It is sad that we can no longer get right through to the Wey and to the Thames.

There is an engaging little book called *The Thames to the Solent by Canal and Sea, or the Log of the Una Boat 'Caprice'*, by an Edwardian gentleman who made the voyage – J. B. Dashwood.

For Arundel itself, it is the most resolutely feudal place in the south of England. Even the medieval religion has been retained there. The castle descends from one built by the Saxons. Bevis the Giant threw an axe from Bevis's Tower and asked to be buried where it fell. He had a horse called *Hirondelle,* hence the name Arundel, thus the unlikely legend. King Alfred probably built the castle, the Conqueror gave it to Roger de Montgomery, one of his divisional commanders at Hastings. The Inner Gateway of the present castle is from Montgomery's time. There is a fine Norman keep, but the castle got very knocked about by Sir William Waller and his Parliamentary forces when they took it from the Royalists just before Christmas, 1642, and again when it was recaptured by the Royalists under Lord Hopton because they were able to creep over the frozen river in the severe winter of 1643, and again when Waller took it back in January, 1644, and thereafter thoroughly dismantled it, that really there isn't much left of it. Not to worry – the whole vast edifice was built again in the eighteenth and nineteenth centuries in a most resolutely castle-like fashion. It is comparable with Bamburgh, in Northumberland.

The Dukes of Norfolk, Earl Marshals of England, got it in the sixteenth century and have hung on to it ever since. The present duke, adept at stage-managing coronations and all that, has deserted the castle itself for a fine mansion that he has had built for himself in the grounds. In the castle there are fine Holbeins, Gainsboroughs and Van Dycks, and we can go in and see it all in the summer, and there is much to see. The grounds are huge and fine, and contain perhaps the most beautifully sited cricket pitch in the world, and a big racing stable. The staff is numbered in hundreds. The whole place, castle and town, has something of the flavour of Gormenghast.

The parish church, which is a delightful building, as it is at present casts an interesting light on contemporary Christianity. In 1880 the 15th Duke claimed it for Rome, being Roman himself, there was a great lawsuit, the Anglican vicar won, by the judgement, the body of the church, but the Fitzalan Chapel, at the east end, was awarded to the duke. This noble immediately set about cutting it off from the rest of the church by a brick wall. He offered, in decency, to pay for the west side of the wall to be plastered, but this offer the vicar indignantly refused, and raw brick it remained for ninety years. The present duke, filled with ecumenical zeal, had the wall pulled down so that the unity of the fine building could be restored again. But the parish council, less ecumenical, insisted on walling it off again, so that none of the heat that they provided should go to warm the Papists beyond. You can go into the chapel via the castle.

The Roman Catholic Cathedral, built by the present duke's father in 1873, is vast and dominates the town even more than the huge castle itself. Every year a Corpus Christi procession leaves it, and proceeds to an altar in the grounds of the castle.

Arundel was named as a port in Domesday Book. By 1295 it sent two members to Parliament, in the fourteenth century there were ninety-four houses and a good market. Defoe, in 1722, said the town was decayed, but that a lot of timber was shipped from here to Woolwich, Deptford, Chatham and Portsmouth for building His Majesty's ships and even some to far-away Plymouth. 'The timber shipped off there is deemed the best,' he wrote, 'as it is also the largest, of any part of England.' An Admiralty report of 1728 said that Arundel was eminent for the building of ketches and hoys (i.e. very small warships) because of the quality and quantity of timber. In the latter half of the eighteenth century much timber was being shipped to Lewes and Rye to be turned into charcoal for the iron furnaces.

On the Clymping side of the river down at Littlehampton the craft of shipbuilding, or at least boatbuilding, is still being carried on. William Osborne specialises in high speed sophisticated fibre glass motor boats, including inshore rescue craft and also larger modern R.N.L.I. lifeboats, and David Hillyard still builds really excellent cruising yachts, out of *wood* of all things, an increasingly rare material. Modern boat builders like to tell you that they build of glass fibre because it is *better* than wood. They don't really. They build like that because they cannot get the craftsmen to build in wood, which is a better material altogether.

Places in the district worth looking at: **Lyminster** has a fascinating church which was once the church of Saxon nuns. A dragon lives in a bottomless pit nearby. **Poling** has a Saxon church of about AD 900. There is a piece of wooden window shutter there, from this period.

CHAPTER 12

Clymping to Hayling Island

THERE is a foot ferry across the river Arun from Littlehampton, and beyond it one of the very few unbuilt-up pieces of shoreline on the Sussex coast. A little inland is **Bailiffscourt**, in the parish of **Clymping** (whatever the Ordnance Survey map says – it says *Climping* indeed). Bailiffscourt has undergone a strange transformation. In the 1920s, when money was there to be squandered like water, the Honourable Walter Guinness, later Lord Moyne, built himself a house here to stay in while he attended the Goodwood Races. It is conjectured that he spent considerably more than a million pounds on it. With Amyas Phillips as architect he scoured England for ancient houses, pulled them down, and transported stone and timber to Bailiffscourt, where he caused to be built a house so resolutely medieval that it looks far more medieval than a really medieval one. The place being treeless he caused whole woods to be uprooted, and carried to his estate on lorries, and there transplanted; and so well was this work done that although they were mature trees ninety-five per cent of them survived! He did not have much time to enjoy this egregious folly, though, for in 1944 he was assassinated in Palestine in mistake for somebody else. There is a Norman chapel at Bailiffscourt, which is quite genuine, which once was used as a dairy, and then the bedroom of the maids of a former house, and we are told that their Victorian employer used to lock them in it at night to keep them from engaging in intrigues. At the time of writing the mansion is run by a Swedish lady, a Mrs Birer, as Birer's Hotel. The surrounding estate is let by the owner (who lives in Yorkshire!) to a tenant who keeps countless pigs. These are basically Wessex, with flop-ears so that they don't charge through the electric fencing, living out of doors in small igloos and looking marvellously healthy.

At **Elmer Sands** is a small angling and boating club, which owns a tractor for hauling the boats of members up the beach. We then come, if we are trying to follow the shore, to a large area controlled by **Middleton** Estates where are fearsome fan-defences with spikes and barbed wire for keeping the hoi-polloi out, countless signs saying NO HORSES as though these ferocious animals must

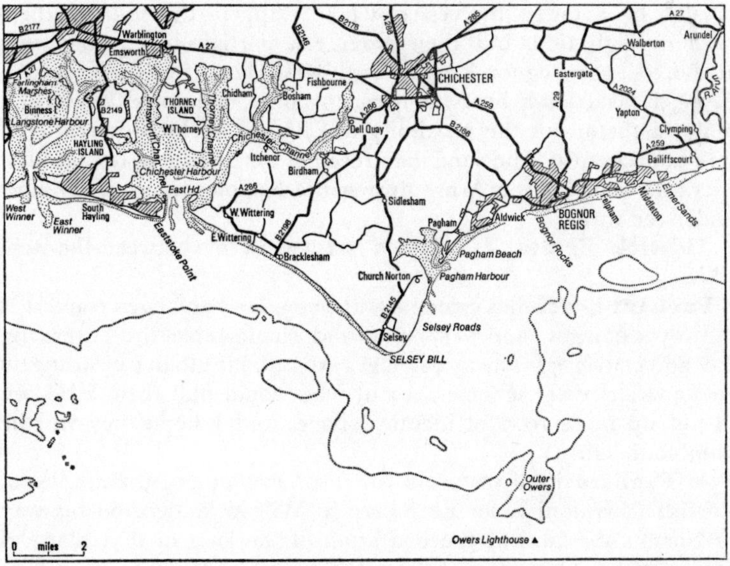

be kept at bay by any means, many exhortations to be BEWARE OF THE DOG, all backed by tasteless houses with lawns in front of them running down to the beach, on which their owners can sit and gaze out to sea and think money.

Bognor Regis, the 'dear little Bognor' of Queen Victoria, is little no longer whether or no it is still dear. It is now a big bustling holiday resort with a huge Butlins Camp and young gentlemen riding up and down the front in black leather jackets on fast motor bicycles. After the somewhat arid respectability of Middleton and Felpham, Bognor is refreshingly full of life. The place was founded, where no place was before, by Sir Richard Hotham in the latter part of the eighteenth century, in an effort to rival Brighton. Princess Charlotte, the daughter of the Prince Regent, came here and George V recuperated here after an illness and gave the place the title of *Regis*. There is a fine pier, first built in 1865 but rebuilt in 1910, plenty of entertainment, and there is Hotham Park where, besides a childrens zoo (that means a zoo with animals in it for children to look at), there is a fine collection of trees and plants. These were collected by W. Fletcher, who owned the place.

The Bognor Rocks (which are of a shelly calcareous sandstone of the London Clay period of the Eocene) dry out at low tide, and should be avoided by vessels whose skippers don't know them even at high tide, but they provide a partial shelter to vessels anchored near Bognor Pier in south-westerlies. Had there been a stronger need for a harbour here no doubt one could have been built on them, but the proximity of Chichester Harbour rendered this unnecessary. The land has receded here, and it is said that barracks built for the Army during the Napoleonic wars are now under the water.

Aldwick Estate is a closed settlement of between-the-wars whimsy.

Pagham Beach has custom-built bungalows and even converted railway carriages, and very snug and comfortable the latter are, too, and converted railway carriages are very nice to live in strangely enough. There are schemers about who would pull them all down to put up more rows of identical boxes and I hope they will be dumbfounded.

At **Pagham** itself we are at, or are near, one of the cradles of English Christianity, for near here St Wilfrid landed, on his way to Northumberland at the invitation of the king of that place to convert the wild Northumbrians. He landed at Pagham in AD 665, but in 681 he returned – having been driven from his see in the north by an uprising. He was granted land around Pagham and Selsey by King Caedwalla, himself a Briton or Welshman although his subjects were English. St Wilfrid built a cathedral, said to be beneath the waves now and needless to say the faithful can still hear its bells ringing from underneath the waves when they are sailing home from an evening at the Crab and Lobster very late at night. But the sea seems to have advanced here: the anchorage or roadstead still called The Parks off-shore is said to have been a deer park of the Tudor kings, now overwhelmed by the waves.

The story that St Wilfrid taught the Selsey men to fish is told by the Venerable Bede in *The Ecclesiastical History of England* (AD 731). Here it is in Leo Sherley-Price's excellent translation from the Latin:

> When Wilfrid had first arrived in the province and found so much misery from famine, he taught the people to obtain food by fishing; for although fish were plentiful in the sea and rivers, the people had no knowledge of fishing and caught only eels. So the bishop's men collected eel-nets from all sides and cast them into the sea, where, by the aid of God's grace, they quickly caught three hundred fishes of various kinds. These they divided into three parts, giving a hundred to the poor, a hundred to those who had lent the nets, and retaining a hundred for their own needs. By this good turn the bishop won the hearts of all, and the people began to listen more

readily to his teaching, hoping to obtain heavenly blessings through the ministry of one to whom they already owed material benefits.

Would that all missionaries would teach their flocks something so useful.

Anyway Pagham has the site of a bishop's palace near its church, and the latter is a fine Norman-Early English Transitional building, and no doubt the bishops of Chichester used to stay in Pagham to get away from the cares of office.

Pagham Harbour, once called Andering or Undering Harbour, had the sea break into it in the fourteenth century to flood nearly three thousand good acres. It is now beset by another sea – a huge caravan park to the east of it but even caravanners have got to have somewhere to go. The 'Harbour' now consists of 698 acres of mud and saltings, and we must bless the gale of 1910 that broke down the sea-walls of the 'inning' of 1870 and let the blessed sea water in again. The mud flats now are much dominated by *Spartina* grass. No doubt the harbour was a port once, and in the memories of men living sailing barges used to nose up to the little quay that still exists beside the Crab and Lobster Inn, at **Sidlesham**, where once was a tide mill, bringing corn to the mill, or coal, or 'London Muck' to spread on the land (manure from London horses and a most important sailing barge cargo), or to take away flour and grist meal. Now the shallow winding creeks are only used by dinghies and a few adventurous larger yachts, and in winter the place is given over to birds, bird-watchers, and wildfowlers. The latter have to be members of the *Pagham and West Sussex Wildfowlers Association*, the number of guns allowed to shoot Pagham Harbour is limited to a hundred, and before a man is admitted to this number he must satisfy a committee that he is a first-class shot, can identify all local birds by their silhouettes in the dark, by the noise of their wing-beats or by their throat noises: in other words that he is not a blundering amateur or a marsh cowboy. The harbour is a fine place for wildfowl: plenty of *Enteromorpha intestinalis* makes good feeding for ducks.

There is a most lovely walk right round the harbour, with the Crab and Lobster conveniently set about half way. There was once a Roman villa near it – what would the Romans have made of the 'Lady Grey Home for Old Horses' which now occupies its site? Inland there is a settlement of the Land Settlement Association: an excellent organisation set up in the Great Depression to settle city people on the land. The city people nearly all went home again, but countrymen moved in, and the Association is still going strong, unsung, unnoticed, but extremely productive and very prosperous.

For a fuller description of the bird life of Pagham Harbour see page 169 under Chichester Harbour.

Church Norton, which is where you end up if you walk round the harbour from Pagham, has what is left of old Selsey Church, built by Bishop Rede from 1369 to 1385 – just the chancel of the old building. The rest of the church was *pulled down*, by the parson in 1865, to be carted off and put up again, in true Victorian fashion, in the modern village of Selsey. But what the vicar left is strange and lonely, set on an ancient mound surrounded by a deep wooded moat, and if this was not once a Celtic *Llan*, or sacred circular enclosure, I would be surprised. It was at this little church that Eddi the Priest, in Rudyard Kipling's story *Eddi's Service*, rang the bell for midnight mass and nobody turned up, because of the wild weather, save a donkey and a bullock. Eddi celebrated mass for them, and when later asked about this strange behaviour said: 'I dare not close His chapel on such as care to attend.'

The shore at this point is shingle, with some sand exposed at low tide, and huge wooden groins have been set up, or are being set up, to prevent further erosion by the sea. Long spits of shingle run out to sea and are dry at low tide.

Selsey is a large and rapidly growing seaside village on that promontory known as **Selsey Bill**. Not long ago Selsey was a fishing village of ancient standing, and recently some of the new residents, trying to flee from London but bringing London with them, had the staggering impertinence to complain of the fact that the fish caught by the surviving fishermen stank of fish! Were not the ancestors of these fishermen taught to catch fish by St Wilfrid in the seventh century? The reply that the fishermen gave them was short, sharp, and very much to the point.

There is a small but vigorous fishing community left here, with about half a dozen decked or half-decked vessels of over twenty-five feet, and perhaps seven small open boats that are fished, full-time, off the open beach and are hauled up by winches. There are also a lot of part-timers. The larger vessels lie out at very heavy moorings, and keep the sea for about nine months of the year, being hauled out for the worst three months or taken round to Littlehampton. The moorings are well sheltered from the west and south-west, and the shoals of the Owers give some shelter from southerlies, but even so in southerlies at high tide, and in south-easters, there can be huge seas. So the moorings have to be strong: generally three anchors of four hundredweight each spider-linked with one-and-a-quarter-inch straight-linked chain.

It is sad that no example exists to-day of the old Selsey Smacks, of which there were perhaps a dozen still sailing in the nineteen-twenties – the last of the line having an engine put in her in 1939. In the nineteen-twenties there were still about fifty boats of different kinds fishing from Selsey, with many small open beach boats beside the smacks.

The Selsey Smack was a very specialised vessel. She was half-decked, about twenty-four feet long, with great beam, long straight keels that hung a foot below the garboard strakes (a few had iron keels but most carried inside ballast), high stems but very low sterns (for trawling), and they set a great spread of canvas. They were true cutter rigged. The mainsail alone was 280 square feet, they set foresails and jibs on very long bowsprits, large topsails, and their booms overhung their counters by several feet. They sailed very fast, and keen races were held every year at the annual regatta.

The fishing then, as now, was mainly lobstering, although the smacks did trawl. There were rich lobster grounds around the Owers, but the Cornish came in great force about four years ago, each boat working up to four hundred pots, and completely cleared the grounds. There is practically nothing left, and the Selsey fishermen are having a very hard time. Selsey boats were small, and used to shoot perhaps thirty to fifty pots, and with these the men could make a very good living. But now that the grounds have been denuded the Selsey men are being forced to buy bigger boats, work more pots, and with all this scrape up a worse living than they had before. And the few remaining lobsters are over-fished. Thus greed, as always, defeats its own end.

The Selsey men drive their small open 'punts' with outboards, and therefore do not like the lute sterns favoured on other parts of the Sussex coast, in fact they will cut off the lute sterns from boats which they buy.

There is a lifeboat, up on a big staging, which gets plenty of work, and which saved a great many aeronauts during the war.

There is a deposit of erratic rocks off Selsey, dumped there by floating ice during the last Ice Age. The glaciers did not get as far south as this then, of course, but there were plenty of ice floes in the Channel nevertheless. Some of these rocks came from as far away as the Channel Islands.

The lightship off the notorious Owers Shoal (on which the English tried so hard to wreck the Spanish Armada) is soon to be replaced by a *Lanby*, or Large Automatic Navigation Buoy. This is an unmanned steel object shaped like a flying saucer, some fifty feet in diameter, with a light on a forty-foot mast on it powered by two continuously running diesels. Fully fuelled it weighs a hundred tons.

It can remain at sea unattended, the diesels never faltering it is hoped, for a year; and if the diesels do falter there are batteries to take over. Normally it will be visited every six months. A Lanby costs £195,000, compared with £500,000 for a lightship, and it costs £3,000 a year to maintain compared with £30,000 for a lightship, so no doubt we shall see more of them. A man on shore can monitor it by radio.

West of Selsey there is quite a long stretch of splendidly lonely beach, with no roads near it, thank God, and here is an exposure of the Bracklesham Beds, a partly marine, partly estuarine, and partly fresh water deposit from the latter part of the Eocene. The Bracklesham Beds were laid down on top of the Bagshot Sands and were overlaid themselves in due course by the Barton Clay. The Bracklesham Beds are deposits of clays, clayey-sands, lignite and pebbles, and were laid down in a shallow estuary which ran eastward into the sea, and therefore near Selsey, that is near their eastward edge, they are of marine origin, while farther west, near Bournemouth, they are of fresh water provenance. They are highly fossiliferous, having yielded crocodiles and sea-snakes and over five hundred species of mollusc. The lonely beach we are now on has many fossils. The full succession of the Beds can be seen best at Whitecliff Bay on the Isle of Wight, while at the other end of the island, at Alum Bay, there is a fine exposure tilted on end so that it can be read like a book.

Bracklesham and **East Wittering** have caravans, bungalows, and a holiday camp. **West Wittering** is where, according to the Anglo-Saxon Chronicle, Aella or Ella and his three sons Cymen, Wenceling and Cissa, doughty Englishmen, landed from three ships, marched to Shoreham, and defeated the Britons on Slonk Hill in AD 495 (some make it 477). In Elizabeth I's time a creek ran past the church door here and there are said to be mooring rings in the wall of that building, which is, incidentally, an old and interesting one with a Saxon font. As late as the nineteen-twenties there were a few working fishermen left at West Wittering, but a hundred years ago there are said to have been seventy luggers fishing from here. Now all belongs to the West Wittering Estates Ltd., car parking 25p and – above all – NO HORSES. Somehow these ferocious animals have to be kept away from our coasts. There is said to have been a famous fig garden planted in 1745 (if indeed not, as some believe, by St Richard in the thirteenth century), and there is a legend that a bird called the *beccafico* flies all the way from Italy to eat the figs. I have seen neither figs nor birds. North of West Wittering is a Roman field system.

We now turn the corner of **East Head**, if we are afloat, or cut within it if we are afoot, into **Chichester Harbour**, a splendid landlocked tidal lagoon of over four thousand acres. There is a bar in the mouth to it, much exposed to all winds between south-west and south-east, and nearly drying at low spring tides, so be careful how you enter or leave.

The whole of Chichester Harbour is now under the control of the Chichester Corporation, under the Act of 1938. It is to be preserved for the recreation of humans and the preservation of other forms of life, and it is now unlikely that the mouth will be dammed, and the whole area turned into a fresh water lake as was recommended by a report in 1967.

The bird life of the harbour, especially in the winter, is rich and interesting. In the winter some three thousand Brent geese come to the chain of tidal harbours along the coast, including Pagham, and this has been estimated as ten per cent of the world population of these birds. Protected now, and attracted by the *Enteromorpha* algae, they are increasing. There are also a few pinkfeet and white fronted geese. There are estimated to be about two thousand shelduck in the three harbours, about one thousand five hundred widgeon (their favourite food, Widgeon-grass (*Zostera marina*), comes and goes, but since 1930 when it all died out – apparently due to the machinations of a fungus called *Labyrinthula* – there has been sadly little of it. It was once used, amongst other things, for sound proofing the walls of B.B.C. studios!), there are mallard, of course, a few pintail, shovellers and garganeys, and the usual teal. There are all the usual waders of this coast: black-tailed godwits, redshanks, curlew, lapwing and as for dunlin – who can count 'em? There are heronries on Old Park Wood (opposite Birdham) and Tournebury Wood, which is a magical place on Hayling Island. **Pilsea Island**, which used to have ten acres of good dry land and a house and garden on it, is now a 'site of special scientific interest', and on it grows the rare Sea Bindweed among other plants.

A most interesting floral phenomenon happened in these harbours about 1870. An American salt-marsh grass called *Spartina alterniflora* was imported to try to bind the mud flats in Southampton Water, but it proved no better than the native *Spartina maritima*. But lo – the American import mated with the native to produce a mule hybrid: *S. townsendii*. This is not quite a mule, in fact, for the females can breed without male intervention. *S. townsendii* proved dramatically more vigorous and hardy than either parent, and colonised the tidal mud flats, and it is covering more and more of the tidal harbours. It looks as though it may cause the complete silting up of the harbours, because its dense meadows cause accretion of mud and ultimately may raise their level above the tide mark. For land-reclamation *S. townsendii* is unbeatable. It does occasionally suffer from unaccountable die-back. It makes fair grazing for sheep and cattle, and can be cut for hay. It is often called Rice Grass.

Itchenor, or **West Itchenor**, had considerable dockyards and shipbuilding yards at the end of the eighteenth century. It now has yachts, yachts, and more yachts. It has (I think) the only *hard* open to the public, down which you can drag a dinghy, or pull one up, or on which you can land, without paying somebody or other, in Chichester Harbour. In Itchenor Reach yachts swing so thickly to moorings that the mariner is hard-put to thread his way between them. There are said to be four hundred swinging moorings in the short length of Chichester Reach alone. Whether one likes that American invention the 'marina' or not, one can see the reason for it. At least it crams hundreds of yachts into a very small space, and leaves the tidal channels for sailing in.

In 1816 18,000 tons of coal and 1,650 tons of other merchandise were landed at Itchenor, put into lighters, and taken up to Dell Quay to be carted to Chichester, or the country beyond. This was because the creek to Dell Quay, traditionally the out-port of Chichester, was silting up.

Charles II had a mistress who used to live in Itchenor House. He named her Fubs, because this was the contemporary slang word for a chubby little boy, which he thought she resembled. He had a yacht built at Deptford, by Peter Pett, and had her sailed to Chichester for the amusement of his lady friend, and he named the yacht *Fubs*. The captain of the yacht, who came with her, was a man named Darley, and there are still Darleys ashore hereabouts.

Just west of Itchenor Hard is Bell Hole, in which Danish pirates dropped the bell of Bosham Church after they had stolen it. The local people tried to drag for it, but with no success, until it was pointed out to them by their priest that the bell was a consecrated bell, and the grappling ropes they were using were not. So a new rope was woven from the tail hairs of white oxen, consecrated, and they tried again. This time, needless to say, they hooked the bell and began to haul it to the surface. But, alas, the rope broke. It was then pointed out (by the same priest no doubt) that the rope had one black hair in it, and that that hair belonged to the Devil. The bell presumably is there still: a challenge to consecrated skin divers.

Birdham had a tidal mill (the pound of which is now a marina for 220 boats), and salterns – or lagoons in which the sea water was allowed to evaporate for the making of salt. **Dell Quay** up the creek is a pretty place, and was once the out-port of Chichester.

But if we go back to Birdham (assuming we are not stuck on the mud, of which there is a *vast* amount here), to the enormous marinas at this spot (there is the Birdham Shipyard Company and the even larger Chichester Yacht Basin, opened in 1966 with berths for 610 yachts and a dredged channel to lock gates enclosing it) we find, if we sail into the Yacht Basin, the entrance to the Chichester Canal. This, as we have seen, was a component of the great waterway that once ran all the way from Portsmouth to London. We *should* be able to sail up it right into Chichester, but people who were either knaves, or fools, or both, built in 1928 low bridges over it (under the B 2201 it is *piped*) and have allowed the canal to decay. So now if we want to go along it we have to walk along the towpath. It was from the bank of this canal that Turner did his great painting of Chichester Cathedral with a ship in the foreground. The original is in Petworth House, where Turner was staying at the time that he did it as a guest of George O'Brien, third Earl of Egremont. We have dealt with the construction of this canal in Chapter 11 (p. 158). In 1972 I watched forty-six fat pike hauled out of this canal by nets by the local angling society from a length of four hundred yards.

The canal takes us into what should be a most delightful canal basin near the middle of **Chichester**, and one day perhaps the local people will have enough good sense and pride to insist that this canal be opened up again whatever the expense (as it should never have been closed), and seafarers will be able to sail from any part of the world and lie comfortably within view of the cathedral, and within a few hundred yards of the centre of this noble little city. When this canal basin was being dug Roman handmills, a funeral vessel, 700 *denarii* and other coins, lamps and pottery were unearthed.

Chichester is an example of what a place for humans to live in should be like. One can see why Eric Gill published a map of it in his autobiography comparing it with a slummy part of Brighton to explain an important part of his spiritual development.

It was named Noviomagus by the Romans. The Celts had had a big fort four miles to the north of it, near what is now Goodwood race course, on a hill called the Trundle. Their king, Cogidubnus, thinking discretion to be the better part of valour, submitted to the Romans without a fight, and they confirmed him in his chieftainship, and he built a Roman-style Regnum, or capital, at Noviomagus. It was Cogidubnus's defection from the British cause which enabled the legions to conquer Britain so easily, for when Claudius advanced north against London he knew that his vital left flank was secure because of the friendly kingdom of Cogidubnus, and later, when he drove into the West Country, he had this quisling stronghold to his rear.

Noviomagus became the centre of what has been termed a little Italy in Britain. The Romans found that the climate here, the fertility of the land, the comparative proximity to the rest of the empire, the many good harbours, much to their liking; and villas, palaces, ports and castles and temples sprang up around. Stone Street, a good Roman road, went straight to London.

Soon after the Romans left the English began to arrive, and they found the Britons (whom they termed the Welsh) quite unable to defend themselves, for they had endured over three hundred years of being a subject nation and had not borne arms for that period. Aella, or Ella, and his three merry sons arrived as we have seen, and Cissa, one of the sons, settled at Noviomagus and this soon became known as Cissa's Ceastor, later commuted to Chichester.

Chichester had early become a port. The Romans had a port at Fishbourne, and by the tenth century the English had turned Chichester into an important trading centre, which they called 'The Port of Horemouth'. The River Lavant was the little creek that brought the ships to their quays. But difficulties are sure to beset any port up a shallow creek. We always say: 'the creek silted up'. But what also happened is that ships got bigger. To sail well to windward ships got deeper in draught, and what had been an adequate port became inadequate. And at Chichester, as in many other ports, a certain very vicious spiral set in. Sailing ships which had to sail from one port to another with no cargo had to take in ballast: generally sand, or shingle, or rock depending upon the most easily available material heavy enough to give them stability. When a ballasted ship tried to get up a shallow channel such as Chichester's she would come aground and the easiest course for her crew was to fling out the ballast. And out it went, into the creek, to make the latter even shallower than it had been before. Plenty of rules were made to try to stop this practice, but, like the rules we have now to prevent ships discharging waste oil at sea, they were more honoured in the breach than the observance, because such rules are absolutely impossible to enforce. So while in 1350 Chichester was ranked as the seventh port in the kingdom, by 1650 a ship of forty tons could only just get to the quay on the top of a spring tide: which means twice a lunar month, and in 1651 it was reported that a ship carrying ten tons of cargo had difficulty in reaching the port.

Chichester itself then was finished as a port; and it was not until the great Portsmouth to London waterway scheme was started in the early nineteenth century that ships managed to reach the city again. But Dell Quay became the port of Chichester, and in 1800 a hundred ships were registered there. The 1930s saw the last trading ships come to Dell Quay. To the last, one old sailing barge, advertising Beecham's Pills in big letters on her red mainsail, used to come with loads of gravel.

When the seventh-century cathedral at Selsey Bill was overwhelmed by the sea the bishopric was transferred to Chichester, and the new cathedral there was consecrated in 1108. The city got a charter in 1231. The cathedral had two bad fires in the twelfth century. The spire collapsed in 1210, and the one that replaced it then also collapsed – very gently and with hardly a rumble – in 1861. The present spire is of 1866, and was designed by Sir Gilbert Scott: an exact replica of the original. The cathedral was much damaged by Cromwellian troops when the city was taken by Sir William Waller in the Civil War, but it remains a very beautiful building. There are plenty of guide books within, but whatever you do don't miss the two superb panels in the south aisle of the choir, one carved to represent the raising of Lazarus, and the other to depict Christ at the house of Martha and Mary. These have been dated as from the second quarter of the twelfth century – but some experts have dated them as pre-Conquest. They are believed to have come from the Saxon cathedral at Selsey Bill. The other thing not to miss is the monument to the Earl and Countess of Arundel (1346–97) about which Philip Larkin wrote a moving little verse. A map of Sussex by Yeakell and Gardner of 1723 in the North Transept is of great interest.

Other things to see in Chichester are the City Museum (29 Little London), the Guildhall Museum (Priory Park), which has fine Roman objects, a stone let into the wall of the Council House which was dug up in 1723 and which had written on it: BY THE AUTHORITY OF TIBERIUS CLAUDIUS, COGIDUBNUS, KING, LEGATE OF AUGUSTUS IN BRITAIN, and had inscribed again when it was discovered: THIS STONE IS SUPPOSED TO HAVE COME FROM THE TEMPLE OF THE SHIPWRIGHTS OF NOVIOMAGUS. Much of the original Roman wall remains about the town, the Market Cross in the centre is of 1501 and fine, and there is the exciting new theatre, opened in 1962 (most improbably it was the idea of the *Mayor* – lucky city to have a mayor with an idea like this!) in which only the highest standards of theatrical art are admitted. The Vicar's Hall, and the Vicar's Crypt below it, are splendid places to go for a meal or coffee. But it is most pleasant just to wander about Chichester's streets, with their predominantly Georgian houses, paid for, no doubt, largely by those hundred ships that were, when the houses were built, registered in the port.

Recently, in 1973, more Roman diggings have been made in the city, and one pre-Roman discovery, too, for two coins of Epaticcus have been found, and he ruled between AD 25 and 35. A Roman house has been discovered on the site of the Old Gospel Hall in Chapel Street. A Roman kiln, also found in Chapel Street, was fired again by a modern potter in 1970 and it worked perfectly!

A couple of miles west of Chichester is **Fishbourne**, where are the most extensive and interesting Roman remains in Britain. They were only discovered in 1960, when a trench was being dug for a water main, and in 1961 proper excavations started. The whole great palace (thought to have been the palace of Cogidubnus at one period of its existence) covers six acres, which would have been an enormous building in any age. Perhaps Cogidubnus knew what he was doing when he went over to the winning side. The foundations already laid bare have been covered over with an enormous roof, and here we see room after room floored with fine mosaic, and there is a fine museum containing things that have been discovered. The whole place is the most important Roman discovery in Britain, and shows a high degree of luxury and sybaritic civilisation. Early works unearthed include harbour works and granaries. The prevalence of granaries among Roman remains in Britain reminds us that the Roman armies were fuelled on wheat, just as the armies in the Western Desert in the Second World War were fuelled on petrol. Great fields of wheat spread about the countryside here to-day, just as they no doubt did in Roman times. The Romans knew the art of drying wheat by hot air from fires passed through it. This art has been revived in England since the invention of the combine harvester has made it necessary to thresh wheat with a high moisture content. The Celts that the Romans conquered practised another art that has only recently been revived, and that also because of the combine harvester. And that is the enclosing of wheat in airtight containers (in the case of the Ancient Britons holes dug in the chalk, filled with grain, and then carefully sealed with clay) so that the carbon dioxide generated by the grain inhibits the mould that would spoil it. The rocket-like grain silos that are rising up in the countryside now are our modern equivalent. A tiny point shown at Fishbourne is that the Romans knew the correct way to tamp a post in the ground. They filled the hole with clean fine gravel and tamped it hard – they didn't just dump in earth as ignorant people do to this day.

At Fishbourne the *Chichester Harbour Wildfowlers' Association* maintains a wildfowl sanctuary and breeding station.

There is a delightful walk over the fields (through an extensive fruit nursery) to **Bosham**, which the inhabitants never tire of telling you should be pronounced Bozzam. This place has by now quite a long history of being a favourite of yachtsmen who think they are the only ones to have 'discovered' it. It is therefore surrounded with a sprawling residential area, which must be very pleasant to live in, for the expensive houses stand in lovely gardens on this very fertile alluvial soil. The place reminds us of one of the plummier suburbs south of Colombo, in Ceylon. There are mercifully many trees and shrubs.

As far as we can see Bosham, however pronounced, is the oldest known centre of Christianity in Sussex, for Bede tells us that a monk named Dicul with 'five or six brethren who served the Lord in humility and poverty' had a cell here two hundred years before the landing of St Augustine the Romaniser. Dicul's cell is thought to be the ancient vault underneath the church. This is cared for by the local boys, who defend it from desecration by their contemporaries of less couth.

Before Dicul arrived, presumably from Ireland, there were people at Bosham, for in 1832 the foundations of a Roman villa were unearthed at Broadbridge when a new mill house was being erected there. A life-sized marble head was unearthed, and has been identified by experts as being a portrait of either Germanicus or Caligula. There was almost certainly a Roman basilica or temple on the site of Bosham Church: the bases of the chancel arches are thought to be the bases of the columns that supported the temple, and coins of Antonius, and much Roman brickwork, have been found on the site.

An astonishing example of oral tradition is the fact that right down to 1865 the local people believed that King Canute or Knut buried his little daughter under a certain spot in Bosham Church. In that year the vicar, wishing to put an end to this superstition perhaps, caused workmen to dig down on this very spot. They unearthed a stone coffin with the crumbling remains of an eight-year-old girl in it, and experts have dated the coffin at the very time of King Canute. In 1954 another coffin was unearthed, in the centre of the nave, and this contained the remains of a hefty man. Some people believe that Earl Godwin was buried here. It is certain that King Canute stayed at Bosham, which was a royal residence; and nothing will move local patriots away from their staunch belief that it was at Bosham that his celebrated defiance of the tides, or admonishment to his courtiers, took place.

One of the famous things that happened in Bosham Church is depicted in the Bayeux Tapestry. Poor young Harold of England, when a prince, came here to receive the sacrament before setting sail on the hunting voyage which was to prove his undoing, for he was wrecked on the coast of Normandy and made to swear to Duke William that he would hand over England to him should he, Harold, ever succeed to its crown. This is well depicted on the tapestry, with Bosham Church.

As for the rest of Bosham, the quay is owned by the Lord of the Manor, and you have to pay to use it. Barges used to load and unload here, and before them schooners and brigantines. Now there are yachts, yachts, and more yachts. There is a very good and popular pub, the landlord of which has the sense to serve with his beer that good old Saxon refreshment, bread and cheese. If he would supply half a raw onion with it, to the needful, he would merit a knighthood. The creek is terribly crowded with moorings, very shallow and muddy, but nice in winter when most of the yachts are laid up. The West Sussex County Council has an old sailing barge here which is used as a youth centre, accommodating eighteen young people at a time.

Chidham has a scattered village, and a nature reserve belonging to the Sussex Naturalists' Trust, and, afloat, the converted Ham Class Inshore Minesweeper, renamed the *Gerald Daniel* in memory of a young policeman of that name who died while on service with the force in 1970. She was presented by the boy's father to be used as a headquarters of the Police Cadet Corps.

Thorney Island is an island no longer, for the Great Deep that separated it from the mainland has been inned and is now full of fresh water. At the tiny village of **West Thorney** is a tiny Norman church. The R.A.F. has made an awful mess of the rest of the island, but hopefully is soon going to vacate it. Let us hope it does not fall victim to yet more flying machines.

Emsworth rose as a port as Chichester fell, for as the eastern end of Chichester Harbour silted up so the slightly deeper Emsworth Channel got the traffic. Coastal trade developed fast in the eighteenth and nineteenth centuries here, and so did the fishery. Emsworth became a centre for the scallop and oyster fisheries, and oysters were stored in a huge old floating crate nicknamed 'The Ark'. The oyster trade came to a sad end when the Dean of Winchester, and other dignitaries, having regaled themselves on a good old blow-out of Emsworth oysters, unfortunately passed away. A law was passed forbidding the fish. Deep sea sailing trawlers operated from Emsworth, too, and three of them were lost in one North Sea gale which hit the port very hard.

Emsworth is an old port. It was certainly a port in the reign of Henry II. In 1848 a 487 ton ship was built here, so we know that it was a building port as well. There were two big tide mills, the pounds of which are still intact. One of them was turned into a yacht harbour in 1967. The Titular Harbour Master of Emsworth is the Engineer to the Havant and Waterlooville Urban District Council. It would be nice to think that he wears a splendid nautical uniform, but I doubt if he does.

At **Warblington** are huts built in the churchyard, which were to house men on the watch for *nautical bodysnatchers*. The latter gentlemen used to sail up the creek at night, nip ashore, and conduct their gruesome business.

As for **Hayling Island**, it has umbilical cords with England, has much *Spartina* grass on the mud between the two islands, the Royal Oak down by the causeway, sand dunes on its sea-shore nearest Portsmouth, a sandy beach which is covered with mostly Portsmouth people on fine weekends. Large lumps of erratic rocks were dumped here by ice floes seventy-five thousand years ago (as we have noticed at Selsey Bill). There is a big one near the primary school. In Elm Close Estate a mechanical grab, in 1960, brought up a lot of bronze palstaves, armlets, etc., of about 1000 BC, which are now in Portsmouth Museum. Hayling is an old word. In AD 955 King Aedwig granted five hides of land at *Haeglinga* to his thegn Aethelsig. William the Conqueror gave Hayling to some French monks, but their abbey was destroyed by storms in the fourteenth century. Hayling North has a fine Early English church, but most of the village was burnt down in the eighteenth century. Hayling South also has a fine Early English church. There is what is left of a nineteenth-century crescent, built in the grand Bath style, intended to be the start of another Brighton, but it never came to anything.

Hayling Island is being eroded. It once stretched much farther out to sea. H.M.S. *Impregnable* came to grief in 1798 on the Winners, once called the Wolsinars: sand-banks which stretch out to sea from the mouth of Langstone Harbour. And in 1805 there was a most macabre incident, when a ship fleeing from plague-ridden Gibraltar tried to make harbour here after having been denied entry into many other ports. Not being able to pick up a pilot she was stranded on the Pole Sand, and the coastguards were given orders to shoot anybody who tried to land from her. They were spared their powder and shot, however, for a south-wester blew up, the ship was overturned, and the fugitives were drowned, germs and all.

Langstone Harbour is much like Chichester Harbour, although being nearer to Portsmouth it is more spoiled by industrial pollution, but less choked with yachts. It is 5,000 acres. Much of the northern part of it, around the Binness Island, was once inned. There were big oyster layings in the harbour, on Farlingham Marshes the traces of 'oyster houses' can still be seen. Tiny Oyster Island is an artificial island on which a house was built for a man who guarded the oyster beds.

CHAPTER 13

Portsmouth to Portchester

PORTSMOUTH, or Pompey as the Lower Deck have always called it, was for so long the greatest naval base in the world that it must find it difficult to adapt to being anything else.

The Romans had a major naval base here, or at least up the harbour at Portchester. According to Henry of Huntingdon, after they left, two Saxon ships, in the year 501, arrived, commanded by a man named Port, and his two sons Bieda and Maegla. The Saxons landed and routed the Britons, who fought bravely, and settled and named the place Portstun. Many historians, however, think the name is older than this, either Roman or Celtic, and why shouldn't it just be what it says: the mouth of the port (the port being Portchester, of course).

Pompey owes its eminence as a naval base to a variety of circumstances. Firstly, a fleet of sailing ships could lie at anchor or moorings, just outside the harbour, in the roadstead of Spithead, and weigh anchor and get to sea with the wind in any quarter. If they couldn't sail one way round the Isle of Wight they could sail the other, and if it really came on a gale from the south-east they could up-helm and run for the safety of Portsmouth Harbour. Secondly it is in a fine place for commanding the Channel. Thirdly there is ample sheltered water inside the harbour for laying-up ships, for dockyards, building yards, and all the rest of it. Fourthly it is eminently defensible against a landing by the enemy, or attack from the mainland. It was just made by nature to be a naval base.

As early as 1121 Portsmouth was favoured by royalty for a port of embarkation for foreign expeditions. In that year Henry II arrived, spent Pentecost week there, then sailed for Normandy. We read that ten years after a large royal fleet was there, there was no wind, and yet many of the ships were destroyed by some mysterious force.

On 20th May, 1213, King John ordered the Sheriff of Southampton to 'cause our docks at Portsmouth to be inclosed with good strong walls . . . for the preservation of our ships and galleys . . .' But in Edward III's reign, in 1338, a French force under Sieur Nicholas Bahuchet, together with the Scots David Bruce, who was

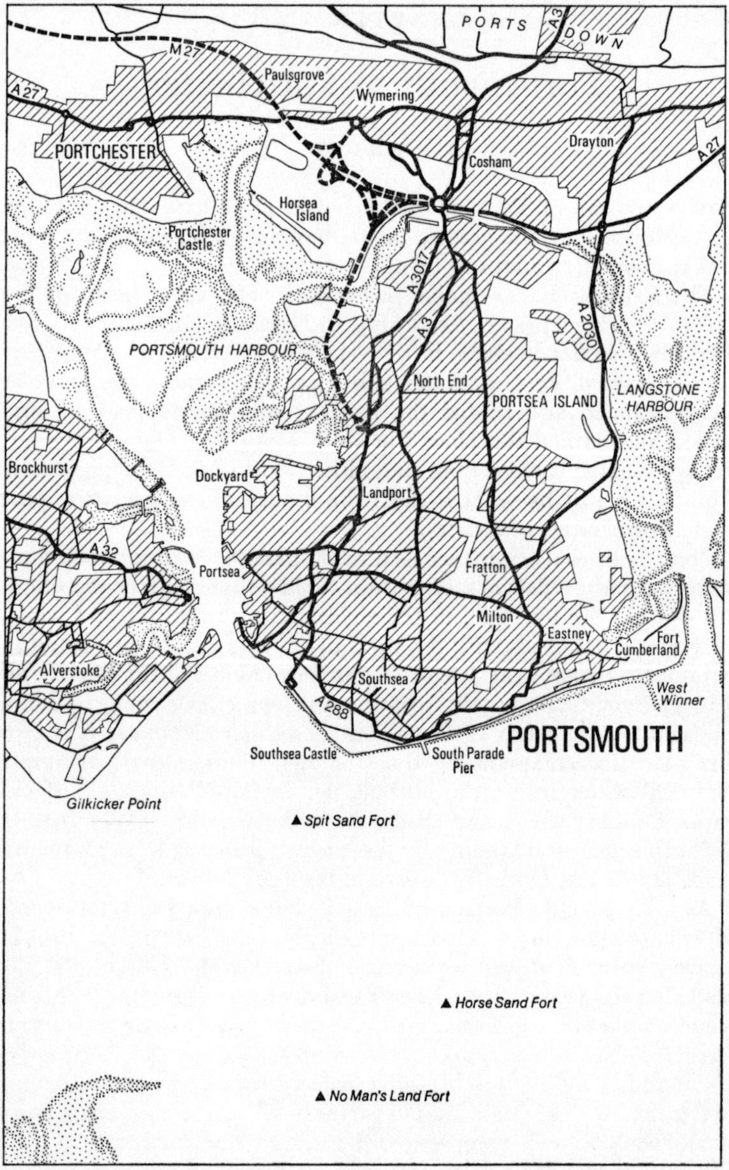
PORTS
DOWN
A3
M27
A27
Paulsgrove
Wymering
Drayton
PORTCHESTER
Cosham
Horsea
Island
Portchester
Castle
A3017
A3
A2030
PORTSMOUTH HARBOUR
North End
PORTSEA ISLAND
LANGSTONE
HARBOUR
Brockhurst
Dockyard
Landport
A32
Portsea
Fratton
Milton
Eastney
Fort
Cumberland
Alverstoke
Southsea
West
Winner
A288
PORTSMOUTH
Southsea Castle
South Parade
Pier
Gilkicker Point
▲ Spit Sand Fort
▲ Horse Sand Fort
▲ No Man's Land Fort

displeased with the English at that time, sailed in and burnt the town down, all except the church and hospital. The French again attacked in 1369, 1377 and possibly also in 1380.

Edward IV started the round towers at the harbour mouth, and they were completed by Henry VIII. Before that Henry V had spent £3,500 on fortifications here, and it was in Portsmouth Harbour that he waited with his fleet to sail for France and Agincourt. His flagship was the *Trinity Royal* and he had a fleet of 1,400 ships and 9,000 men at arms. He sailed to the music of 'pypes, trompes, nakers and clarionnes'. He landed over the other side at Kidecaus, three miles from Harfleur.

By the time of Henry VII Portsmouth was well under way as a naval port. In 1495 one Robert Brygandine was appointed Head of Naval Administration. He had built the first dry dock in the kingdom, entirely of wood, near the place where H.M.S. *Victory* now lies. It cost the king £193 and sixpence three farthings. He also built the twin towers at the harbour mouth and – after Henry VIII had come to the throne – the great ship *Henry Grâce Dieu* – the 'Great Harry'. She was over 1,000 tons burthen, had two decks, was carvel built, four masted, mounted 182 guns, the largest being five-inch fifteen-pounder basilisks, she was manned by three hundred 'shipmen' and gunners, and two hundred and fifty soldiers. She was built between 1514 and 1519. Leland wrote, many years afterwards: 'About a quarter of a mile above the towne is a great dok for shippes and yn this dok lyeth part of the ribbes of the *Henry, Grace Dieu*, one of the biggest shippes that hath been made *in hominum memoria.*' He goes on to add that Henry VIII had built three great breweries in Portsmouth for the men of his fleet. Henry was a monarch who put first things first.

A sad thing occurred during Henry VIII's reign. Another great ship built soon after he came to the throne was the *Mary Rose* – said to have been 'the noblest shippe of sayle and grette shippe in Christendom and the Flower of all the shippes that ever sayled'. She was rebuilt in 1536. On 19th July, 1545, the French sailed into Spithead and set about the English fleet. The wind was blowing from the southward, and there was not enough wind for the English fleet to get to sea to attack the French. But when a wind *did* spring up, unexpectedly, the *Mary Rose* heeled over, and her gun-ports being open and the guns loose the water poured into her and she filled and sank. Henry was watching the desultory battle from the shore, and when he saw his great ship founder he 'cried out like any maid: "Oh my gallant gentlemen! Oh my gallant gentlemen!"' The Royal Navy is nothing if not tenacious of tradition, and on 17th

October, 1917, another *Mary Rose* (ship's crest a Tudor Rose with the motto: 'The Flower of all the Ships that ever sailed') engaged three German cruisers off Jutland, and was sunk herself with only three of her crew being saved. There is now, incidentally, a *Mary Rose* committee working to salvage the remains of the first ship of the name from the bottom of the sea at Spithead. They have to the time of writing recovered one of her cannon, which we shall discuss later on.

By Edward VI's reign Portsmouth was well established as the first naval base in the land, and in 1552 that most unwarlike of monarchs reviewed his entire fleet there with the exception of three ships. On parade were fifty-three ships manned by 7,780 men, with numerous galleys, pinnaces and rowboats besides.

In Charles I's reign the port had to provide one ship of 900 tons, a ship of 800 tons, four of 500 tons and one of 300 tons. This was just the town's contribution. Charles landed here on 5th October, 1623, with the Duke of Buckingham after a tour through France and Spain. In 1627 Buckingham left here with a hundred ships to help the Huguenots who were holding out against the French crown at La Rochelle, but the English returned, having lost 2,000 men and having killed not one of the enemy. Buckingham was assassinated by a man named John Felton with a hunting knife at the Spotted Dog Inn at Portsmouth. Felton was hanged for it.

In the Civil War Portsmouth held out under Colonel Goring for the king, but was soon forced to surrender to Sir William Waller, and the garrison fled by sea to Holland. The loss of Portsmouth 'struck the king to the very heart!'

In 1650 there were about a hundred shipwrights working in the Commonwealth Dockyard. The Commonwealth ship *Portsmouth*, forty-six guns, was launched in that year, three years later the C.S. *Hampshire*, and in 1670 Portsmouth delivered 6,324 tons of shipping to the Royal Navy, and by 1690 31,213 tons.

But kings came back, and on 21st May, 1662 Charles II met his bride-to-be, Catherine of Braganza, at Portsmouth (preferring the city to Southampton, which had been very anti-royalist) and he married her there and then in the Garrison Church. In July, 1671, Charles made the first-ever *yachting voyage* by an Englishman. He sailed from Portsmouth in his new royal yacht, *Cleveland*, a cutter, to inspect the new citadel at Plymouth. Fore-and-aft rig, imported from Holland, was a new thing, too.

Other notable comings and goings of Portsmouth were that Anson sailed in here after his circumnavigation of the globe, Lord Howe sailed in with his prizes after the Glorious First of June (which was just three years after the mutiny at Spithead!), Bligh sailed from here in the *Bounty* to very strange adventures, Hawke, Keppel, Boscawen, Rodney, St Vincent, Nelson, Jellico, Beatty: all sailed from here. In 1784 a 'blackguard horse' nearly killed Nelson on Southsea Common.

Garrison Church was called the 'Military Cathedral of England'. It was originally the Domus Dei Hospital, founded by Peter de Rupibus, Bishop of Winchester, in the thirteenth century. In 1449 Bishop Adam de Moleyns was seized by some soldiers and sailors of Portsmouth after a dispute about the 'abrygging of their wages, they fil on him and cruelli there kilde him'.

Queene Anne made great improvements to the then already substantial dockyards. Under George I the Naval Academy was established for 'sons of noblemen and gentlemen', and the students were taught the use of the quadrant invented by John Hadley, and they had to read Captain Daniel Newhouse's *Whole Art of Navigation.* After the Napoleonic wars the Naval Academy was named the Royal Naval College, and was transferred to Dartmouth in 1863. Maybe it was suspected that Portsmouth was not a very suitable place for young gentlemen to be: one has only to see the lively drawing by Rowlandson of *Portsmouth Point* to see why this should be so.

George III visited the dockyard in 1772 and was rowed out to a ship in a barge by twelve local ladies. We are not told if they were virgins.

The Royal Dockyards were by then extensive, and being built in the age of good taste were, and still are, comely to look at. Part of the Dockyard was burnt by a man named James Aitken, called 'Jack the Painter', because he sympathised with the colonial cause during the American Revolution. He placed an 'infernal machine' between the thousand-foot-long rope walk and some sheds and burnt a lot of buildings down. He was caught at the Raven Inn at Hook, near Basingstoke, and hanged sixty feet high on the mizzen mast of the *Saucy Arethusa* for the encouragement of others of like mind. One of his fingers got used as a pipe-stopper and is said to be in Portsmouth Museum. At least he died for his principles.

There were other disasters. The *Royal George*, 108 guns, just turned over and sank off Portsmouth because, apparently, she was exceedingly rotten and all of her guns had been hauled to one side for cleaning operations. Six hundred and fifty men were drowned and many officers, and down with them went no less than 250 ladies! Most of us had to learn at school that plonking poem about the tragedy, but this made no mention of the 250 ladies.

And on May Day, 1797, the whole town was shaken when H.M.S. *Boyne* blew up at her moorings at Spithead.

The last great naval review of the wind-driven navy was held at Spithead in 1842. Alas – the end of sail was in sight. In 1845 at Spithead the paddle steamer *Alecto* and the screw steamer *Rattler* were tied stern to stern and both ships went full ahead. The *Rattler* won the contest, and the screw propellor proved its superiority over paddles.

In 1856 there was another great review, in which were twenty-four ships of the line, hundreds of lesser ships, nineteen of which were screw frigates and paddle-wheelers. At the review of 1897 a prize exhibit was *Turbinia*, invented and owned by Sir Charles Parsons, the world's first turbine-driven vessel. She now reclines in a museum at Newcastle upon Tyne.

The last naval review was held in 1914: ominous date. And Kaiser William was there as a guest. He saw sixty-eight battleships (and there were fourteen on the stocks), 218 destroyers (twenty on the stocks), twenty-six submarines (twenty on the stocks). Seven of the battleships were dreadnoughts, supposed to be unsinkable. During the ensuing war, in 1916 and 1917, two more, the *Queen Elizabeth* and the *Royal Sovereign* were launched.

But 'Pompey' always went from strength to strength. The naval base that had served King John served George V. The main battle fleet in the First World War might be kept out of harm's way in Scapa Flow, but Portsmouth was still the great naval base. In the Second World War *J Assault Force*, the 3rd Canadian Infantry Division, sailed from Portsmouth on D Day. Southwick House, seven and a half miles north of Portsmouth, was the headquarters of General Eisenhower during the Allied invasion. His invasion map is still preserved there as a relic.

As for Pompey now, the Navy may have shrunk as to numbers of ships, but in fire power it has greatly increased. For the main armament now is the immensely powerful rocket. The day of the dreadnought with her sixteen- or eighteen-inch guns is over, and now a very small ship can give a terrible punch. And there are fewer sailors. But Portsmouth is diversifying her industries fast, and anyway is becoming part of the enormous conurbation that is rapidly filling the whole of the Solent basin. Government policy and natural economic forces are forcing population and industry into this area.

Thus the history. What is there to see in Portsmouth to-day?

Well, there is a long succession of castles and forts. There is the Square Tower, at the seaward end of High Street. It was built in 1494 – one of the first forts specifically designed for cannon warfare, and at first it was probably the residence of the governor. During the Civil War it became a powder magazine, and Colonel Goring threatened to blow it up if he did not get good surrender terms from Waller. In the 1700s it was converted into a meat store for victualling ships, and in 1812 a semaphore station was established on it, for communicating, through a chain of other such devices, with London. In about 1850 the roof was concreted and three eight-inch guns mounted on it. The original gun-ports can no longer be seen. Near the inland side of it is a fine bust of Charles I, put there to celebrate his return from France and Spain. When first put there everyone had to salute it. How it survived the Civil War is a mystery to me, at least.

East of the Square Tower we get the Ten-Gun Battery and the Saluting Platform: the former probably seventeenth century and the latter fifteenth. Farther into the harbour is the Round Tower, probably started in 1426 with a counterpart on the Gosport side. In 1522 a chain was stretched across the harbour to stop enemy ships coming in. A link of this mighty chain (which had to be renewed every hundred years) can be seen inside the tower. It is always stated in guide books and such that there was a capstan to haul the chain taut at each end, but such an arrangement would seem to this writer to be slightly crazy. My supposition is that there was one capstan at one end only. In the Round Tower now is an interesting museum, and the tower is also used by the Fort Cumberland Guard, a fine body of enthusiasts dressed up like the soldiers of the 1840s, who go through all the correct drills, and occasionally fire a cannon off.

Southsea Castle, one of Henry VIII's forts, also has a museum in it, and this is interesting because in it can be seen the successive modifications adapting the castle for warfare from the sixteenth century to the twentieth. Fort Cumberland, commanding the entrance to Langstone Harbour, is still in military use and you cannot go into it, but it looks impressive from the outside. It was started in 1746, enlarged to what it is now between 1794 and 1820, mounted a hundred cannon and could contain 4,000 troops. It is now known that the French knew about it and were deterred from attacking Portsmouth because of this knowledge.

The Landport Gate still stands, north of St George's Road and west of the High Street roundabout. It was built in 1760, on the site of a much older gate, and once had bastion-type fortifications outside it – no longer there.

But Portsmouth was perhaps the most elaborately fortified place in the British Isles, and its fortifications would take a dozen volumes to describe and years to study. The report of a Royal Commission in 1859/60 advised spending ten millions on coastal forts, and induced Palmerston to build massive fortifications at Dover (which we have seen), Portsmouth and Plymouth, and as far west in fact as Milford Haven. His idea was to push the fortifications out farther from the vulnerable dockyards and harbour entrances to allow for the increased range of contemporary weapons. He had built a great ring of massive forts right round Portsmouth, all of which are still there to see, from a line of forts standing on top of Portsdown – the high ridge of chalk hills inland – to forts standing in shoal water out at sea: Spitbank Fort, Horse Sand Fort and No Man's Land Fort. The building particularly of the inland forts caused people to talk of 'Palmerston's Follies' because these forts faced inland, away from the enemy. Well, having seen position after position of the Italian defences in Ethiopia taken by the simple expedient of sending a small force round behind it I think Palmerston may have been wiser than his critics. Whether static fortification was necessary at all in the nineteenth century is another question. Certainly none of these forts was used. But, anyway, the student of fortification can see examples of every period of his art from Iron Age to Rocket Age in Portsmouth or within a very few miles of it. *Portsmouth – A Guide to Places of Historic Interest*, published by the city and on sale at all the museums, is an excellent little guide to these fortifications, and *Fortifications in Old Portsmouth* by Arthur Corney, published by the City Museums, also deals well with the same subject. Southsea Castle has a little guide of its own.

Of museums there is Eastney Pumping Station, which houses a pair of Boulton and Watt reciprocal steam pumps installed in 1887. This is right over to the eastern side of the seafront. Cumberland House, on St Helen's Parade, deals with the natural history of the region. Charles Dickens Birthplace Museum, 393 Commercial Road has a lot of Dickensiana and Victoriana in it, and the City Museum and Art Gallery, in Alexandra Road, has good glass, bad modern art, some local painting, a few really outstandingly good modern primitives such as 'Ringnet Fishing' by James Dixon of Tory Island, and a painting by Alfred Wallis, the Devonshire fisherman turned St Ives scrap dealer, the fine engraving 'Portsmouth Point' by Thomas Rowlandson that I have already mentioned, which shows what a bawdy jolly place it was, and there is the 'Prize Cattle Corner', which should be seen by all prize cattle lovers.

Southsea, which is just a part of Portsmouth which has been tricked out as a holiday resort, is great fun, with a noisy pleasure park, and most notably *Billy Manning's Original Electric Rodeo and*

Animal Cars, which is a really splendid show of twentieth-century folk art.

From near here small hovercraft hover off to Ryde across the water. Like most devices of doubtful utility they are abominably noisy.

Portsmouth was gutted during the Second World War, and what Hitler failed to do the planners have done since, and one of those horrible faceless post-war shopping centres has grown up in the middle of the city: huge department stores built in that wishy-washy debased neo-Georgian of post-war reconstruction. But the old part of the city around the Camber is still attractive, and the Camber has real ships coming into it and discharging real cargoes, and there is a small fleet of old wooden trawlers, some of them elderly Scots vessels bought by local men. There doesn't seem to be much heart in the Portsmouth fishing community, though. Probably there is too much other work in the port. The Solent Fishermen's Association has moorings in a fine old graving dock under the power station.

There are still bits of the town of Nelson's day left, and also some grand Victorian pubs, no doubt all scheduled to be knocked down to make way for those High Temples of the twentieth century: glass and concrete office blocks. Landport Terrace, now full of lawyers, was once a rope walk. There are still pubs to be gazed upon in wonder, such as the Borough Arms in St Paul Street, the flamboyant front of which brings to our attention: BRICKWOOD AND COS' BRILLIANT ALES AND RUM, WHISKY, BRANDY, AND OLD TOM. It is sad that the New Theatre in Commercial Road, hideous as it is, is on the way out, but the City Hall, bombed and rebuilt, stands up in old glory resplendent with mighty lions, corinthian capitals gone crazy, and a horrendous clock.

In days gone by the Spithead Wherry was the famous local boat, used in great numbers for taxi work between the fleet in Spithead and the shore, and also for the run over to the Isle of Wight. The First Class Wherry was thirty feet overall and was half decked. Some wherries in fact went up to thirty-four feet. Under the foredeck they mounted a small coal stove, stepped a main mast which was kept short so as not to foul men-of-war's rigging, a mizzen, was sprit-rigged on both masts. They stowed from three to four tons of iron ballast, plus half a ton of iron in pigs with handles on them, which could be shifted to windward every time the boat went about. By Act of Parliament of 1822 a wherry with one man as crew could charge five shillings to sail between Portsmouth and Ryde, and seven shillings if she had a crew of two or more.

What has survived at Portsmouth, and which all will wish to see, is that astonishing survival from another age: H.M.S. *Victory*. Whether we like the idea of hundreds of men having their legs blown off and their guts shot out makes no difference as to whether we can appreciate the power and beauty of this mighty ship. Launched at Chatham in 1765, she is an example of the summit of the ship-builder's art, and also of the aesthetic taste of the English: English architecture, ashore as well as afloat, reached a peak then from which it has steadily retreated. Look at the great stern of the *Victory*: it resembles a very beautiful Georgian three-story town house, not part of a fighting ship. But as a fighting ship she was supreme, and the elegant furniture of the admiral's and captain's cabins could be hustled out of the way and mighty iron guns trundled into position to take its place. It is calculated that over two thousand mature oak trees were felled to build her, or the crop from fifty to sixty acres of woodland. Ships like this had to be of enormously sophisticated design besides being immensely strong. One of her sailors stated that she steered like a fishing boat – 'one spoke and a half was sufficient on a wind and two turns of the wheel would spin her round like a top!' She carried a hundred of the largest guns of her time. Her career, and the career of Nelson, with whom she was so closely linked (he once spent two years aboard her with hardly a turn ashore) sound like the story of a great dramatist rather than the writings of fate. Nelson's death at the most critical point of the shattering victory of Trafalgar, a victory which gave Britain suzerainty of the seas for a hundred years, had the dramatic inevitability of high drama, and if Shakespeare had lived at that day would have formed the story for his greatest tragedy.

But there are naval guides aboard to show the curious, or the patriotic, around the ship, there is a fine *Victory* Museum ashore beside her, plenty of books and pamphlets large and small, and it would be redundant to go here further into her history. She is there for all to see. The trouble is to get to do so, for the queue to get aboard, in holiday times, can stretch twice as long as her 186 feet. Go off-season, or not at all. The museum on the quay has a fine collection of that vigorous genre of folk art: the ship's figurehead.

We mustn't forget the old *Foudroyant*, another wooden wall, currently being repaired for her job as a training ship in Portsmouth Harbour. She was built much later than *Victory*, in 1817, and belongs to the *Foudroyant* Trust.

To return to the original *Mary Rose* – Henry VIII's 'Flower of all ships that ever sailed' – that so unfortunately turned over and sank in 1545. One of her cannon has just been salvaged at the time of writing. It has been put in a hydrogen furnace with a flowing mixture of ten per cent hydrogen and ninety per cent nitrogen. This has the peculiar effect of turning rust back into iron. After this the iron will be impregnated with a low-melting-point polyvinyl chloride, which will stop it turning to rust again.

Portsmouth Harbour is much like the last two natural 'harbours' we have discussed, except that it is more full of shipping, and more surrounded with dock-works and industry. There are plenty of gentlemen in motor boats, descendants of the skippers of the 'Spithead Wherries' no doubt – who are eager to 'take you round the battleships', and a very interesting voyage it is, too. Local men go forth on the harbour in small boats and put set-nets across the creeks in the mud for silver eels, fattened as they are after their seven years up Hampshire rivers, and on their way to cross the Atlantic to their spawning grounds in the Sargasso Sea. A couple of years ago a man could catch here twenty or thirty nice flounders on a hook and line in a few hours. Now some poison has put an end to all but a few survivors. There is a vast land reclamation scheme going on behind **Horsea Island**. Huge factories are to be built there, including one for I.B.M., so that ever more thousands will be drawn to this underbelly of England.

Portchester Castle dominates the harbour, now as it did when the Romans built it. Instead of entering the building immediately, it is pleasant to stroll around the foreshore first, and appreciate the mighty Roman wall from the outsider's point of view. The old sailing barge *Black Prince* lies on the foreshore, with a sad superstructure plonked on her lovely hull. The private landing stage that has been – well – *conjurated* to serve the M.T.B. *Silver Mist* and her companions should have a preservation order clapped on it immediately. It is unique.

Now we turn to the long, faceless, impassive walls of the Roman fort, which are extensive enough to enclose a small town. Besides the two gates, and the Norman keep, this wall is broken only by the ejection orifices of the medieval monks' *necessarium.*

The Roman Portus Adurni is almost certainly modern Portchester, and it was a fairly typical fort of the Saxon Shore, such as we dealt with at some length under Dover in Chapter 4. Portchester was fairly similar to Richborough, and probably built at about the same time, that is in the last quarter of the third century. The fort was probably built by the usurping sailor-emperor Carausius (although some theories place it earlier under Probus). Allectus, the man who killed Carausius and made himself emperor, was occupying Portchester when he was attacked by Constantius Chlorus, who had landed to the west of him and who beat him and brought Britain back to within the Roman fold.

According to Professor Cunliffe, who excavated Portchester, the first military occupation only lasted twenty years. This was followed by a period during which the fort may have been used as a concentration camp for the followers of the rebels Allectus and Carausius, for rubbish and squalor were then piled up against the walls. About 340 the fort was refurbished for military occupation, but about 369, under Count Theodosius, the functions of Portchester were transferred to Bitterne, then called Clausentum, and Portchester was substantially abandoned as a fortification.

When the Romans left the Saxons came, and there is strong evidence that Portchester was settled by them. Unfortunately only limited excavation can be done. If the south-east quarter of the castle garth was sacred ground in Saxon times (and is now a graveyard) the north-east corner is sacred ground now – *for it is a cricket ground*, and cannot be disturbed on any account. So it may be hundreds of years – maybe never – before we know what lies beneath it. But there is very little doubt but that the Saxons built a church here, and that this was a mission station of early Christianity. Whether the Romans had had a temple here, too, is not known, but it would have been most unlikely for them not to have done.

At all events we know that before 904 Portchester belonged to the Bishops of Winchester. After 1100 Henry I had a great Norman keep built in the north-west corner of the Roman fort, an inner bailey round it, and he replaced the Roman Land Gate and the Water Gate with well-fortified Norman gates and gatehouses. It is surely remarkable that eight hundred years after the Romans had built those great walls they were still good enough for the Normans to use as the outer bailey of their castle, and remarkable, too, that eight hundred years after the Normans they still stand up straight and strong. The Normans and early Plantagenets used the place as a royal castle, a departure point for Normandy, and a hunting lodge for the Forest of Bere. Prince Louis of France, who, as we have seen, failed to take Dover when he was invited in by the barons who were rebelling against King John, did not fail to take Portchester.

Richard II built a palace in the inner bailey (the first range of buildings you see on your left as you go through the gate into the inner bailey). Henry V stayed here while he was waiting for the wind to set fair for France and for Agincourt.

Henry VIII could find nothing better to do with Portchester

but to use it as a naval storehouse, for Portsmouth had by now become the naval base. Parliament took the castle in the Civil War and used it as a barracks, and in the Dutch wars of the seventeenth century, and the many French wars of the eighteenth, it was repeatedly used to hold prisoners of war. The latter carved their names on the walls in many places, and their bones, and the bones of American prisoners who followed them in the revolutionary wars, are still sometimes dug up in Urchin Meadow to the west of the castle, and in the mud flats and saltings to the east. Only three prisoners of war are marked in the parish register as having been buried in consecrated ground.

The inner bailey and the keep are well worth seeing. The latter is a massive building, with story after lofty story and a fine view from the top. From here we can survey all of Portsmouth Harbour, including the great new reclamation works going on inside Horsea Island to make room for yet more factories.

But whatever you do, do not miss the church, which is in the south-east corner of the Roman fort, for it is one of the finest Romanesque buildings in the area. It has a very urbane, clean-cut and civilised air about it for a Norman church in the English countryside. It was built to serve both the parish, and a priory of Augustinian canons. There were conventual buildings to the south of it which have completely disappeared, and the area can't be excavated because of the graveyard. The west door is quite stunning, the arches of the crossing superb, and the font – with those monsters and man-monsters with their tails tied in inextricable knots over an arcade of blind arches – is quite remarkable. Alas, the south transept has been pulled down.

And, to the north-west of the castle, the little organic village of beautiful old houses which was Portchester winds away along its main street, with the great red tide of modern housing estates washing right up to the bottom fences of its gardens – as though determined to break through this flimsy barrier and overwhelm the little village, the castle, and spread out over the very tidal harbour itself.

Here I might mention that curious phenomenon of the Solent area: double tides. There are four tides in every twenty-five hours and not two as is usual elsewhere. In every twenty-four hours there are from seven to eight hours of fairly high and slack water, which make the working of big ships much easier, and is a big advantage for a tidal port. Many people think that this peculiar circumstance is caused by the way the tides race round both ends of the Isle of Wight. They are quite wrong. The double tides are caused by the fact that this stretch of the coast of England is the meeting-point of the tidal surge coming up-Channel, and the one coming down-Channel from the North Sea. Poole Harbour, not affected by the Isle of Wight, has double tides, too.

The phenomenon is not new. The Venerable Bede wrote: 'In this sea comes a double tide out of the seas which spring from the infinite ocean of the Arctic which surrounds all Britain.'

CHAPTER 14

Fareham to Southampton

CALLED Fernham in Domesday Book, **Fareham** had two mills, and one, Cam's Mill, was there in Saxon times and it took the 1920s to knock it down. Fareham was a free port. Sir John Coke, in 1630, recommended that it should be made a naval base, but nothing came of it. (Nobody but a farmer would ever have thought it would have been any good for this purpose anyway.) In the sixteenth and seventeenth centuries there was a good trade of wine in and timber out. Coal was still coming in five years ago, then the trade was stopped and the coal carried on the already groaning roads. It is

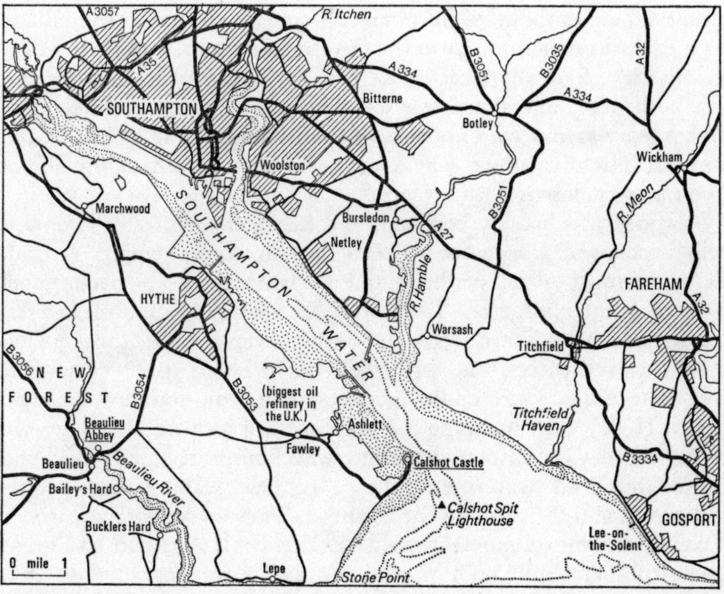

still a tiny bit of a port, though, because the old coal wharf is used for landing shingle from three little dredgers. Fareham, and Cam's Lake, which is a reach of the creek lower down, are very busy and crowded with yachting, and there are yacht-building yards ashore.

Thank God the little peninsula that Cam's Hall stands on is not being built on, for there is a pleasant walk around it.

Fareham is now being made the administration centre of a vast area of the red flood. The whole of that once-favoured piece of very fertile country between the Downs and the sea is being turned into a vast conurbation. The fine Georgian houses of the High Street are being preserved, like a pearl in an oyster. There is a watchmaker in the town named Oliver Cromwell.

Titchfield, nearby, is even more to be regretted, for it is a noble little place. Just north of it are the rather splendid remains of a thirteenth-century Premonstratensian abbey, built of stone carried from the Isle of Wight. Richard II and his queen stayed here, and so did Henry V when he was waiting for the wind to set fair for France, or at least when he wasn't in Portchester or – as Shakespeare tells us in his play about him – having the Earl of March's head cut off at Southampton. Henry VI waited here for Margaret of Anjou (there is still an Anjou Bridge). In 1538 the abbey was dissolved. Thomas Wriothesley, later 1st Earl of Southampton, built a 'ryghte statelie House embatalid' here, and the parish church in the village has a grandiose monument to the family, and a tablet to little Mary Wriothesley, four years old. The first earl's son welcomed Queen Elizabeth here, and it was *his* son who was such a good friend of Shakespeare's, and who appears in such an ambiguous light in the Sonnets. Titchfield once was a port, but the mouth of the River Meon was enclosed.

Gosport was heavily bombed, and hence the centre of it now is utility post-war department store architecture, which is sad, because it must once have been, like Portsmouth, a rip-roaring port town of great character. T. H. Rogers writes, in *Gosport Records*, that around 1800 there were just under seventy pubs, three coach houses, two theatres, one bridewell (or prison), three breweries, two flour mills, fourteen bakehouses, one iron foundry (a man named Henry Cort invented a new process of iron puddling here in 1776), there were also malthouses, warehouses and wharves, and several hundred watermen whose business was rowing people backwards and forwards in the harbour. There were many prisoner of war hulks out on moorings, old wooden walls that had had great superstructures built on top of them, and were degraded to that horrible occupation. And, of course, then as now, the Royal Navy was in full swing. The place was a big commercial port, too: a merchant named Erasmus Carver, as one example, had a fine fleet of ships during the eighteenth century, in which he used to carry captured French guns and other material obtained from the Navy to West Africa, to exchange for slaves for America, to exchange for sugar home. In the 1840s it is said that upwards of 1,900 ships could be seen lying in the roads off Gosport at one time. And, of course, the place was a most important victualling port for the Royal Navy, and still is.

Then there was, and is, Camper and Nicholson. Amos Camper started a boat-building yard here early in the nineteenth century. He took on Benjamin Nicholson as an apprentice, took him into partnership in 1843, and, by dint of keeping up with the times or a little ahead of them, became the biggest builder of yachts and small craft in the country. Outside the gate of the Hornet Naval Yacht Centre stands *Coastal Motor Boat 103*, kept as a memorial to the famous Motor Torpedo Boats of the First World War. She was built by Camper and Nicholson in 1918. The shore station H.M.S. *Hornet* was commissioned in 1925, and was the M.T.B. base until 1958. There is a war memorial to the Coastal Forces here, and when some German 'E' boats came in after the war on a courtesy visit their crews went ashore and chivalrously placed wreaths upon it. H.M.S. *Dolphin*, the main submarine base, is at Gosport, too.

In 1873 William Froude built a tank for testing models of ships at **Haslar**, and it was the first in the world. It was 400 hundred feet long by twenty feet wide by nine feet deep. Froude was tired of being laughed at by the people of Totnes, in Devon, when he used to carry out his experiments in the Dart. He invented a dynamometer to measure the resistance of the water to various shapes of hull. To keep the water clear in his tank he inserted eels, and one man of his staff was appointed Official Keeper of the Eels and had to feed them on cat's meat. Now the clearing is done with chemicals, and there has been a sad break with tradition.

Alverstoke is an interesting survival of a place. Besides the inevitable fort it has the inevitable golf course, and this one is unique in that the conception of that abstract officer *Colonel Bogey* was conceived here, the gallant gentleman being named, in 1892, from a song which went: 'Hush hush, here comes the Bogey Man!'

Robert Cruikshank was the driving force behind non-golfing Alverstoke. He, like many others elsewhere, tried to repeat the success of Brighton. He called his creation *Angleseaville*, after the Marquis of Anglesea, the one who left a leg at Waterloo. He built the Crescent about 1820, and it is still there. This was meant to be one of many such terraces, but the scheme never came off. He built a bridge over Haslar Creek (bombed 1940), he tried hard to build docks and a railway at Gilkicker Point, and a ship canal to connect the docks with the railway. He did succeed in establishing a 'floating bridge' (a chain ferry) across to Portsmouth to replace the light foot ferry formerly used. He had to force this through in the face of bitter opposition from the hundreds of Gosport watermen. He died in 1853, and most of what he started came to nothing.

There are two great houses at Alverstoke. One is Bay House, built by Lord Ashburton around 1839. Thomas Carlyle often used to stay there. In 1870 this became a naval college, and Queen Victoria's second son, Prince Alfred, lived here while he was a pupil at Burney's Academy, and many another naval gentleman was trained here, including Admirals Beatty and Togo, who gave respectively the Germans and the Russians such hard times.

Alverbank House, built by John Wilson Croker, Secretary to the Admiralty in 1842, was another great house. Sir Robert Peel, the Duke of Wellington, and other Tories used to go there.

The Royal Naval Hospital at Haslar is an old establishment. Dr James Lind (1758–83) discovered the value of lime juice for preventing scurvy here, and earned for British tars the sobriquet, across the Atlantic, of 'limeys'.

Last but not least, Queen Victoria had a special railway line, and railway station built, so that she could sail from it to her house at Osborne on the Isle of Wight, untroubled, as she said, by 'excited crowds of patriotic citizens or gazing rustics'.

Lee-on-the-Solent is a residential seaside resort, much inhabited by naval personnel. The Bracklesham Beds reappear here at the base of the cliffs and it is a good place to look for fossils. Gosport is underlaid by these beds, and the Bagshot Beds, and their combined thickness is from two to three hundred feet.

At **Browndown** Lieutenant C. Hawkey of the Royal Marines, and Captain Seton of the Eleventh Dragoons fought the last duel in England. Seton, who had been enamoured of Hawkey's wife, was mortally wounded.

And after crossing Titchfield Haven, and a long walk along a refreshingly unbuilt-up shore, we come to **Warsash** and the **River Hamble.** And if you like the sight of simply lots and lots of fabulously expensive yachts – then the Hamble is the river for you. One estimate recently made placed the value of the yachts in the Hamble River at £32½ million! There they lie, moored as closely together as they can be moored without banging into each other, all the way up to Bursledon, and more above the bridge as far as Botley (although the reach above Bursledon Bridge is devoted to water skiing), and yet more packed into the marinas that are springing up on all sides, and the most striking thing about these great fleets of so expensive vessels is that so few of them ever seem to go to sea. You go there on a fine bank-holiday weekend, or in the middle of Cowes Week or any other week, and there they still lie, in their hundreds, with just the occasional bit of activity as a yacht here and there gets under way, always under engine, of course, and motors out towards the sea. One feels that their owners are so busy earning money up in the City to pay for them that they very seldom have time actually to *sail* them. Most of them are just great big floating sacred cows. Representing the last thing in naval architecture, filled with every kind of gadget and invention of our technological age – including electronic navigational systems of the utmost sophistication – they lie there, most of them for at least eleven months of every year, simply advertising their owners' wealth and the fact that, in a more robust age, he would have been a pirate. A *few* of them, of course, actually do go cruising. Some of them go round the world. But the ones that get across the English Channel are a minute proportion.

The boats that *do* put to sea and in vast numbers, although they don't go very far, are what are rudely called 'bum-hangers', the small racing class boats that are hauled up in vast 'boat parks' when they are not racing, when the rattle of their metal shrouds on their metal masts in the wind makes a strange sort of tinny noise that can be deafening. It is nothing to see a thousand sail of these out on the Solent on a fine day in summer. There are said to be forty-two yacht and sailing clubs in the Solent area.

There is still, amazingly, a small fleet of commercial fishing boats operating from the Hamble. They are simple craft built of wood, and although their operators manage to go to sea in practically all weathers for twelve months of the year, they seem to manage without any electronic equipment at all. They dredge for oysters, rake for cockles, and some hardy men grope about in the black mud over on the Wight side for clams. Some go trawling, mostly for soles. They make a living. In 1890 there were twenty-two boats and eighty men engaged, largely in spratting. Some of the boats were old Colchester oyster dredgers brought over. By 1920 there were only three of them left, but now they are on the increase again.

There was once a fleet in the Hamble of *Well Smacks*: decked fishing boats that had perforated bottoms so as to let the water flow into their watertight holds and thus keep the fish alive. These sailed at first to France to bring back crayfish and lobsters. Seeing that nowadays a large proportion of lobsters caught in English waters are flown straight to France this may seem strange; but a hundred years ago there were still rich lobster grounds on the French side, and the English were still wealthy enough to eat lobsters. Now the French fishermen have denuded their coasts of everything that crawls or swims, and the French are the ones who can – and will – pay for good food, and so they come here and buy our shell fish. Even *winkles.* The import trade into the Hamble from France ended in 1885, and then the Well Smacks started going to the West Coast of Ireland, and buying lobsters off the *curagh* fishermen there. The lobsters were kept in great floating crates called *carbs.* They were either sent to London as demanded, or else put aboard the luxury liners sailing from Southampton.

At Warsash is the Southampton School of Navigation. The embryo of this was a private school in Bassett known as the Gilchrist Navigation School. It was taken over by the University of Southampton in 1932, transferred to Warsash between 1943 and 1946, and relinquished by the university and transferred to the City of Southampton in April, 1972. It trains cadets and midshipmen, and also has courses for masters and mates. Of interest to yachtsmen (sea-going) are evening classes held during the autumn and spring terms to prepare people for certificates of competency as Yachtmaster (Ocean) and Yachtmaster (Coastal).

The school has the auxiliary ketch *Halcyon* for sea training, and also the 108 ton motor vessel *Somerset*, which is specifically for instrument training. A famous episode of great drama was the end of the *Halcyon*'s predecessor, the yawl *Mayana.* This fine little ship, built in 1899 as a yacht, won the Torbay to Lisbon Sail Training Race of 1956, and then encountered an exceptional gale on her way home to England. When her captain found that she was being blown back on to a lee shore of France, and could make no headway to windward, and that her young crew of cadets was exhausted, he radioed for help and the crew was taken off her by the *Clan Maclean.* The yacht herself was taken in tow, but sank as she was being towed and that was the end of her.

The sixty-year-old Brixham trawler *Terminus* is to terminate her days as a club house for the Mercury Yacht Harbour, part of a marina. She is to be kept properly rigged aloft, but is to be all 'fitted carpets, imitation oil lamps and louvred doors' below.

Botley, up-river, is a boat-building and yachting place, but is also the centre of a big early strawberry growing area.

The coast from the Hamble to the River Itchen is entirely built up. **Netley** has an abbey, founded in the thirteenth century by Cistercians from Beaulieu. Henry III endowed it, and went to the dedication of it with his queen. At the Dissolution it went to the First Marquess of Winchester, who was also Comptroller of the Royal Household, but in 1719 was sold to one Walter Taylor, who only wanted to pull it down, cart the stone to the Isle of Wight (where no doubt much of it had come from) and build himself a mansion there. He dreamed that a monk came and warned him that if he did pull it down a stone would fall on his head and kill him. His dream came true. A piece of the great west window came down on top of him and put an end to his nefarious schemes. The ruins thus spared are fine and romantic, and predominantly Early English. Henry VIII converted the gatehouse of the abbey into one of his shore castles, and in the nineteenth century this was in turn converted into something also very typical of its age: a Victorian 'Gothic' folly. It is still there. Jane Austen describes making an excursion to Netley by boat, landing at the hard there, and picnicking in the beautiful ruins of the abbey.

At **Woolston** Vosper Thorneycroft ply their trade, turning out 'frigates' and mine-hunters galore, both for this country and for oil sheikdoms over the sea. John I. Thorneycroft came here from his works in Chiswick in 1904. At the Training Centre (for shipbuilders) at Woolston is preserved *C.M.B.4*, a forty-foot coastal motor boat, in which Lieut. A. W. Agar, R.N., won the Victoria Cross in the Baltic in 1919. Hubert Scott-Paine was the pioneer here in designing high speed boats, and from his work the R.A.F. air-sea rescue launches were developed.

The famous Schneider Trophy-winning Supermarine sea-planes were designed and built at Woolston, and the Spitfire, which, whether we like it or not, saved Britain and democratic government in 1940, was built here until the works were completely destroyed by enemy action, when manufacture was dispersed. We will discuss the Schneider Trophy planes when we get to Calshot, which is where they flew.

The **River Itchen** has a human history stretching far back into the past. It was used by boats in the Bronze Age and has been used by boats ever since. The Romans built Clausentum, a fort on a ness or promontory formed by a bend in the river, at what is now **Bitterne**. The river was at that time navigable as far inland as Winchester. The Antonine Itinerary lists Roman roads from Clausentum to Chichester and to Winchester.

Southampton was a great landing place of the marauding Danes. They arrived in 857, in thirty-five ships, were beaten off again, but came back in 860 and captured Southampton, which already must have been a town. King Alfred drove them out again, they returned in 980 under Olaf of Norway and Sweyn of Denmark, marched in and captured London and ravaged far and wide. They then came back to Southampton, to be near their ships, and waited for the *danegeld* promised them by the wretched Ethelred. After the flight of that unready monarch the Witan, or Parliament, met here and offered the crown to Cnut, Knut or Canute. This was in 1016. There is still a Canute Street here, and Southampton people claim that it was here that Canute had his famous encounter with the tides. There is a theory that what he was actually doing was observing for himself that strange and very uncommon phenomenon – the Solent's double tides. At all events, however scholars may argue about this very important matter, the landlord of the Canute Hotel in Canute Street suffers no doubts. High up on his hotel wall is written: 'In 1028 near this spot Canute Reproved his Courtiers'. That puts Bosham in its place.

A Saxon and a Danish town grew up on the bank of the Itchen. When the Normans came they preferred the gravel ridge overlooking the Test, and there they built a great castle, a palace, churches, and, in 1224, the Priory of St Denis of the Black Canons was founded.

When the English kings lost their holdings in France, Southampton lost its importance as a port of embarkation for Normandy, but it gained as a naval seaport, for afterwards followed almost constant war. On Sunday, 4th October, 1338, a fleet of Norman, Genoese and Spanish ships sailed in, led by the son of the King of Sicily, and took Southampton, driving the citizens out. But next day the people of Hampshire rallied, counter-attacked, and killed the King of Sicily's son and three hundred others. Stow, the Elizabethan historian, describing this battle, wrote that the Sicilian prince cried: 'Rançon! Rançon!' to the man who was attacking him, 'notwithstanding which the husbandman laid on him with his clubbe till he had slaine him, speaking these words, "Yea," quoth he, "I know thee well enough: thou art a *Francon*, and therefore thou shalt die;" for he understood not his speech . . . Wherefore the residue of these Genoways, after they had set the towne on fire and burnit it up quite, fledde to their galleys, and in their flying certain of them were drowned. After this the inhabitants encompassed it about with a great and strong wall.'

This wall, now the 'Arcades', still stands in part. It was built with the stone from the King's House.

The foreigners came back again, not once but several times; for after all Southampton was a very rich prize. They attacked and were repulsed in 1340. After then, and the Battle of Sluys, where the French fleet was practically destroyed, England had command of the Narrow Seas and there was far less trouble. But history – *English* history at least – does not tell us how much trouble the *French* had over the other side.

In 1345 Edward III collected 32,000 troops in Southampton,

and the town itself contributed twenty-one ships and 576 men for the Creçy campaign. In Henry V's reign two great ships were built here: the *Grâce Dieu* and the *Holy Ghost*, and Southampton was the main base, together with Portchester, in which he mustered his army of 30,000 and 1,500 ships to sail for Agincourt. He addressed his letter to the French king demanding his French dominions back from *Chastel he Hantonne au rivage de la mer.*

As far as more peaceful pursuits went, Southampton was a prosperous commercial port, in the Middle Ages as it is now. By 1215 it was second only to London for the import of wine – in 1272 it imported 3,147 tuns compared to London's 3,799. In the fourteenth century a great trade grew up with Venice, for the import of goods brought from Asia Minor in Venetian bottoms. Once a year a great fleet of Venetian galleys used to sail from Venice for northern Europe, with great ceremony, bringing goods from the east, and taking back wood, cloth, wool and leather. In 1378 Richard II allowed the Venetians to make Southampton their port of call, and it is said that because of this there are still Italian names in old Hampshire families, because a permanent settlement of Venetian families grew up in the city, much as did a settlement of English wine merchants in Portugal much later. But the discovery by Vasco da Gama of the Cape Route to the east sounded the knell of Venice as a mighty trading power. It was much cheaper to bring the silks and spices of the Indies around the Cape by sea than to buy them from Arab traders who had carried them across the great deserts on camel-back. The last Venetian galley came to Southampton in 1532.

In 1447 Southampton was created a County Borough with a sheriff, so it was by then a great city. Flemish immigrants replaced the Venetians, many arriving in 1567, when permission was granted for weavers and other craftsmen to come and establish factories, provided that each one employed two English apprentices and taught them the trade. One English journeyman, too, had to be employed for every foreigner.

But by Tudor times Southampton's trade had taken a turn for the worse. The rise of the west country ports: Dartmouth and Plymouth and Falmouth and many more – was Southampton's loss. Henry VIII had to remit some of the city's debt for taxes. Queen Mary gave the city protection in both import and export trades, and Elizabeth carried on this protection. Southampton managed to get a small share of the three-cornered Newfoundland trade: salt and trade goods to Newfoundland, salt cod to Portugal or the Mediterranean, wine back to England. (The other great three-cornered trade: trade goods to West Africa, slaves to America and sugar back to England had been much cornered by Bristol, and the west country.) In 1620 the *Mayflower* sailed from here to Dartmouth, Plymouth, and America. By the end of the eighteenth century the port was very much in decline. In George III's time, however, it began to rise as a 'watering place', and it looked at one time as if it might rival Brighton. Pope, Swift, Horace Walpole and Jane Austen all used to frequent the city. Needless to say some foul-tasting 'mineral water' was found welling up somewhere, and was said to be medicinal. The present Union Castle Steamship Company's office is on the site of the Gloucester Baths. The Dolphin Inn, now a Trust House, was used for balls and rallies. In 1766 a Long Room was built, a theatre opened in 1766 in French Street, Mrs Sarah Siddons, the great actress, owned a house in what is now Portland Street and later bought Freemantle House near the shore.

The fact that the port was much used in the Napoleonic Wars helped to build up prosperity again and in 1795 there were plans to link the port with London because French privateers were reaping such a harvest in the Channel, but the Navy cleared the privateers out and so the scheme was abandoned.

Then in 1803 came an Act to build docks and after this development was rapid and continuous:

1836: Dock Company floated.

1838: Work started reclaiming 216 acres of mud at the confluence of the Test and Itchen.

1839: Tidal dock, sixteen acres, largest in England, entrance 150 feet wide with 18 feet of water at Low Spring Tides completed. This is now called the Eastern Docks.

1838: A railway to London was building.

1842: P and O steamers started using the port.

1843: The Outer Dock was opened – 16 acres, 2,621 feet of quay, 18 feet of L.W.S. This is still in use.

1857: Inner Docks completed (10 acres, 2,575 feet of quay).

1876: The Itchen Quays for the South Africa trade were completed.

1879: Extension to the Itchen Quays was made.

By this time there were four graving docks.

1890: The Empress Dock was opened on 26th July by Queen Victoria. 18½ acres, 3,880 foot quayage, 26 foot L.W.S., 165 foot entrance.

1892: At midnight on 21st October the docks were transferred to the ownership of the London and South Western Railway. The tail was wagging the dog.

1893: On 4th March S.S. *New York* of the American Line sailed into the Empress Dock. Southampton was now without question the main port for the Atlantic run.

1895: Prince of Wales Graving Dock opened: 745 feet by 91: the largest dry dock in the world.

1905: The Trafalgar Dry Dock opened, 915 feet by 100 feet, even bigger. Ships were getting bigger so dry docks had to.

1911: Ocean Dock opened for the largest liners afloat. 15½ acres, 3,807 feet of quay space, 40 foot Low Water Springs, 400 foot entrance. The White Star Line deserted Liverpool to come here.

1914: Embarkation Port for No. 1 Expeditionary Force.

1923: Railway Company was amalgamated with the Southern Railway.

1927: Huge dock extensions begun. Completed in 1934 with 7,543 feet of quays.

1932: The New Docks, now Western Docks, opened.

1933: The King George V Graving Dock opened 26th July. For ships of up to 100,000 tons. Unfortunately it happened to be on an artesian well and pumping had to go on night and day. This made seven dry docks in all.

1939: Chief port of embarkation for Expeditionary Force. By the Battle of Dunkirk 800,000 men and 375,000 tons of stores had been shipped to France.

1940: 30th November first really big air raid. The city was to be largely destroyed during the Second World War.

1942: Combined Operations raid on Dieppe sailed from here.

During the latter part of this war the great dry docks were used for the construction of the Mulberry Harbours. Some components weighed 5,000 tons. In the thirty weeks following D Day 1,600,000 tons of stores were shipped out of Southampton.

But, of course, once very big ships came in it was inevitable that Southampton should become a major port. Southampton Water is a drowned valley, inundated about 20,000 years ago, it has plenty of depth of water naturally, and as its contributary rivers run over chalk they bring very little sediment to silt it up. Also it has the phenomenon of four tides a day (instead of two as most places in the world get) and this gives it many more hours of high tide than other harbours. Now, as aircraft have replaced ships for carrying passengers, so Southampton has lost trade. But more and more diversified industry has come to the city to take its place, and there still seem to be plenty of ships, and large ones, too, at the wharves.

The shores of the Itchen River are now crowded with the infrastructure of big industry, but there was once a most picturesque fishermen's and watermen's village here, and this was the home of the famous Itchen Ferry Punts and the Southampton Fishing Hoys. Both punts and hoys were broad-beamed, quite round in section, cutter-rigged with a huge spread of canvas – a long running bowsprit, jack-yard topsail and a loose-footed mainsail. In 1822 an Act of Parliament laid down the fare from Southampton to Cowes for a boat with two men at 12/6d, and for a boat with four men at £1.15.0. But the Red Funnel Steamers came and knocked these boats right out. The Red Funnel Line was formed in 1861 by amalgamation of the Southampton, Isle of Wight and South of England Royal Mail Steam Packet Company Limited. And the Itchen men, as ferrying and fishing declined, turned to serving as yacht hands in the huge new yachts that were being built by both old- and new-rich in the nineteenth century.

A Southampton family of great note was the Taylors, of block-making fame. There were Walter Taylor I, W.T.II, and W.T.III. Walter Taylor II has been called the father of mass production. He started life as a ship's carpenter, was captured by the French in 1746, and while a prisoner of war in Rouen contrived to make an electrical machine out of an ostrich egg! When he got home he set up as a block maker, with his son Walter Taylor III. He had seen, in gales in the Mediterranean and other places, how inefficient the blocks in use at the time were.

A block is what the landlubber might call a pulley. It is a block of wood, nicely shaped, with a groove cut through its centre through which a rope might run (or more than one groove in the case of multiple blocks). Inside each groove is a sheave – a wheel with a grooved rim for the rope to run round, and through the middle of each sheave is a pin, which is driven through the middle of the block and serves as an axle for the sheave to turn on. The purpose of blocks is to obtain mechanical advantage in hauling ropes (a rope through one single block, termed a 'whip', gives a mechanical advantage of two-to-one, etc.). A ship of the line, in days of sail, needed 1,400 blocks, and pre-Taylor they all had to be carved out by hand.

The Taylors began to develop machinery for making them, working in secret at first, and the whine of their circular saw in the basement where they kept it made people believe they were having parley with the Devil! Gradually they elaborated the most complex machinery for cutting out the shapes they needed. Much of this machinery can still be seen in the National Maritime Museum at Greenwich. Their first block-making machine, completed about 1755, has been called the first-ever piece of mass-production machinery.

Captain Bentinck, R.N., was the first master to try the new blocks out, and he fitted his command, H.M.S. *Centaur*, with them throughout. They proved satisfactory. In 1770 a fire destroyed the old-fashioned Admiralty block shops in Portsmouth, and the Taylors were able to make up the lost production. In 1794 their machinery was driven by horse-gins, but they moved to Weston Mill in 1770 and there used water power. They also manufactured ships' pumps. Their contract with the Admiralty ended in 1803, the founders of the firm died out, and their offspring rapidly squandered the fortune they had made by trying to keep up with the Regency bucks.

Another local inventor was Captain George Peacock, Dock Master at Southampton, and a fine marine engineer. He devised a new system of navigation buoyage for Southampton Water in about 1860, and he did surveying work with the Royal Navy in connection with the Panama Canal. But he is chiefly remembered for the invention of an anti-fouling paint (a paint to keep marine growth off the bottoms of ships, buoys, etc.). He made it in a factory at Millbrook, and in South America, we are told, anti-fouling is still called *Picoco*.

As for the city to-day, this is outside the scope of this book. But there is a fine maritime museum in the fourteenth-century Wool House, Bargate is a fine medieval town gate, Tudor House, where Henry VIII and Anne Boleyn are supposed to have stayed, is a museum, there are some fighting towers left: Catch Cold (fifteenth century) and Arundel (fourteenth century). But the city spreads and spreads and bids fair to join up with Portsmouth and become one of the major cities of the world. It is a little surprising, when you think of it, that London was chosen as the site for the capital of England, and not Southampton. London is miles up a shallow, winding, muddy river, and when you get there it's built on clay land that was once swamp. Southampton is much more accessible for ships from all over the world, it is in the middle of the south coast, and would have been in many ways a far better site for a capital city than the present Wen.

The arms of 'The Town and County of the Town of Southampton' are to be described thus:

Per fesse argent and gules three roses counter charged of the field.

CHAPTER 15

Hythe to Lymington

HYTHE, reached by fast and frequent foot-ferry from Southampton, might have been a big port, too, for the edge of the mud is not too far out at high tide, but that it is the wrong side of the estuary. What trade was there to and from the New Forest? It could also have remained a very pleasant place: a charming little Georgian and Victorian river port but its inhabitants seem to have been hell-bent on spoiling it. St John's Street, even now, could be saved and made charming again but anybody can see that the Town Fathers have already consigned it, in their minds, to the bulldozer. There is a fine little artificial harbour, now surrounded by sleazy-looking factories which make no use of the harbour at all and could just have well been built inland. The harbour is beset with notices saying Keep Out and Beware of the Dog. The place seems to have a sort of death wish.

Hythe was the base for Imperial Airways flying boats during the short life of this sensible form of aircraft. The British Marine Navigation Company was formed in 1923, and in September of that year a service started to St Peter's Port in Guernsey with 'Sea Eagle' flying boats. In 1924 came government support and Imperial Airways was founded, in 1935 twenty-eight Short S.23 flying boats were ordered, in 1936 the first S.23, a 'Canopus', was launched into the Medway at Rochester and two days afterwards made her maiden flight. She was all-metal and powered by four Bristol Pegasus radial engines, her payload was one and a half tons of mail and twenty-four day passengers, or sixteen sleeping passengers in comfortable berths and then three and a half tons of mail.

On 4th February, 1937, regular services were started to Sydney, on 28th June the same year to Durban, and by 1938 there were the following services: seven a week to Egypt, four to India, three to East Africa, two to South Africa, two to Hong Kong, two to Australia.

And on 30th September, 1958, the whole thing was brought to an end, and the great fleet of large and luxurious ships of the air sold to the Americans, who appreciated them.

Now the United States Army Marine Fleet has a base which

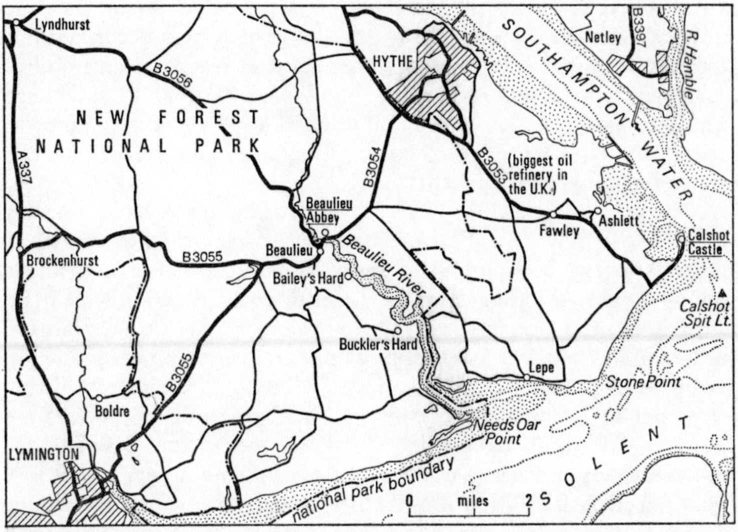

takes up a long stretch of the foreshore at Hythe, and weird flat-bottomed vessels with cranes on them are moored off-shore.

Groves, the Weymouth naturalist, first discovered *Spartina townsendii*, the new hybrid marsh grass, on the mud-flats at Hythe in 1878. This hybrid was a mule – that is it could not breed by sexual reproduction. There seems to have been a mutation since then, though, which is allowing it to breed sexually.

Fawley is a small and ancient village, mentioned in records at Winchester as early as AD 971, now absolutely overwhelmed by the biggest refinery in Britain. Its little church is interesting, one Saxon window rebuilt into the east wall, interesting interior, the chancel had the distinction of having been blasted by an *Italian* bomb during the Second World War (the only Italian raid there was over England – although the Italians, apparently, have disclaimed the honour of having dropped a bomb on Fawley church) and in the south aisle there is a model of a *Long Boat* from Tristan da Cunha. She has a strange-shaped mainsail with the clew held out by a short boom the inboard end of which is lashed to a thwart. There is an actual Tristan da Cunha longboat in Greenwich Maritime Museum.

The reason why the model is in Fawley church is that the islanders lived in the Married Quarters in the old R.A.F. camp at Calshot when the volcano threatened to blow their island up. They lived there from January, 1962, to October, 1963. A few of them, who had married local people, elected to stay behind when the rest returned to their island (one works as a very popular roadman hereabouts) but it is noteworthy that most of the thirteen families who arrived in England announcing their intention to stay here went back again. A year and a half in Calshot Camp was apparently enough. A. C. Cossor, of electric valve fame, was buried by the gate of the churchyard in 1918.

As for the refinery it was started way back in 1920 when refineries were blessedly few, and the ones there were, were small. It was built by the Atlantic Gulf and West Indies Steamship Company, taken over by Anglo American Standard Oil in 1924, now known as the Esso Petroleum Company, and the enormous expansion programme was begun in 1949 and substantially finished in 1951, making Fawley the biggest refinery in the British Isles. In 1958 the first of Esso's petro-chemical units there came on stream, and in 1966 Esso Chemical Ltd took over this side of the operation. Fawley can process sixteen and a half million tons of crude oil a year – that is if it can get it. A limitation now is the growing size of tankers. Esso, in conjunction with the Southampton Harbour Board, has dredged the Nab Shoal and the approach channel at a cost of two million pounds so as to be able to take ships of 100,000 tons' dead weight. But tankers are getting much bigger than this, and Milford Haven and other very deep water ports are likely to go ahead of places like Fawley.

At **Ashlett**, near the village, there is a fine tidal mill, and the refinery makes use of its old mill-pounds for containing its cooling water. By raising the temperature of one of these they have caused a growth of a tropical white coral on the sluice gates. The Jolly Sailor Inn at Ashlett is a jolly good pub, and the magnificent mill building has been taken over as a club-house for Esso employees. This tidal mill once had four pairs of stones each pair of which could grind four hundredweight of corn in an hour and the four together could easily grind a ton on a tide – that is two tons a day and not a penny to an Arabian oil sheik.

At **Calshot Spit** Cerdic and Cynric, two jolly Saxons, landed in AD 498 for a raid. As early as 1823 there was a *steamer* service from here to the Isle of Wight. Later the Spit was used by the R.A.F. for their Small Craft Maintenance Base.

There is a very strange pub in Calshot named the Owl and Moon, which used to be the R.A.F. Officers' Mess. Around the walls of the public bar are many photographs of Supermarine seaplanes. These were made over the water at Woolston, but were flown from Calshot. The Supermarine story is dominated by the name of

R. J. Mitchell, who was that rare being, an artist as well as a scientist. Mitchell came to Supermarine in 1916. Seaplanes were already being built by the firm at Woolston: Pemberton-Billing had already designed several before the First World War and in 1916 a two-seater seaplane was already in production for the Admiralty. After the war the Schneider Cup races began, and Mitchell's Supermarine *Sea Lion II* won the cup, for the fastest flying machine, at Naples in 1922 by flying at 145.7 miles an hour over a course of 200 nautical miles. In 1927 Britain won again with an all-metal *S.5* monoplane, 875 horse-power, flown by Flight-Lieutenant Webster at 281.49 miles an hour. Next year there was no race, but Flight-Lieutenant Kinkhead dived his Napier *S.5* into the Solent and killed himself after having achieved 300 miles an hour. Speeds went up after this: 319.57 in November, 1928, and then 357.7, this with the *S.6* with a 1,900 horse-power Rolls-Royce engine. On 13th September, 1931, Flight-Lieutenant Boothman won the Trophy for Britain with 340.08 miles an hour and on the same day Flight-Lieutenant Stainforth managed 379.08. On 29th September he flew 407.8 with a 2,600 horse-power engine. This aeroplane is preserved in a shelter at the entrance to the Royal Pier at Southampton.

Mitchell designed the Spitfire, of course, and died in 1937, before he could see western civilisation saved by a few young men flying the aeroplanes he had developed.

The old flying boat and seaplane base on the Spit is now an Adventure Centre run by the County Council, and there is an artificial ski-slope, a wall of death, and many other delights. The public is (at the time of writing) as rigorously excluded as if the place were a plague hospital, but it is rumoured that the Henry VIII castle on the Spit is soon going to be opened to us all.

West of Calshot the shore is guarded by the sort of defences formerly used to keep the Nazis out. These are put there by the local Scottish landowner to keep out the Sassenach. They didn't keep this Sassenach out, though, and there is a delightful walk along the shore round **Stone Point** to **Lepe**, where Joe Spering lives and knows more about the birds of this bird-haunted shore than anybody else.

From Stone Point it is said that there was once a causeway to the Isle of Wight, and that over this the stone was brought to build Butley Abbey. I don't believe this for two reasons. Firstly the depth of the water in the Solent is such that I don't believe it could have been that shallow such a short time ago. Secondly it was far easier, pre-motor-lorry, to transport things by water, and even if there *had* been a causeway the monks would have carried the stone by ship.

To sail up **Beaulieu River** is a delight. There is Needs Oar Point to port, with the Bull's Run to seaward of it, a great gulls' nesting place between Bull's Run (which is a creek) and the sea, large lakes half a mile farther up with hundreds of Canada geese on them (and many other birds), an off-shoot of the Royal Southampton Yacht Club at a place called *Gins* (does this give a clue to the members' proclivities?) and just up the lane from it are the ruins of St Leonard's Chapel, thirteenth century, with what is left of an enormous barn: once the barn of the grange of the monks of Beaulieu Abbey. Then we come to woods on both banks, to port the site of where a *Phoenix* – a concrete caisson that formed part of the Mulberry harbours which were placed on the Normandy coast after the landings in the Second World War – was built, and we then turn sharp left-handed to come to **Buckler's Hard**, which played such an important part in our maritime history.

Buckler's Hard built ships in the time of Henry V, but then fell into a deep sleep until awakened to life by the War of the Austrian Succession.

John, second Duke of Montagu, took over the Beaulieu estate in 1709 after his father died and decided to build a new town on his estate at Buckler's Hard (a *hard* is a hard causeway over soft mud built by dumping stone or other means) and this town was to be in conjunction with his farther-flung estates in St Lucia and St Vincent Islands in the West Indies. Sugar was to be grown on the islands and brought home to be refined at Buckler's Hard. The West Indian end of it fell through, though, for the settlers sent out were intercepted by the French, but the Buckler's Hard town, to be called Montagu Town, was laid out with wide streets and on a grid plan, and above all with a shipyard. The latter, right there in the middle of the New Forest with its plentiful oak trees with their *crooks*, so beloved of shipbuilders, rapidly became large and famous, and by the end of the eighteenth century was employing four thousand men – not bad for a tiny village in the woods in those days. Among the famous and mighty wooden walls of Old England built there were: *Illustrious*, 74 guns, *Agamemnon*, 64 (she was Nelson's flagship in the Mediterranean until 1796 and his favourite ship although it was in her, off Corsica, that he lost his eye), *Vigilant*, 54, *Indefatigable*, 54, *Swiftsure*, 74, *Euralus*, 36, *Greenwich*, 44, *Sheerness*, 44, and many more – including a substantial part of the fleet which fought at Trafalgar. Between 1745 and 1822 fifty-five men-of-war were launched from Buckler's Hard and two fire ships and in addition, and perhaps more usefully, fifteen merchant ships.

James and Joseph Wyatt were the master-builders of the first period, John Darley took over in 1746 but went bankrupt, and Henry Adams, who had been sent there first as an overseer by the Navy Board, took over the firm and he and his two sons kept the yard going until 1821, when the last of the shipbuilding sons died, the yard continued building merchant ships for a few years and then ceased, knocked out by the coming of iron, and other factors.

Now there is a very good maritime museum at Buckler's Hard. There is a splendid model in it of the old village and shipbuilding yard, with two great ships on the stocks, great piles of timber, and lovely country and people's vegetable gardens all mixed up with it. Would that industry still looked as *comely* as this. There is much material in the museum about shipbuilding, and ships, Nelson, and Sir Francis Chichester, who began and ended his circumnavigation from Buckler's Hard. There is a good hotel, called the Master Builder's House Hotel, and it is indeed in the old Master Builder's house. There was a limited revival of the old industry at Buckler's Hard during the Second World War, when a wooden minesweeper was built and launched into the river at **Bailey's Hard** just up-river. Wooden ships had a short come-back when it was found that steel ones were blown up by the magnetic mine.

Beaulieu is, of course, the place for you if you like simply lots and lots of old cars, and if you don't mind paying quite a lot of money to go and see them and millions of people apparently don't. There is an enormous bus and car-park to accommodate all the vehicles of all the people and in the summer at least it is often very nearly full. The museum is very large, and very interesting.

You can wander in the abbey grounds if you have paid to go into the museum, and it is well worth it. The abbey is now picturesque ruins. It was the only one founded by King John, supposedly as a result of a dream. One story is that he had ordered that a group of Cistercian monks be trampled to death by horses because they kept asking for things, and he had this dream in which he was told to build them an abbey instead. The site was called *Bellus Locus.* The abbey was completed in forty-five years, and consecrated in 1249, Henry III, his queen, and many nobles attending the ceremony. The king was so pleased with it all that he let the abbot off a fine which had been imposed on him for poaching the royal deer.

Pope Innocent III granted the abbey important rights of sanctuary, and several important people found sanctuary there, Anne Neville, widow of Warwick the Kingmaker after the latter had been killed at the Battle of Barnet (she had to hide her head at Beaulieu for fourteen years), Margaret of Anjou, and Perkin Warbeck, who stayed here two years before surrendering himself to the forces of law and order.

In 1537 the abbey was dissolved, and Henry VIII pulled most of it down and used the stone to build Hurst Castle. At the Dissolution there was much dismay at many wide boys and fugitives who had been living there in a sanctuary that was suddenly taken away from them.

The parish church of Beaulieu is orientated north and south, because it was once the refectory of the abbey. It has Early English windows, thick buttresses, and the fine carved pulpit was once the reading lectern for meal-time sacred reading.

The outer wall and four towers around the abbey grounds were built in the eighteenth century to keep out French privateers. There was a witch at Beaulieu in the eighteenth century who could turn herself at will into a hare, an owl, or a black cat. A wine press still exists in the grounds, for the monks made as well as drank wine, and it is significant that there is now a large modern vineyard just outside the abbey grounds. Palace House, the present home of the Montagus, was the old gate house.

Lymington has changed from being a yachtsmen's paradise into being a place where there are just far too many yachtsmen. This is sad because it is such a splendid little town. The High Street runs straight and wide up-hill, honest Georgian both sides of it, the church with its offset tower just rightly sited at the top of it, and in the big house just before the church the Clerk to the Verderers of the New Forest has his being, for Lymington is the capital of the forest. Quay Hill, winding and cobbled and blessedly car-free, is perfect. On Saturday mornings there is a street market, to which the denizens of the forest come to do their marketing.

In the fourteenth century Lymington had a good shipbuilding trade. In 1345 the town supplied more ships to fight the French than Portsmouth did. But *salt* was the mainstay of Lymington for a long time. South of the town, along the indeterminate shore, was a complex of salterns which supplied much of the salt used in the south of England. An excellent pamphlet called *The Salterns of the Lymington Area*, by A. T. Lloyd, gives a full description of this once-important industry.

Briefly, the method of salt-making was to admit sea water into broad, very shallow lagoons and allow sun and wind to evaporate the water. As the brine became more concentrated it was allowed to run into successive *pans* as the lagoons were called which contained stronger brine. When the specific gravity of the brine had been increased by evaporation to the point at which it would float a specially made glass bead it was pumped by windmill up into an iron pan under which coal was burnt. According to one contemporary account half a chaldron of coal (eighteen bushels) would boil out two tons of salt. You can see this boiling process being carried out in exactly the same way in the Lion Salt Works at Middlewich, in Cheshire, but there the brine comes from a borehole down into the salt measure and not from the sea.

The 'bitter water', or 'bittern', that drained away from the crystallising salt was kept in tanks until the winter, when salt-making out of doors became impossible, and then boiled up again and allowed to crystallise. The resulting crystals were Epsom salts.

The industry was bedevilled by the most savage taxes imposed on any product of men's labour. In the 1860s the industry died, not as a result of taxes but as a result of competition from the north of England: the salt of the Zechstein Sea being easier to obtain than that of the English Channel. But if you go down to the Keyhaven and Pennington Marshes to-day you can discern traces of the old pans, even on land which has since been reclaimed and put under the plough.

There is a small fishing fleet working from Lymington. Several of the boats have turned to oyster dredging in recent years. This is free in the Solent, but skippers are asked to exercise restraint. But restraint is a thing that it is hard to exercise if you are a fisherman trying to make a living in a competitive world. The authorities should make the same law that they have in the Falmouth Estuary: anybody can dredge for oysters, in the season, without let or hindrance provided he does not have an engine in his boat. This would ensure, as it does quite successfully at Falmouth, that the oyster stocks were not depleted nor the grounds damaged (see *Companion Guide to the Coast of South West England*). At Falmouth any man who is prepared to work hard, with sail and oar, can make a fine living. The motor dredgers will not take very long to destroy the Solent beds.

CHAPTER 16

The Isle of Wight

LYMINGTON is a port for the Isle of Wight, with frequent car ferries, and this would be a good point of departure for us to take a look at the island. It will be a cursory look, for the Isle of Wight should no more be part of England than the Isle of Man is. Isle of Wight people call themselves Corkheads, and us Cocklers or Oveners.

The island is twenty-three miles by thirteen and has sixty miles of coastline. Two hundred and fifty thousand years ago, when Palaeolithic Man was in the land, it was part of the mainland of England, and land spread far out to the south of it into what is now called the Channel. A large river, named by geologists the Solent River, rose somewhere in what is now Somerset, flowed through Poole Harbour, and cut its channel through the soft rock between what is now the Isle of Wight and the mainland to run on eastward until it debouched into the sea about seven miles south of Brighton.

By the time Neolithic Man came Wight was an island. They have left their remains at Bonchurch, and the leavings of their feasts, consisting of horse, ox, deer and pig bones, winkles, limpet shells and other molluscs. The Beaker Folk arrived about 1900 BC; at Nunwell, near Brading, a round-headed skull with very worn teeth was found (worn because of eating quern-ground flour?). On Chillerton Down, south-west of Newport, there is an Iron Age fort. Vespasian conquered the island in AD 43. In 530 the West Saxons Cerdic and Cynric, having carved out a kingdom on the mainland, sailed over and united the island with Wessex. After Cerdic died the island needed conquering again, and a nephew of Cerdic named Wihtgar (from him the name Wight) and another man with the splendid name of Stuf were the ones that did it. The island came under the rule of Aldewach, King of Sussex, but he was killed by Caedwalla. It is difficult to believe that this gentleman was not Celtic in origin, having such a Celtic name. He was a Christian and in surely a rather un-Christian way slaughtered such of the inhabitants as were not of his faith and made a *present* of the rest of them, their lands and appurtenances, to Bishop Wilfrid of Selsey.

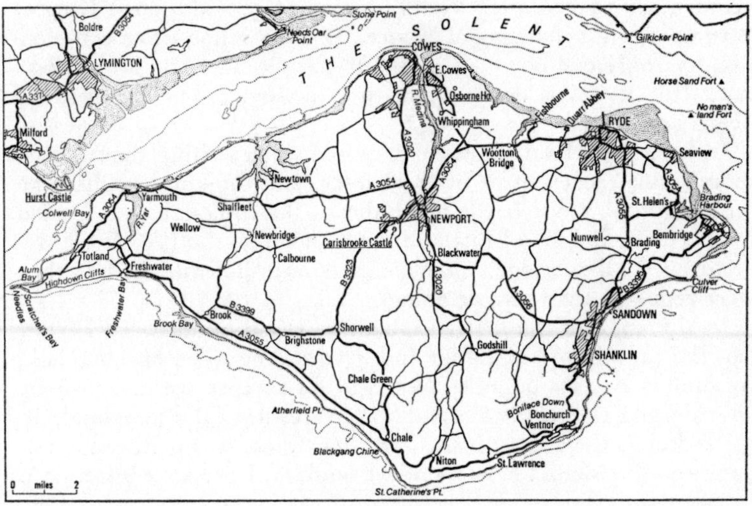

The Danes began to come in 896, six shiploads of them landing at Brading. Nine of King Alfred's galleys cut off their retreat, however, the Danes were pursued inland, caught, and hanged at Winchester. But in 1048 twenty-five shiploads landed and this time they had it their way.

William the Conqueror gave the island to Fitz-Osborn, who allocated estates to Fitz-Sturs, Fitz-Azors and Hugh de Oglandres, whose descendants hold their estates to this day, although in 1874 the family died out in the male line. A cousin then succeeded the last Sir Henry. In Stephen's reign Baldwin de Redvers held the island for the Empress Maud, was defeated by Stephen, but later forgiven and reinstated as the governor of the island. In Edward I's reign Isabella de Fortibus sold the island, lock, stock and barrel, to the Crown, in which it has been vested ever since.

The French attacked the island on numerous occasions in the fourteenth century and the Hundred Years War, and cut off from help from the mainland, the island was an easy target. In 1377 they managed to burn Yarmouth, Newtown and Newport. Carisbrooke Castle held out but the garrison had to bribe the French with a thousand marks to go away. Before this they inflicted fairly severe losses on the French invaders, though, and the French leader was killed by a *quarrel* from a crossbow fired by one Peter de Hey. They came back again in 1402 but were repulsed. In 1488 a return match was played by a party of forty gentlemen and four hundred yeomen, who sailed away from St Helens to give aid to the King of Brittany against the King of France. The expedition was a complete disaster: only one boy came home to tell the tale, and after it was said: 'the island is desolate and not inhabited, but occupied by beests and cattel'.

In Henry VIII's time, as we discussed when writing about Portsmouth, the French came in great force, and the king watched the indeterminate naval battle in Spithead. But although they landed not on the mainland of England they landed on the Isle of Wight – at Seaview, Bembridge, Shanklin and near Bonchurch, but they were repulsed after stirring doings.

In the reign of the first Elizabeth good old Sir Edward Horsey was the captain of the island, and lived in fine style, his household consuming two fat bullocks and eight fat sheep a week. It was he who stocked the hareless island with hares from the mainland. In the seventeenth century it was said that 'there was neither fox nor papist on the island'. Now there are both, for foxes were introduced by sporting squires.

There is the melancholy story about how Charles I came here, trusting to the good faith of Governor Hammond, after he had escaped from the Army. Hammond, rather understandably, sat on the fence, was horrified when he heard that the king was coming but allowed him to come and at first treated him as an honoured guest, but came off the fence somewhat after it had been disclosed that the king had been intriguing with the Scots to try to get them to invade England and restraints were then imposed upon the king. He was securely lodged in Carisbrooke Castle. He tried to escape twice: on 20th March he managed to get himself stuck in a window, through which his head would pass but his body wouldn't follow. Files and acid were sent for to cut the bars and a second attempt was made, but a traitor (to the king) sprang the plot and Hammond entered the king's apartments at the last moment with a facetious comment that he had come to take leave of His Majesty as he had heard that he was going away.

After the Second Civil War it was decided that the king should retain his throne but as a constitutional monarch, but the situation changed and hardened, by 29th November, 1648, two thousand troops had landed on the island, the king was arrested, taken to Hurst Castle, thence to London, tried and executed.

His two children, Elizabeth, then fifteen, and Henry, ten, were brought to the castle. Little Elizabeth died of a chill caught playing bowls with her brother. In 1793 her coffin was unearthed under the old church in Newport. As for Henry, after two years of incarceration he was allowed to go and join his mama in Paris. The regicides at least were not infanticides.

Carisbrooke Castle is well worth going to see. It has defensive elements from Roman times to the outer bastions put up at the Armada scare, a good museum, much of interest (including a donkey walking round and round inside a wheel to draw water from a well) and a sumptuous Georgian Roman Catholic chapel.

But to get back to **Yarmouth**, where we landed, it is a tiny town on an estuary crammed with yachts, it has one of that obsessive castle-builder Henry VIII's castles (you can go in it, guide book on sale within), a large Victorian fort, Carey's Sconce a mile to the west, another beyond that, which with Hurst Castle over the water command very effectively the straits into the Solent. In Yarmouth's seventeenth-century church are the Allenby paintings, late seventeenth-century English primitives, very fine but hung so far up you can't see them.

The George Inn was once the home of Sir Robert Holmes, the 'Hero of Yarmouth' and a doughty privateer against the Dutch. In the church is a magnificent statue of him. At least the head is his: the body is said to have been done by an Italian sculptor for the French king. When the headless statue was being shipped to France for completion Sir Robert seized the ship that it was in, and made the sculptor finish it in his own likeness. It makes a fitting monument to a pirate king. Sir Robert entertained Charles II here. Sir Robert ravaged the Dutch settlements in West Africa, and the gold he brought back from there was struck into a new denomination of coins called the guinea. Not only did he bring gold back from the Guinea coast but also, we are told, a Great Baboon. He captured New Amsterdam from the Dutch and renamed it New York, after the Duke of York, who was Admiral of the Blue. It is still called by that name. Charles II had to imprison him in the Tower for a short while, when peace was made with the Dutch, in order to placate them. But he soon let him out again and made him Governor of the Isle of Wight. He was very popular locally, and used to entertain his guests in two caves in Scratchell's Bay, and these are still called 'Lord Holmes's Parlour and Kitchen'.

George Morland, the painter, in 1799 was *frog-marched* from Yarmouth to Newport by over-zealous Isle of Wight Fencibles, who thought he was a spy. They had every reason for thinking so, for he had a drawing of a spaniel on him, which they took to be a map.

In Domesday Yarmouth was called Eremud (the mouth of the Ere), later changed to Eremue, and the old bells of Yarmouth church are said to be in St Paul's at Boulogne, and they have the name Eremue engraved on them. They were taken in a raid of 1524. James I made Yarmouth a borough, and it sent two members to Parliament until it was extinguished in 1883. Needless to say, from its position, Yarmouth was a great smuggling place. One over-zealous revenue official was sewn up in sail cloth, taken across the Channel, and dumped on a lonely part of the French coast, quite unharmed. His wife was informed that he had gone on holiday. When the Council built a steamer pier, and put gates across the harbour against the wishes of the local fishermen, the latter 'sold' their boats to friends so these could not be seized for debt and then destroyed the gates.

Newtown, to the east, is on a lovely little retired estuary, and it is hard to believe that this tiny village once also sent two members to Parliament (until 1832) and was once the chief port of the island, accommodating ships of up to 500 tons. It is now the centre of a vigorous and growing shell-fish industry, run by a Mr Lucas, who brings in oysters from near and far, purifies them in tanks, and exports them, and cockles and clams, too, to the insatiable French.

Cowes takes its name from one of two forts that Henry VIII had built to guard the entrance to the Medina. One was called the Cow Fort. The short history of Cowes may be said to be the history of English yachting.

In the eighteenth century Cowes was noted for two things: the building of very fast smuggling luggers and the building of very fast revenue cutters to try to catch them. It was from the competition between these two types of vessel that the fast light sailing craft was born. Cowes also built fast pilot cutters. Speed was needed for them because they, too, lived in a competitive world: the one that got down-Channel fastest got her pilot aboard the incoming ship. It is noteworthy that none of these classes of craft had to be big weight carriers (even the smugglers') but they all had to be fast. I once heard the owner of a twelve metre boasting to the skipper of a sailing barge that the former's vessel was faster. 'Yes,' said the bargeman, 'but you can't carry a hundred and seventy-five tons.'

At the beginning of the nineteenth century wealthy people began to come to Cowes for holidays. In 1811 the Duke of Gloucester arrived, and he, and other wealthy men, began to amuse themselves by placing bets on local working boats when these used to have unofficial races, as such boats in sailing days always did, up or down the river. In 1813 the duke organised a formal regatta, and the 'gentlemen' themselves began to take a hand. First they began to charter boats and back the professional seamen who sailed them, then actually going to sea themselves in the smacks, and then commissioning the building of yachts, or boats specifically built for pleasure. Yachting was not a new thing then, after all Charles II had a yacht, and the Royal Cork Yacht Club was founded as early as 1720, but yachting on this *scale* was new. And Cowes was perfect, near London, plenty of sheltered water (with four tides a day), but most important, plenty of boat builders used to building fast light boats, and good sail makers ashore, too.

In 1815 they formed a yacht club, commodored by the Honourable Charles Pelham, later Lord Yarborough. Yarborough had a yacht built on the lines of a naval twenty gun corvette, the *Falcon*. She was fully armed with cannon, and he made his crew sign articles to the effect that they didn't mind being flogged if in the master's view it was necessary to preserve discipline. In 1817 the Prince Regent joined the club, and as soon as he became king changed the name to the Royal Yacht Squadron. Not only the *Falcon* mounted guns, and by the 1840s the total armament of the squadron was four hundred guns: it was a powerful naval force of its own, owned by the aristocracy of the country. Elaborate ritualistic customs were evolved, a complicated flag-etiquette which to break was social death, and the squadron was the most exclusive club in the world. A casual inspection of the ugly church of the Holy Trinity just behind the R.Y.S. revealed memorials to two dukes, two marquesses, two viscounts, nine baronets, and one wretched knight who one feels must have crept in there by mistake. A much appreciated touch in Cowes is the butcher who – amid the plethora of traders proclaiming themselves to be 'Purveyor to Her Majesty' – announces over his shop, quite simply: 'Purveyor to Her Majesty's Subjects'. The Prince of Wales, son of Queen Victoria, became Patron of the Squadron in 1863, Commodore later.

And, of course, other yacht clubs sprang up for the hoi-polloi. There was the Royal Victoria Y.C. at Ryde (1845), Royal Solent at Yarmouth (1878), Langstone Sailing Club (how low can you *get*?) (1883), Bembridge S.C. (1886), Island Sailing Club at Cowes (1889), Seaview Y.C. (1893), East Cowes S.C. (1912), and the Royal Corinthian, of Burnham on Crouch, opened a clubhouse at Cowes after the Second World War. At Cowes Week the congestion of yachts afloat and yachtsmen and women ashore has to be seen to be believed.

W. A. Souter and Son, together with the Maritime Trust, have recently towed the J Class Yacht *Endeavour* from her muddy resting place at Southampton to their yard in Cowes, and she is to be restored and kept on show. She is just 129.7 feet, displaces 143 tons, draws just under fifteen feet and used to set 7,561 square feet of canvas. She tried so many times to win the America Cup back from America, where it so stubbornly remains to this day.

East Cowes is very much an industrial town, with the huge factory of British Hovercraft, where Saunders-Roe used to build *Walruses* and other seaplanes before production ceased in 1944.

Up-Medina **Newport** is still a port, although the port part of it is currently being hideously disfigured by a horrible by-pass bridge. There are some fine nineteenth-century brewery buildings and warehouses at the top of the river, with distinguished and distinctive cast iron window frames in them. The Vectis Isle Shipping Company still operates a small fleet of coasters, bringing goods to the mainland, and a little ship that was theirs, the *Vectis Isle*, owner and captain Bob Roberts of sailing barge fame, still has her base there although her voyagings take her all over northern Europe.

Hard by East Cowes is **Osborne House**, built between 1845 and 1848 to the design of Thomas Cubitt, egged on by the Prince Consort, and now belonging to the nation and open to the public. It is the very throbbing heart of Victoriana. The Durbar Room is the idea of Imperial India expressed in a riot of carved teak, and everything in the extraordinary Antler Room is made from the antlers of stags slaughtered by royal bullets in the Highlands of Scotland. The Swiss Cottage, in the grounds, was built expressly for the royal children. **Whippingham Church** nearby was designed chiefly by the Prince Consort, and looks like it.

Fishbourne and **Wootton Bridge** are on another little bite the sea has taken out of the Oligocene clays and marls. **Quarr Abbey**, just east, is not ancient, having been built in pink Belgian brick for French Benedictine monks at the beginning of this century. But it is on the site of an old Cistercian abbey. In the fifteenth century the abbot had his own fleet of ships for importing wine.

Ryde is a large seaside resort, mostly built in Victorian times. From here now frequent hovercraft come and go to and from Portsmouth, and more traditional (and much quieter) vessels ply backwards and forwards, too, quite quickly enough. Owing to the hovercraft it is possible to live in Ryde and commute to London or, I suppose, vice versa. To make the commuters feel at home old London underground trains ply out to the end of the pier, and back the other way across the island to Shanklin.

A Captain Boyce lived at Apley House near Ryde. He was a very successful smuggler, and made enough money to live in some style. He once bought £500 worth of books, although it was said that he could hardly read. When eventually he was caught red handed and sent to prison it was found that he had £40,000 invested. But with brandy fourteen shillings a keg in Cherbourg and fifty shillings here there was something in it.

Seaview is a charming little town, with a delightful beach, a prosperous yacht club with a fleet of *Mermaids* (that is a class of boat – actual mermaids are no commoner at Seaview than anywhere else) and its very own class of dinghies.

St Helen's once had a cannon to warn the inhabitants of the arrival of the Press Gang (being very near Portsmouth), and it was a considerable victualling station for the Navy. And here lived the lovely Sophie Dawes, daughter of a smuggler and oyster fisherman who died untimely, and Sophie was sent at the tender age of thirteen to work with a farmer. This was not her bent, and she quickly left him for higher things and before long she had graduated through several *situations* until she became mistress to the Duke of Kent. That nobleman lost her in a game of cards to the Duc de Bourbon, who took her back to France where she lived in enormous style, and led him a hell of a dance, and took her entire family over from St Helen's to live in his palace, and eventually came back to England to die a rich woman.

Brading Harbour once made **Brading** a port, but the Yar (yet another Yar) has silted up, and much of the mud has been inned, and Brading is no longer a port. **Bembridge** is a pleasant little yachting place. Off-shore is St Helen's Fort, and still farther out the extraordinary Nab Tower. This remarkable object was to be one of a line of six such, sunk to the floor of the Straits of Dover and connected with anti-submarine net to stop German U-boats getting into the Channel in the First World War. Two of the towers were started, as we have seen, at Shoreham. One was never completed but broken up again. This one, redundant because the war was over, was towed to its present position on a calm day in 1920 by two aged paddle steamers and sunk. It replaced the Nab Light vessel and it can act as a fort in time of war.

At **Culver Cliff** we leave the Oligocene and Eocene clays and soft rocks and come suddenly on the hard chalk which forms the backbone of Wight: chalk highly tilted and greatly distorted, all this area having been folded and distorted, along an east–west axis, by the waves of pressure that came from central Europe when the Alps were being formed some fourteen or fifteen million years ago: the great Alpine Storm.

Sandown, Shanklin, Bonchurch and **Ventnor** are largish seaside resorts, climatically much favoured because they are sheltered from the north and west but exposed to the mild English Channel. Keats stayed in Shanklin, so did Longfellow. Swinburne is buried at Bonchurch, so is De Vere Stacpoole the novelist. Macaulay lived at Madeira Hall on the road to Ventnor. Ventnor is particularly well sheltered, with St Boniface Down to the north of it, 785 feet high and the peak of the island. The town is built higgledy-piggledy down the steep cliffs of the undercliff, like the rest of these resorts resolutely Victorian and very prosperous.

Niton was a great place for smugglers. They used to *row* to Cherbourg in six-oared galleys, for a galley could generally outpace a sailing vessel to windward. Sometimes the sailing luggers would rig standing rigging of spun tobacco as a way of eluding the customs. Ralph Stone is a man whose name is remembered for being leader of a successful smuggling crew.

St Catherine's Point has a spectacular undercliff, where the Lower Greensand under the great chalk downs has slipped and crumbled. St Catherine's Tower up on top was originally a fourteenth-century oratory and light beacon built by Walter de Gadeton as penance for receiving wine from a wreck belonging to a religious house, but was rebuilt to commemorate the visit of Alexander I, Tsar of All the Russias, in 1811. There is an unfinished lighthouse near it known as the Pepper Pot, but the real lighthouse is down on the Point, built 1840.

Blackgang Chine is a weird extravaganza in a cleft in the steep cliff near **Chale**, all tricked out like a Walt Disney wonderland.

Fourteen ships were wrecked near here in one night in 1757, and in the graveyard of Chale church are the graves of the men who were recovered drowned when the full-rigger *Clarendon* went ashore in the last century.

At Atherfield Point, at three o'clock on the misty and stormy and rainy afternoon of 9th March, 1888, a coastguard heard a ship's siren, and looked to sea into the mist and thought he saw a rain-squall approaching from the sea. Suddenly he realised with horror that what he saw was not a cloud of rain but a cloud of canvas. It was a full-rigged ship, sailing on to the terrible reef of rocks off this point. He raced off and called out the Brighstone lifeboat, the *Worcester Cadet*. She put off into the sort of mixture of mist, high wind and raging sea that you sometimes get in the Channel, at four o'clock when the light was already beginning to weaken. Her thirteen man crew got her into the lee of the vessel, which was the 1,590 ton full-rigger *Sirenia* homeward-bound from San Francisco, and they managed to rescue the captain's wife, children, their nurse, and a young apprentice. The lifeboat was rowed back to the shore, where the rescued were landed, and the same crew immediately put to sea again. By this time it was pitch dark and a raging sea was running, and most of the oars on one side were smashed as the boat was put alongside. However, a grapnel was got aboard, and three of the crew taken off when a wave got the boat just wrong and overturned her. She self-righted, and all got aboard again save the coxswain and his mate and two of the rescued men. The men who got back in the boat were not only soaked, of course, but terribly bruised and shocked, but they carried on a search for the missing men (although each man in his heart must have known it was hopeless) for several hours and then rowed back to shore.

A relief crew immediately took the boat out again – by now there was a severe south-westerly gale blowing, and at the wreck they found the lifeboat from Brook, about five miles along the shore. A huge wave washed three men of the *Worcester Cadet* overboard but two got back. The *Sirenia*'s captain refused to let the lifeboat rescue any more of his own men until a search had been made for the missing man, who, of course, was not found. The Brook boat anchored to await the dawn, but the *Worcester Cadet* managed, after the abortive search, to get alongside and take off the rest of the *Sirenia*'s crew and get them safely ashore. The Brook boat then had a five mile slog to windward, in the teeth of the gale, to get home. There are a great many stories about *wreckers* operating round the coasts of England and the Isle of Wight – people who lured ships to their doom by tying lanterns to donkeys' tails and the like. Hardly any such cases have ever been authenticated and most were the inventions of Victorian and earlier novelists, few of whom had ever been to sea. Before we trouble ourselves with spurious stories about *wreckers* we should consider the true story of the rescue of the crew of the *Sirenia*. The two crews who manned the *Worcester Cadet* could have had no hope of monetary reward beyond the few shillings' launch money. There could be no hope of salvage. Their only possible motive was to save the lives of complete strangers to them. They lost three men drowned that night from their tiny community. This *true* story can be paralleled by others in practically every other fishing village around the coasts of the British Isles. In the fifty years up to 1933 there were twenty wrecks on the 'Back of the Wight' involving total losses, and nearly every one brought serious peril on the lifeboat crews of the island, and never once did a crew fail to respond.

In **Brook Bay** fossil tree stumps are said to be visible at low tide.

Freshwater, almost on another island because the western Yar nearly cuts it off from the rest of the Wight, is full of memories of Tennyson, who lived for years at Farringford House, eighteenth-century Gothic, and now a hotel. They say his study is the television lounge.

At **Highdown**, over Scratchell's Bay, was Britain's chief entry into the Space Race, before she had the sense to leave it to other people. In 1956 duffel-coated boffins appeared and turned the place into the testing ground for Black Knight rocket. Twenty-four rockets were made at East Cowes by Saunders-Roe, tested here without being fired, one was resonance-tested to destruction, one was sent off to the Science Museum, and the other twenty-two sent off to Woomera in Australia to be fired into the stratosphere. The Black Arrow Satellite Launching Programme was also developed here. A fully operational satellite was actually successfully put into orbit, in 1971, from Woomera. Then the whole expensive business was abandoned.

The **Needles** show how resistant chalk can be, especially when up on edge. These island-pinnacles are at one end of a gap torn in the once-continuous chalk ridge by the sea, before it flooded in to inundate the old Solent River Valley to form the Solent. The other end is at Old Harry, just north of Swanage.

Alum Bay is an extraordinary geological phenomenon. A great thickness of the Eocene Beds has been chucked up here on end by the Alpine Storm, and there it stands, stratum after stratum, to be read like a book. A long interval had evidently elapsed before these Eocene Beds were laid down upon the chalk, the latter having become eroded down considerably during a period of dry land conditions before the formation of another sea here, known to geologists as the Anglo-French-Belgian Basin. These weird Alum Bay deposits were laid down in this, in many varying conditions, in shallow seas and deep ones, salt water and brackish, in many kinds of climate and with intervals of dry land, and with different life-forms which have left us different fossils. An astonishing twenty-nine different strata have been named at Alum Bay by geologists, from the Reading Beds butting up against the chalk in the south, through ten layers of different sorts of rock in the London Clay series, four strata of the Bagshot Sands, nine of the Bracklesham Beds (which we met at Bracklesham), and then Barton Clay. We then move into a later era – the Oligocene – here the Headon Beds, and these were laid down after the great Alpine Storm which up-hove the chalk and the Alum Bay beds into a nearly vertical position. Therefore the Headon Beds are still horizontal, as they were laid down, and at nearly right angles to the Barton Clay up against which they butt. These Oligocene deposits make up the soft, flat north of the Isle of Wight. The famous coloured sands of Alum Bay, which the tourists go so far to see, and which look like all eventually being taken away in bottles, comprise the Bagshot Sands and Bracklesham Beds series.

There is a monument to Guglielmo Marconi here because in 1897 he established here the first wireless station in the world. At **Totland** there are pilot boats to take pilots out to ships bound into the Solent. At **Colwell Bay** are beautiful fossils of the Oligocene, mostly shells.

And so we return to Yarmouth, and can return by ferry to Lymington, assuming that we have not got our own boat, and it was on this crossing that Tennyson is supposed to have written *Crossing the Bar* (although this would be hotly contested by the inhabitants of Salcombe in Devon).

CHAPTER 17

Hurst Castle to Bournemouth

Hurst Castle can be got at by boat, by frequent ferry in the summer from Lymington, or by walking along a mile and a half of shingle spit, which is what the caretaker does twice a day every day of his life. Hurst Castle is *enormous*. It takes half an hour to walk round it, plodding through deep loose shingle. The first castle was built, like many another, by Henry VIII, and completed in 1544. Parliamentary forces occupied it during the Civil War, Charles I was immured here for a short time on his way to London from the Isle of Wight, and to his trial and execution, the castle was much strengthened in the Napoleonic wars but the biggest changes came in 1873. It is now a fine example of a very large and strong fortification of that period. It looks as if it would stand up to anything short of an atom bomb.

Milford-on-Sea, Barton-on-Sea and **Hinchcliffe** are seaside resorts, very 'residential', whatever that means, and really part of the huge Bournemouth conurbation.

The strata of the cliffs here dip eastward, therefore the most recent strata are to the east near Milford: the Unio, Crocodile and Chara Beds of the Lower Headon Series, passing through Upper, Middle and Lower Barton Beds as you go westward and coming back to our old friends the Bracklesham Beds at Mudeford. The whole is overlaid unconformably with Plateau Gravel, and cut in places with deep eroded clefts locally called *bunnies*. These would be called *chines* on the Isle of Wight, *wykes* in Yorkshire.

Mudeford is one of those ancient fishing communities buried but not destroyed by the red brick flood. Some thirty fishermen work out of here in the summertime, aboard some score of thirty-foot or so flush-decked smacks. Most of them work the Solent, and from Solent harbours during the winter, and more and more for oysters. Oyster dredging only restarted in the Solent in 1972. The establishment of more effective purifying tanks for oysters has made it possible to market these succulent bi-valves from heavily polluted waters.

Another form of fishing at Mudeford is the netting of salmon inside Christchurch Harbour. There are twelve licences which

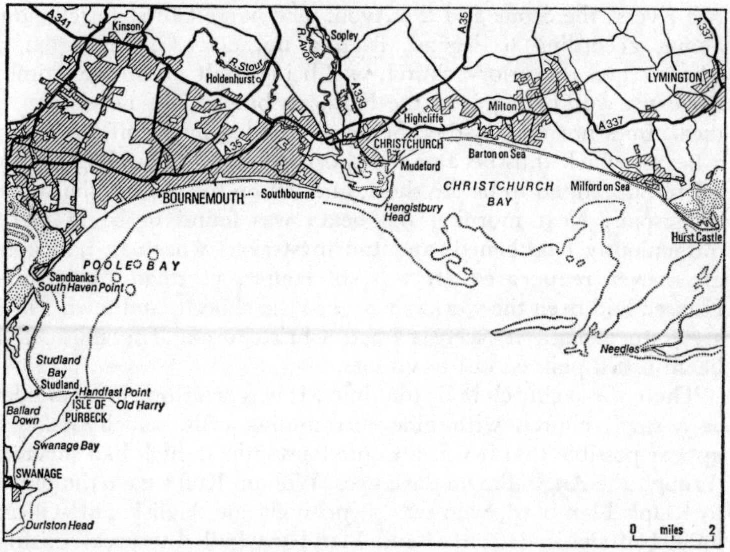

allow fishing from the 1st of February to the last day of July, but not at weekends. A curious activity that I have met nowhere else is winkle-dragging. Winkles are normally picked up off the rocks or hard mud at low tide by wise old gentlemen with big moustaches and long overcoats, but here they are dredged for from boats.

Christchurch has this beautiful little natural harbour which communicates with the sea through the Run at Mudeford, and the town itself has charms, although so near to Bournemouth as to be virtually part of it. The harbour only just escaped being developed commercially when the Earl of Clarendon, in 1665, being Lord of the Manor, commissioned Captain Arthur Yarranton to survey the natural harbour and the River Avon with a view to making the latter navigable up to Salisbury, improving the harbour, building an iron works making use of the Dogger iron ore at Hengistbury and charcoal which was to be shipped down the river to smelt it, building a shipbuilding yard to use timber likewise barged down-river from the forests inland, and to protect it all there was to be a fort on Hengistbury Head. A start was made by the cutting of a new mouth to the harbour, but then the whole venture fizzled out and came to nothing. The new mouth didn't last long and the sea soon returned to the old.

Christchurch was once called Toinham, which came from Twynham, and had reference to the fact that the town is placed between two rivers: the Stour and the Avon. The name Christchurch came about, according to legend, from a miraculous intervention of Christ when the priory church was being built in Norman times. An extra workman joined the builders, but he was never seen at meal times nor on pay-day. Someone cut too much off the end of a beam, which thus became too short to span the building. It was offered up, found to be too short, and left on the ground that night in despair. Next morning the beam was found to be in place, miraculously lengthened, and the mysterious workman had gone and never reappeared. It was, of course, assumed that Christ Himself had been the workman and so the church, and town which grew up around it, were named Christchurch. The miraculous beam is still pointed out to visitors.

There was a church in Saxon times. It was described in Domesday as a small church with nine surrounding cells, which makes it appear possible that it was a Celtic foundation which had survived through the Anglo-Saxon dark ages. William Rufus gave the parish to Ralph Flambard, who was surprisingly an Englishman – if not indeed of Celtic descent – and Flambard built the great existing church. On Rufus's death he was deposed, but later came back into favour and was made Bishop of Durham and he built the cathedral there, which has striking similarities architecturally to Christchurch.

The church as it is now was built over several centuries. The nave and triforium are finest Norman; although the roof over the nave is modern, the transepts are Norman and Early English, the Lady Chapel, which was built as the manorial chapel, is Perpendicular, the choir was originally fourteenth century but had to be renewed in the fifteenth century because the spire collapsed and fell down into it. The fifteenth-century choir roof-vaulting is magnificent. The lovely reredos of 1320 is all that is left of the original choir and repays close inspection, and so do the misericords in the choir. The whole building is very beautiful: it is an extraordinarily fine church. Unusually, but like Wymondham in Norfolk, this church was shared by Town and Gown: the Augustinian canons who occupied the priory from 1150 to the Dissolution used the choir as their church while the parishioners used the nave. One of the canons acted as parish priest and for this, we are told, he received seven loaves of bread a week and twenty-one *gallons* of beer! We are put in mind of Prince Henry's remark in Shakespeare's Henry IV Part One: 'Oh monstrous! but one half-pennyworth of bread to this intolerable deal of sack!' In the tower of the church is a fine memorial to the poet Shelley, inscribed with the noble verse from *Adonais*

Above, the superb Norman Chantry at St Aldhelm's Head, once a beacon for sailors. *Below,* Chapman's Pool, where the sea has cut into the soft Kimmeridge clay.

Above, Durdle Door, cut by the sea in the Portland Stone. *Right*, East Lulworth, and some fine examples of Dorset thatch.

which begins: *He hath outsoared the shadow of our night.* Less nobly the initials *Wm. RI* in the visitor's book were put there by the monarch familiarly called by the English Kaiser Bill.

There are the remains of a castle near the church. This was built by de Redvers, whom we have already met on the Isle of Wight. The castellan's house in the garden of the King's Arms is a fine example of Norman domestic architecture and its circular chimney one of the earliest domestic chimneys extant in England (there are several circular chimneys in South Pembrokeshire, built by the Norman colonists there, which may well be contemporaneous with it). At the end of the seventeenth century William Jackson, the parish priest, nobly saved the house from some human jackal who had already ripped the roof off it for building material. King John held his court in the castle: most other monarchs preferred the comfort of the priory.

North of Christchurch there is St Catherine's Hill, once called Kattern's Hill, said by a local antiquarian to derive from the Celtic Kader Ryn which I should guess is from *cadr rhyn*, which is Welsh for a strong hill. At all events up there was an early British hill town. A *burgh* was built at what is now Christchurch by the English (what a good site it was for them – defended by two rivers and with a fine harbour from the sea) and the Anglo-Saxon Chronicle tells us that after King Alfred's death Ethelwold the Aethling seized Tweoxna, or the place of two rivers.

We are told that in 1760 or thereabouts two large luggers landed so much contraband in Christchurch that it took fifty wagons and three hundred pack ponies to carry it all away. Good luck to them!

Hengistbury Head is interesting geologically, botanically, zoologically and archaeologically, but it is but a small piece of wild country near to the middle of a large conurbation and therefore very vulnerable to the trampling of the feet of thousands. Besides Mesolithic flints, Bronze Age barrows of from 1500 to 1200 BC have been found, and also much Iron Age material such as round houses, pottery including imports from Gaul and Glastonbury, iron smelting remains, signs of silver extraction and coins and jewellery in silver, bronze and gold. Cutting the headland off defensively from the mainland is a fine Iron Age double dyke.

In a more modern iron age, in fact in 1848 or thereabouts, a Christchurch coal merchant named Holloway got permission from the Lord of the Manor to dig out the iron ore on Hengistbury Head. The rationale of this was that he could load it as ballast into his coal barges, which brought coal from the ships in Southampton Water, and there it could be transhipped into the colliers, which had to load ballast anyway, to be taken to South Wales where the colliers were returning and there smelted. This iron ore, exploited as it had been in such very early days, was the stone Doggers of the Eocene Hengistbury Beds, and it was very rich in iron, up to thirty per cent, which made the trade profitable. But alas, the removal of the hard shelves of Doggers from the foreshore let the sea advance and caused erosion, and by 1856 Holloway was stopped from dredging up any more. But the damage had been done, and the Head was only saved from being completely washed away by the building of the big groin in 1936. Holloway's Dock, at which he loaded his barges, can be seen in the lagoon which cuts into the Head from the harbour. All this, and an excellent account of the natural history and ecology of the Head, with a complete list of animals and plants found there, can be found in a booklet put out by the Bournemouth Education Committee, edited by C. E. Pepin and sold for 25p.

Bournemouth, about which nobody could say that it doesn't exist, didn't exist a hundred and fifty years ago. In 1826 the Earl of Malmsbury claimed that he once shot a blackcock on the very spot where St Peter's Church then stood, and in 1795, after the Duke of Rutland and a friend had ridden over the site of what is now the middle of Bournemouth, the duke could write: 'on the barren uncultivated heath where we were there was not a human being to direct us.'

But the gallant Captain Tregonwell patrolled Bourne Chine as a cavalry man between 1796 to 1802, and he liked the place so much that he built a house on that barren heathy spot and called it Exeter House. This is now part of the Royal Exeter Hotel.

The sea here had cut a broad shallow bay out of the soft deposits that had been laid down in fresh water and shallow sea conditions in Tertiary times, and which had once been protected by the same ridge of chalk that once joined Ballard Down, north of Swanage, to the Needles on the Isle of Wight. The sea broke through this and gouged out the softer stuff behind. The site was ideal for a big seaside resort. Useless for agricultural land the barren sands and spewy gravels of the Bagshot Beds here could be extolled by the housing developer as being well drained and therefore healthy, the foreshore was of the sand so beloved of the holidaymaker, the coast was sheltered from the wild south-west by the hard high Jurassic and Cretaceous rocks of the Isle of Purbeck and from the even wilder south-east by the Isle of Wight. And withal it was only a hundred miles from London and fifty more than that from Birmingham.

The only trees that would really grow were conifers. At first Scots

Pine was planted, but later Corsican, Remarkable, Black Austrian, Maritime, Weymouth and Monterey Pines became more rampant. The town became noted as being the town amid the pines. The foreshore is deeply cut in places by chines or bunnies, and this saves Bournemouth from the awful monotony of so many English seaside resorts. It is a very civilised place. There is, of course, the Bournemouth Symphony Orchestra, there are the Winter Gardens, the vast Pavilion, plenty of theatre, music, ballet and the rest of it. The Rothesay Museum, No. 8 Bath Road, has a good maritime collection, and the Russel-Cotes Museum has a splendid collection of High Victorian art, including some telling *erotica.*

Writers of note have lived at Bournemouth. R. L. Stevenson came here in 1884 and rented several houses before settling in one which he named Skerryvore in honour of the fact that some of his ancestors had built Skerryvore lighthouse. Unfortunately this house was destroyed by a bomb in 1940. Stevenson wrote *Dr Jekyll and Mr Hyde*, *Kidnapped*, *The Merry Men* and *Underwoods* at Bournemouth. He left in 1887 to go to the Pacific and died in Samoa in 1894.

Olive Schreiner, that undervalued if unprolific writer (author of that fine novel, *The Story of an African Farm*) lived at Bournemouth for a few months, as did Shelley, Galsworthy, D. H. Lawrence and, going from the sublime to the bathetic, P. C. Wren.

A fossilised forest was unearthed when the pier was being built, and came to light again when the West Undercliff Drive was constructing. It is interesting that some of the fossil timber that has been found in the Bagshot Beds around here has had the holes of the Teredo Worm in it, showing that either it had been floated to where it is by a warm sea, or else that it was overwhelmed where it was growing by an encroachment of the sea. The sands of these Bagshot Beds incidentally derive from some large mass of granite that once joined the existing granite uplands of Cornwall and Brittany. The predominantly quartz grains that make up this sandstone are coated with iron oxide, which gives the rock its yellowish colour.

Alum was worked in what is now known as Alum Chine (where Stevenson's Skerryvore was) by James Blount, 9th Baron Mountjoy, in 1567, probably the first time alum was extracted in Britain. (For a detailed description of the alum industry see *Companion Guide to the Coast of North-East England*). The enterprise, at Bournemouth, was short lived, as was the one, later, at Alum Bay on the Isle of Wight. On the north Yorkshire coast it altered the face of the countryside.

Before Bournemouth was built this lonely coast was an important smuggling place. At **Kinson** broken coping stones at the top of the church tower were caused by men hauling contraband to the top of the tower to conceal it. In the churchyard here is the grave of Robert Trotman, with an inscription which tells us that he was barbarously murdered on the 'Shore near Poole the 24th March 1765:

> A little Tea one leaf I did not steal
> For Guiltless Blood shed I to God appeal . . .'

But Isaac Gulliver was the king of the smugglers hereabouts. He led a gang of fifty men, whom he had the audacity to dress in white livery. They were known as 'The White Wigs'. It was Gulliver who planted the clump of trees on the great earthwork at Eggardon Manor to act as a seamark for his landings, and he once came ashore at Bournemouth with three big shiploads of cargo which took a horse convoy two miles long to carry inland, and Gulliver rode at the head of the convoy on a 'spirited white charger'. He revealed a French plot to King George III, who is supposed to have said, in gratitude: 'Let Gulliver smuggle as long as he likes.' Gulliver is buried at Wimborne Minster.

CHAPTER 18

Poole and Wareham

Poole, alas, is now joined on to Bournemouth, although it is in a different county and Poole men have a fierce independence. But the old town of Poole, before it was choked with modern 'development', must have been a fine and lusty seaport. Even now the quay and the small area of streets behind it retain something of the old atmosphere. The quay, when seen from the harbour or from Hamworthy Point, is charming, marred only by the horrible great Royal National Lifeboat Institution office building. But we who go down to the sea in small boats can forgive the R.N.L.I. for quite a lot of aesthetic spoliation. There is a row of noble pubs along Poole waterfront. The Poole Arms, with its façade hung with bright green tiles made by Carter Tiles Ltd – a predecessor of the famous Poole Pottery – is a lovely building, first class inside, too, and the landlord is one of nature's landlords and will give you a raw onion with your bread and cheese if you ask him, the Portsmouth Hoy with its Gothic look and crazy chimney, and, over the creek at Hamworthy, the Shipwright's Arms is a real waterside pub, surrounded as it should be with port installations, and much given to far-out folk and jazz music on certain occasions.

But to get away from the pubs (sometimes difficult in Poole) the *raison d'être* of Poole is, of course, its fine natural harbour. This is part of the drowned valley of the ancient Frome–Solent River, which we have mentioned several times and in particular while discussing the Isle of Wight. The sea, after it had broken the great chalk barrier that for long kept it out, cut easily into the soft alluvial plain here and formed this magnificent natural harbour. It is fourteen square miles, with a coastline of ninety miles, so that naturally it is much easier to see it from a boat than on foot. Sharing with the Solent the 'double high tides' it has high water for from six to seven hours on every tide and can be said to be available for shipping for about seventeen hours out of the twenty-four. It is not, in fact, very deep.

The Romans had a settlement on the strange little peninsula of Hamworthy, and so did the Celts, and the English obviously did from its present name. The Danes first sailed into Poole Harbour in

787 and came several times afterwards. At that time Wareham was the chief town on the harbour – Poole hadn't been invented yet. Poole Harbour is unfortunately silting up, and commerce moved to Poole about 1145 when Wareham, farther inland, was found to be getting too difficult to get to with the ships of the day. In 1248 Poole got a charter from William Longspee, Lord of the Manor, for which Poole had to pay Longspee seventy marks. This allowed the

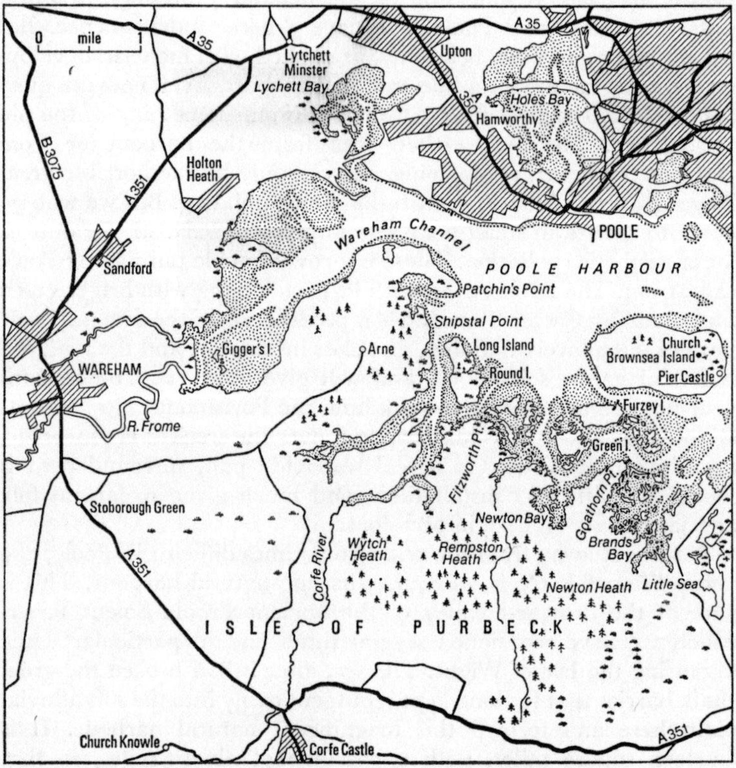

place to go ahead as a port. Poole managed to supply four ships for the Siege of Calais and she became an important base for privateers (not to mention the word *pirates*) in the fourteenth century.

The famous Harry Paye, or the infamous 'Arripay' if you happened to be a Frenchman or a Spaniard, brought great fleets of captured shipping into Poole Harbour. A Spaniard wrote of him (in *Cronica dell Conde de Pero Nino Conde de Buelno*): 'This Arripay came often upon the coast of Castille, and carried away many ships and barks; and he scoured the channel of Flanders so powerfully that no vessel could pass that way without being taken. This Arripay [*sic*] burnt Gijon and Finisterra . . . and much more damage he did in Castille, taking many prisoners and exacting ransomes . . .'

On one famous occasion, in 1404, 'Arripay' was out with a fleet commanded by the Duke of Somerset, and they were set upon by a combined French and Spanish fleet that had sailed out of Harfleur. Seventeen enemy ships were taken, but Harry Paye himself was captured by the French. Paye and his crew were bound and battened below, and their ship was sailed off towards France with a French crew on board. The prize crew, however, abandoned themselves to looting (and the wine lockers, one presumes, were not unstocked) and suddenly 'Arripay's' war cry rang out and up came the Poole men with loosened fetters, retook the ship and furthermore attacked and took the French ship that was sailing with them as an escort. Nor was this enough. Instead of sailing straight back to Poole as Paye might have been forgiven for doing after his unpleasant experience he sailed up the Seine, flying French colours, and did damage to French shipping there. And that same year he captured a Spanish vessel with 'a mule, two silver girdles, robes, and gold and silver to the value of five thousand nobles.'

In 1405 Paye and Lord Berkeley intercepted a French fleet off the coast of South Wales. The French had been going to the aid of Owain Glyndwr, who had taken Haverfordwest from the English. The French were scattered and fifteen of their ships taken and burnt. From the time of Edward I it was the English command of the sea that made Welsh resistance to them hopeless.

But in the same year of 1405 the Spaniards and the French got some of their own back, sailing into Poole and doing great damage to shipping and the town. The Spaniards, under their leader Pero Nino, killed Harry Paye's brother before they were repulsed. Next year, though, Harry had his revenge, bringing into Poole a total of a hundred and twenty prizes, laden with salt, iron, oil and Breton wine. Paye was made a Vice-Admiral of the Cinque Ports. He died at Faversham in 1419.

In 1497 John Cabot came back from having discovered Newfoundland, Basque ships were fishing for cod there by 1504, and about a century later the great cod fishery by west country ships came into full swing: pioneered largely by Dartmouth men who had hitherto been fishing the dangerous Icelandic waters. Poole entered early into this trade, and it is said that most of the great prosperity of the port in the seventeenth and eighteenth centuries was founded on it.

By 1815 four hundred English ships were fishing in Newfoundland waters.

Ships would leave all the west country ports, including Poole, on 1st March. It was against a rigidly enforced custom for a ship to leave earlier and there was a very good reason for this. It was a big advantage to get to Newfoundland first, for if you did you could pick the best landing place to set up your oil presses and salting sheds and the rest of it. But if the sailing date were left to individual choice captains would leave earlier and earlier until more and more ships would be lost to bad weather or ice. As it was, a race was made of it, and captains drove their ships as hard as they would go, often through iceberg-infested waters and poor visibility.

Having got there a landing stage was erected, the salt that the ship had carried across was put ashore, salting sheds were built (often women were taken to do the cooking and help salt the fish) and the ship herself would sail off – sometimes straight for the Grand Banks after cod, sometimes for a few weeks' sealing first. Cod or seal skins would be put ashore, the latter treated, the former pressed for oil (which was known as *train oil* and was a valuable item of trade) and then salted. At the end of the summer the ships would load up with their cod, oil and skins and sail, not home but to the Mediterranean. There the captains would sell the cod to the cod-hungry south Europeans, spend the money they thus obtained on wine and dried fruit, and sail back to England. They would then spend the rest of the winter resting and seeing to the fitting out of their vessels and the three-cornered trade cycle would start again next March.

As time went on specialisation set in. It was found that the big cargo ships for the Atlantic crossing were not the best for the actual fishing, and so men moved out to Newfoundland with their families and settled there permanently, operating with locally built cod smacks. The English ships took salt and trade goods to them in the spring and sailed away with their salt cod in the autumn. Thus Newfoundland was settled with west country men, and there are many Poole names among the inhabitants there now.

Meanwhile Poole merchants developed a trade with South Carolina, taking manufactured goods out and rice and other produce back. But these trades dwindled and died away with changing circumstances. By the middle of the nineteenth century the Grand Banks were being fished by Yankee and Portuguese hand liners and the fishery became less profitable for Poole men.

Fortunately a clay export trade came to save the Poole fleet of ships. Deposits of good quality ball clay are found in the Bagshot

Above, the Bill of Portland, off which runs the notorious Portland Race.
Below, the fourteen mile long Chesil Beach, seen from the Isle of Portland.

Above, the splendid little artificial harbour of Bridport, now misnamed West Bay. *Below*, the beach at Charmouth, looking towards Golden Cap.

Beds about the harbour: the felspar constituent of the granite uplands which as we have seen once joined Cornwall and Brittany and provided the quartz sand which comprises the bulk of the Bagshot Beds. This clay was dug in many a pit round about, hauled to the waterside in horse-drawn carts, loaded into barges, and sailed to Poole for transhipment into the brigs and brigantines and other coastal sailing ships that would take it either to Runcorn, in Cheshire, to be transhipped into horse-drawn narrow boats for taking to the Potteries up the Trent and Mersey Canal, or to various places on the Continent: even as far away as Italy. It is said that by 1820 twenty thousand tons a year was going via Runcorn to Stoke-on-Trent, and that by 1840 a third of the clay used for pottery in England came from Poole Harbour. Even in the 1920s Italian sailing ships were sailing into Poole to load clay for Italy.

And a local pottery industry grew up, too: an industry that can honestly trace its origins back to Neolithic times. Roman kilns have been unearthed at Hamworthy, and Hamworthy pottery has been found as far away as Hadrian's Wall. Even earlier than this there is evidence to show (although I have to confess I do not know what it is) that the Phoenicians were shipping clay if not made pottery out of Poole as early as 800 BC.

But to get down to more easily verifiable facts, a man named Jesse Carter came to Poole in 1873 and bought the East Quay Works, a tile-making firm that had been founded in 1860. 'Carter's Red' tiles soon became famous. Carter's went from strength to strength, opening another works in Poole itself as opposed to Hamworthy for the making of pots, and importing craftsmen from Staffordshire to help get it going. Harold Stabler and John Adams joined the firm after 1919, the latter bringing new ideas from Stoke-on-Trent, and the name of the firm was changed to Carter, Stabler and Adams. Gradually, however, the firm became known as Poole Pottery *tout simple*, and that is what it still is called. After the Second World War the East Quay Works became the main pottery again, and Poole Pottery is one of the mainstays of commercial Poole.

The **Port of Poole** is still flourishing, *malgré* the tremendous subsidies that are given to road transport these days (shipping has absolutely no government assistance, let alone protection), and over one million tonnes of goods came into the port in 1972, oil the biggest item (861,500 tonnes), ballast second (151,900), coal and coke (77,300), grain and cattle food (16,400). Outward-bound there was clay (14,100), petroleum by-products (16,400), 4,900 tonnes of grain and some other goods.

There is shipbuilding and repairing (including specialising in strange one-off craft like salvage vessels and ferries) and yacht building. The Shipwright's Arms is not named for nothing.

There is still much savour of the sea about Old Poole (although the miles of dreary suburbs that have sprung up around it savour of nothing except boredom). The last British square-rigger to keep in trade was launched broadside-on from Bolson's Yard about 1876. She was the barquentine *Waterwitch*, and her master was a Cornishman named Charles Deacon from Port Isaac in Cornwall. She was employed in the china clay trade from Cornwall to the Mersey, carrying coal back. She was sold to Esthonia as a coal hulk.

As for fishing, in 1908 there were about thirty small sailing trawlers fishing out of Poole, working mostly in Bournemouth Bay and off Christchurch Ledge. These were smacks of some thirty feet – Poole never went in for the grand seventy-footers of Ramsgate or Brixham. Now there are only about four small trawlers really fishing full-time and perhaps fifteen lobster and crab potters. In the season there is some pair fishing for sprats. Many small boats take anglers out to sea. The 'Fishermen's Shambles' is an odd little harbour-within-a-harbour.

The oyster industry is reviving in Poole now, and this looks like becoming more important. There was an attempt in 1958 to lay oysters in the Wareham Channel and elsewhere in the harbour, but this was nullified by the hard winter of 1961–2 which killed the oysters. Now, after several mild winters, the free oyster beds are looking up again, and are fished by the Poole Oystermen's Association, and they also dredge outside, in 'the Main', as they call the sea. But more significant perhaps are the activities of the Poole Oyster Company, which has laid down a hundred acres of *Crassostrea jigas*, the Pacific Oyster, in a protected area of the harbour. These oysters lend themselves to intensive cultivation, and they mature at the astonishingly early age of eighteen months. They can be, and are, artificially bred in tanks, the spat is placed in bags which are laid on rafts in the estuary until the oysters have grown big enough to be scattered on to the mud. There they lie until they mature and fatten, and are then either picked up by dredging or picked up by hand at very low water. The old custom of importing spat from Portugal and Brittany is dying: this spat has become too polluted to survive in sufficient quantities. The Pacific Oyster, although it needs some expertise to breed it, may well bring the oyster back into general use as a food again. It is about the most efficient producer of high quality protein that there is, and uses up no valuable dry land.

The Poole Harbour *punts* are a famous breed of estuary craft, evolved in the past for wildfowling and estuarial fishing, and there are still plenty left. As we circumambulate the coasts we are constantly being surprised by new and bizarre forms of fishing. Here we get men in punts *dragging* for rag worms, with strange little dredges with iron hooks on them. The rag worms are sold to the ever-increasing army of sea anglers, who, of course, pay far more for bait than they ever catch the worth of in fish.

There are a few fine old buildings left in Poole. The Guildhall in Market Street, built 1761 and now used to house a small museum, is one. The Old Town House, also now a museum, was probably a guildhall before the present one was built, it became a pub, then a private house, then tenements, then nearly fell down, and then the Society of Poole Men bought it and is saving it from ruin. In it is a Bronze Age canoe which was discovered in the harbour, in two bits, in 1964, and has to be displayed under water in a special tank to keep it from drying out and powdering away. Then there is the 'Town Cellars', now being excavated, fifteenth century, once the Wool House.

The Custom House is of 1813 and good looking. Its predecessor was involved in the famous incident when the smuggler John Diamond ran two tons of tea in from Guernsey, the run was seized by the Revenue men and impounded in the Customs House. Diamond, at the head of sixty men, attacked the Customs House, carried it, and took away thirty-seven hundredweight of the impounded tea (they didn't touch any other goods). But alas, next morning when they were riding inland with the stuff they came upon a customs officer in the company of an informer on his way to report to the magistrate. Incensed at the informer's treachery they killed him, and then killed the customs officer for good measure. One Thomas Kingsmill, who had led the storming party at the Customs House, was later hanged for this, together with nine other smugglers.

The Harbour Office is a fine building of 1727, and there are some fine warehouses down by the quay, unfortunately not being used any more for their proper purpose.

There is much industry in the new Poole, some of it connected with the sea, such as *Seagulls*, who produce their fine outboard engines here. Perhaps the most bizarre of Poole's industries is one of the many activities of Messrs Harveys' Marine Services. These are willing to take what is left of you, after you are past reading this or any other book, outside the three miles' limit, encased in a lead-lined coffin and draped with appropriate flags, and consign you to the deep.

The tour of the **Harbour** can only reasonably be done in a boat, and that a shallow draught one, but what a delightful tour it is.

The *vast* lighters that disfigure the Wareham Channel off Gold Point belong to the United States of America. The French had the benefit of them until they left NATO and now we have to put up with them. You can sail up to **Wareham**, which is well worth doing for it is a fine little honest town that doesn't try to angle for the millions and has a long and honourable history, good pubs and two fine Saxon churches, or at least churches with Saxon elements in them. One is Lady St Mary, on the site of a nunnery which was old, it is said, even in 705 when it was reformed by St Aldhelm, the Bishop of Sherborne. The nunnery was destroyed by the Danes in 876, rebuilt in 915 by King Athenstan, destroyed again by the Danes in 998, and again, by King Cnut, in 1015. Cnut spared the church that time, but the Victorians didn't spare it: they savagely cut it in half in 1842 because they thought its acoustics didn't do justice to their rector's beautiful voice. Behotric, a king of the West Saxons, is probably buried here, and Edward the Martyr once was but was dug up and transposed to Shaftesbury. He was murdered by his stepmother when he rode over to see her at Corfe. There are sixth- and seventh-century engraved stones, a fine twelfth-century lead font, and a simple and moving effigy of the Lady Mary, modern, in the porch.

The other church is St Aldhelm's Chapel, or St-Martins-in-the-wall, and it stands where St Aldhelm built a church about AD 678. The existing building may be substantially of 1030, although the north aisle and the chancel arch are Norman, the north arcade thirteenth century, and there are later windows and other details. There are fascinating murals within, and the famous effigy of Lawrence of Arabia made by Eric Kennington. Lawrence took an interest in restoring this church in the 1930s (it was rededicated in 1936). Misguided people have said that the effigy looks out of place in this ancient building. It does not, it looks bang-on.

Wareham was an important place in Saxon days, which is why it was so repeatedly and savagely attacked by the Danes. There were Saxon earthworks on three sides of the town, which were brought back into fortification in 1138 when Robert de Lincoln seized the town for Matilda, and Stephen took it back again in 1142. There were great doings here in the Civil War. In 1644 Sir Anthony Ashley-Cooper took the town by storm for Parliament. In 1762 much of the old town was burned, so much of it dates to after this date. Sometimes the gardens of the Tudor-period Old Priory are opened to the public.

The southern shores of Poole Harbour are wild and lonely, more or less jealously protected from the public by private large landowners, although the Forestry Commission, which has large holdings here, seems to have abandoned its policy of keeping we tax payers off our own land with our own servants who are paid with our own money. These barren heaths are still uncultivated, unspoilt (unless you object to conifers – and no other trees would grow here very well) and un-built-on. The Natterjack Toad is said to natter here, the Sand Lizard and the Smooth Snake coexist with more usual reptiles, and that rare bird, the Dartford Warbler, is to be found and arouses strong passions in the breasts of bird watchers. On the waters and mudflats of the harbour there are all the ducks, waders, grebes, and gulls that you might expect to find in such shallow tidal muddy waters, including less common birds such as the Purple Sandpiper and, I am told, very occasionally the Slavonian Grebe has been seen.

The mudflats are being rapidly colonised by *Spartina*, or Rice Grass. Townsend, in his *Flora*, recorded *Spartina townsendii* in Poole Harbour in 1904. Because of this, and other factors, the harbour is slowly silting up.

All along the very indented shore are the decayed remains of old wharves. Sometimes the name is the only thing that is left of them. There is Shipstal Point, near **Arne**, Middlebere Farm, Wytch Farm, Fitzworth, Goathorn, Ower. All these were loading places for clay, and Ower, in particular, was the port of embarkation for most of the Purbeck Marble that found its way all over England in the thirteenth century to make those Early English pillars. Newton, now one lonely house, was as its name implies a town: one of those planned by that great town planner Edward I. This was to be a port for the exporting of the marble. Whether it came to anything in Edward's day I do not know, certainly it has not come to very much now.

The islands are fascinating places. **Long Island** is said to have been a hideout of 'Arripay' when hard-pressed by his enemies. **Brownsea**, like the others sand and heath, but this also has woodlands, is a favourite resort now of people from Poole, who can get over all summer in motor launches which operate from the quay. On old maps this was called Branksea (from Old English *brunc*, the side of a hill, and *sey*, an island). The monks of Cerne Abbey had a chapel here in the twelfth century, Henry VIII built one of his innumerable block-houses to keep the Pope out, Parliament garrisoned the island in the Civil War, Sir Robert Clayton started up a copperas works here in Charles II's time (it was closed in 1700). In 1852 one Colonel Petrie Waugh bought the island and –

egged on by his wife, who was an amateur geologist – opened a clay works. He built a village, a church and school, inned some marshes, rebuilt the block house which he renamed the castle, and went bankrupt. There are broken tiles, pots, and clay pipes on the western beach to give sign of this activity. The Cavendish Bentincts then took over, and during their reign the island had the glory of having held on it the first-ever boy scout camp. In 1907 Lord Baden Powell went over with twenty boys, mostly sons of friends of his, to camp for a week and teach the boys 'woodcraft, observation, discipline, health and endurance, chivalry, saving life and patriotism'. Thus was founded the Boy Scout Movement. Then came Mrs Bonham Christie, who ruled with a rod of iron until she died in 1961, rigorously excluding all visitors and employing, there were rumours, hefty female gymnasts to guard her domains. She let the island go back, more or less, to jungle. Then, in 1962 came the National Trust, who cleared much of the jungle, helped by the Dorset Naturalists' Trust and the Nature Conservancy. They made a nature reserve of St Andrew's Bay and the two lakes. The public can go to the island but no one may camp or light fires, which seems sad on the holy ground of the Boy Scout Movement. There are Shakespeare plays out of doors every summer, with mosquito repellent handed out with the programmes and it is sorely needed.

If, in your wanderings along the shores of the harbour, you wandered up the Corfe River you would come to **Corfe Castle**. This is a dramatic and spectacular place – the castle built on a little hill which commands the one good pass through the up-edged chalk of the Purbeck Hills. The builders of Corfe Castle had never heard of the Alpine Orogeny, but they knew where to build their castle.

There was a castle pre AD 978. Then Elfrida, stepmother of Edward, had a hunting lodge here. She lured Prince Edward, who was heir to the throne, to come and see her and then, while he was sitting on his horse drinking a stirrup cup, either stabbed him herself or had him stabbed. He was buried first at Wareham, then dug up and taken to Shaftesbury. Elfrida's guilt was made manifest by the fact that when she tried to follow the corpse to the second burial she was miraculously prevented. The tragedy of the whole thing is that, although we do not know what sort of a king Edward would have made, we do know that the usurper who supplanted him – Elfrida's own son, who earned himself the name of Ethelred the Redeless, or the lacking in council, commonly now called Ethelred the Unready, was everything a king of a country facing foreign invasion should not be. Unready to fight, constantly caught unprepared, he had to resort to paying enormous bribes to try to keep the Danes out but, of course, each bribe caused the enemy to ask for another. If Edward the Martyr had become king, and had been a good king, who knows: the Dane might have been kept at bay and, later, the Norman might have been beaten, too, and England would have remained English.

The Norman Baldwin de Redvers seized the castle from the Norman Queen Matilda during her war with Stephen. Under King John the castle was used as a royal prison and gained an unsavoury reputation. The modern totalitarian states didn't invent beastliness. King John put twenty-four knights he did not like in the dungeons of Corfe and let all but two of them starve to death, and about the same time he immured Princess Eleanor, sister of Arthur, in Corfe for forty years until she died. She did, however, have the companionship of two Scottish princesses whom John managed to lay his hands on and who were imprisoned in Corfe from 1209. In 1212 one Peter de Pomfret rashly prophesied that the king would lose his throne on the next Ascension Day. To teach him not to make rash prophesies John had him dragged behind horses from Corfe to Wareham and back and then drawn and quartered. Later Edward II was kept here a prisoner after his downfall, his jailer being Sir John Maltravers.

In the Civil War Lady Bankes held the castle against the Parliamentary troops while her husband, Sir John, was away at the wars. First Sir Walter Erle attacked her, and eventually forced her to surrender but on honourable terms. She was obliged to give up her four small cannon, but was allowed to remain with her people in the castle. She took advantage of this by re-arming her garrison, re-supplying the castle, and, when attacked by Sir Walter again, she managed to hold out for six weeks. The attackers mounted their guns on the church tower, melted the lead roof of the church to cast bullets, and used the very organ pipes for holding powder and shot. The siege was raised by Royalist troops, but the Roundheads came back in 1645 under Sir Anthony Ashley-Cooper and, after Lady Bankes had been betrayed by one of her own officers, Colonel Pitman, who rode out saying he was going to bring in reinforcements but in fact came back with a hundred Roundheads from Weymouth, the castle was taken and slighted. There is a good account of Lady Banke's gallant and dogged defence in the *History and Guide to Corfe Castle*, obtainable for 15p at the Post Office.

The church at Corfe Castle is good and whatever you do don't miss the gargoyles.

CHAPTER 19

The Isle of Purbeck

THE **Isle of Purbeck** is not an isle, but would be if the sea broke through at Arish Mell and cut through the soft Tertiary rock east of East Lulworth to join the Frome. As it was, in ancient times Purbeck was effectively an isle so far as men were concerned, because the only effective land route to it was through the pass guarded by Corfe Castle. In Norman times the Constable of Corfe exercised despotic control over the people of Purbeck. No Purbeck person, for example, was allowed to marry anyone from outside the 'Isle' without the constable's permission.

If we are travelling the coast by land we may well reach the Isle by the ferry – that carries the country bus as well as everything else – from **Sandbanks** in Poole to South Haven Point. We enter a lonely land of marsh and sand dunes, there is the Little Sea, now a lake, once part of a channel from the sea to the harbour, which, we are told, 'Arripay' used to sail to get away from – or at – his enemies. The Little Sea is now a nature reserve. We round the shores of the magnificent Studland Bay to Studland.

Studland has a beautiful Early Norman church, not to be missed on any account. The church, built on Saxon foundations, is said to be very similar to old churches in Normandy over the water. It is one of the most beautiful Norman churches in Dorset. The **Agglestone**, within walking distance, is a four hundred ton lump of sandstone perched up on softer rock which has eroded away. There are, as there should be, plenty of stories about its miraculous provenance and magical properties and people have resorted to it to improve their fertility, with what result I do not know. Certainly the surrounding country is underpopulated.

Studland Bay is much resorted to by yachts in the summer time, and with the wind with any west or north in it, it is perfect. If it does suddenly pipe up from the south-east you can always slide round into Poole Harbour: it is thus a much safer anchorage than Swanage Bay. There used to be a jetty at Studland at which boatmen from Poole, locally called 'the Gondoliers', used to land passengers. Studland Bay was used for the filming of *The Ship that Died of Shame*, and the jetty was damaged and has never been rebuilt. Studland

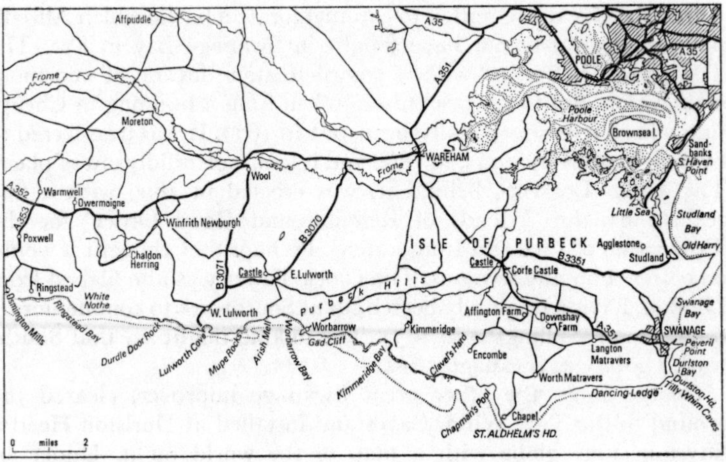

itself, as a village, strikes me as being a non-village: mostly residential hotels closed down in the winter.

South of Studland we come to the great up-ended chalk ridge of the Purbeck Hills. These are the northern limb of a monoclinal fold which was thrown up between fourteen and fifteen million years ago by the Alpine Orogeny: the great earth-storm that threw up the Alps and the waves of which caused rock folding all over Europe. This ridge of chalk continued across to what is now the Isle of Wight until the sea broke through in fairly recent times. The Needles are part of the Wight end of the gap and Old Harry is the Purbeck end. Old Harry had a wife once but, alas, she fell into the sea in 1896 and Harry became a widower. There are Bronze Age and Iron Age remains all along the spine of the Purbeck Hills.

Swanage lies at the end of a valley of Wealden Clay that lies between the chalk of the Purbeck Hills and the Jurassic limestones to the south. The sea has cut a bay into this soft Wealden Clay, which is protected from further erosion by the limestone of Peveril Point. Swanage was once a port for the shipping out of Purbeck Stone and Purbeck-Portland and Purbeck Marble, and then became a seaside resort in Victorian times. As a resort it was very much moulded by two wealthy quarrying families: the Mowlems and the Burts. It has been said that they had more money than taste, but their taste was considered the right taste in the Victorian era, and at least their works show a certain bizarre exuberance. John Mowlem, who died in 1869, built the Mowlem Institute and the

Alfred the Great Memorial, to commemorate a battle which Alfred's navy may or may not have fought in Swanage Bay in 877. The Town Hall is fronted with a complete stone façade of enormous elaboration, not to say pretension, taken from a building in Cheapside where it had originally been put in 1670. It was transferred to Swanage, stone by stone, in 1882 and it looks splendidly out of place. The Town Lock-up, behind it, was erected in 1803 with a fine realism by the 'Friends of Religion and Good Order' for the 'Prevention of Vice and Immorality'. Perhaps they thought it would be better than any sermons. The Clock Tower was also filched from London, having originally been built at Southwark to commemorate the Duke of Wellington in 1854. The unkind might say that Southwark's gain was Swanage's loss.

George Burt, the other great Swanage improver, cleared the ground to the Tilly Whim Caves and installed at Durlston Head a fifty-ton stone globe with a map of the world on it. Under an enthusiastic description of himself he caused to be added the words: 'He Made the Stars Also.' Stone benches around the globe provide astronomical data, and some blank stone slabs have been thoughtfully provided for compulsive *graffiti* carvers.

The Tilly Whim Caves consist mostly of underground quarries which were used for the extraction of Purbeck-Portland Stone, Tilly having been the name of a man and *whim* meaning a crane or windlass for hoisting stone. And here we might discuss the whole fascinating business of Purbeck Stone quarrying.

We can still see at Swanage light railway tracks running along the front, and in front of what is now the Information Office were once huge dumps of stone blocks which were there split and riven into smaller blocks which could be humped on men's backs to waiting boats, which carried the stone to ships which sailed it away to London and other places. These dumps were called the Bankers. The stone was of three main divisions: Purbeck Marble, Purbeck, and Purbeck-Portland. The Alpine Earth-storm, about which we have talked so much, hoisted the Jurassic Limestone of this area, which had been laid down from a hundred and twenty to a hundred and thirty million years ago, and overlaid by subsequent depositions, into a ridge which has been exposed again by the erosion of later deposits upon it and which forms the coastal cliffs and plain of the country here. This limestone, some of it laid down in the sea and some in fresh water conditions, and then compressed and contorted by the Alpine storm, just happens to make magnificent building material. It is a freestone – in other words it cleaves not only along the lateral planes of its original bedding, but also along planes of weakness almost at right angles to this and at right angles to each other. Thus it can be cloven into cubes or rectangles. It is fairly soft when first exposed, and can be sawn or guillotined, but it hardens with exposure to the air.

At Peveril Point the uppermost layer of the Upper Purbeck Beds can clearly be seen outcropping in the cliffs. The famous Purbeck Marble, which is not quite a true marble because it has not been metamorphosed sufficiently by heat and pressure, is the uppermost stratum of these beds. It was laid down in fresh water and is largely composed of the shells of a fresh water snail, once named *Paludina*, now called *Viviparus*. It is a beautiful greenish or bluish rock, with a fine texture and will take a fine polish but will not stand up to weathering. It was used extensively in the thirteenth century for what we call 'Early English' architecture, forming very many of those small pillars which are such a feature of that style, and being used extensively in monuments. It found its way all over England. The Romans used it, and some of their work in it has been found at Colchester. The rock is only a thin vein, and it outcrops right along the southern edge of the Vale of Purbeck, being overlaid there with the Wealden Clay on which Swanage is built.

The men who worked Purbeck Marble jealously preserved their privileges, with their craft guild called *The Marblers and Stonecutters of Purbeck*, and these men still meet, every Shrove Tuesday, at the Town Hall of Corfe Castle, and, after certain ceremonies, they present the Lord of the Manor with a pound of peppercorns. In former days they had to prove their manhood by carrying a brimming tankard of ale across the road in Corfe without spilling any, then kicking a ball of some sort all the way to Ower. The purpose of these strange rites was to keep open the right of way to the shores of Poole Harbour, for it was from those sheltered waters that, in days gone by, they used to ship most of their marble. Purbeck Marble seems to be out of fashion now, which is sad because it is a beautiful stone and we don't have to import it.

Most quarrymen in Purbeck now quarry the Upper and Lower Building Stone of the Middle Purbeck Beds. These measures were laid down partly under fresh water and partly under salt. The rock is covered in most places by a few feet of overburden, and this nowadays is removed by a contractor with an excavator, it not being economical for a quarryman to own one of these machines. The quarrymen then drill horizontal holes (I use the word horizontal for convenience: in fact the beds have quite a dip to them and the driller follows this dip) put in very small quantities of a slow explosive and gently *bump* rather than blast the rock, just so as to shake it loose without shattering it. The old method of thus splitting the rock out was the use of the *plug and feathers* (what a name for a pub incidentally). A hole would be drilled in, horizontally or vertically, whichever was convenient, the two feathers – which were narrow flat slivers of metal – placed in the hole and the plug, which was a steel wedge, driven between the two feathers with a sledge hammer. A row of such plugs and feathers would be driven along one line of cleavage and hammered in together when suddenly the rock would split. The huge block thus broken out from the bed of rock would then be split in convenient pieces by further treatment.

The whole Middle and Lower Purbeck series can be seen well exposed in the cliffs of Durlston Bay, and H.M. Stationery Office booklet, *The Hampshire Basin and Adjoining Areas*, in the *British Regional Geology Series*, describes them in detail. In the 1850s W. R. Brodie caused digging to be undertaken in what is now called the Mammalian Bed near Durlston Head and remains of many of the very first mammals, besides crocodiles, were found.

Below the Purbeck Series, and separated from it by a thick layer of Marl, lie the Portland Beds, and owing to a spectacular fault just behind Durlston Head these outcrop at the base of the cliffs all along the south shore of the Isle of Purbeck until you get west to St Aldhelm's Head. It is in these Purbeck-Portland measures that you find the picturesque and fascinating underground quarries, or stone mines, such as Tilly Whim, Dancing Ledge, Seacombe and – possibly the finest – Winspit. The intrepid quarrymen drove their levels into the cliffs – laboriously hacking out a narrow crevice above the layer of stone they were trying to win so as to allow the block they were operating on to split upwards when they drove their plugs in below, or let off their small charges of powder. They had to leave pillars at intervals to support the great weight of the roof above, but one cannot help wondering how they knew exactly how much pillar to leave! In places such pillars support the weight of huge chunks of lofty cliffs above them and they often look very slender for the job.

The blocks of stone thus won would be hauled out to the bottom of the cliffs by ropes and windlasses and then lowered by crane into ten-ton open boats below. There was no shelter whatever for these tough little boats, and they had to lie right up against the hard rock-face and take whatever buffeting that came. Formerly the boats or barges were then rowed out to ships of from sixty to a hundred tons called 'stone ackers' that lay at anchor perhaps half a mile off and into these the stones were transferred. The ackers would then sail the stone to its destination. Between the wars a steam tug came to be used, and this would tow a string of loaded small barges into Swanage Bay, where the stone could be more safely transferred into ships or sailing barges. Later still a steam wagon came into use, for taking the stone away from Winspit, which was the last of these shore quarries to be worked. This hauled the stone away inland, and it no longer went by water. There is still plenty of magnificent building stone left in these cliffs to be worked, and if men ever start building with stone again there is no reason why these quarries should not open again.

But there are several actively working quarries inland: there is one very actively worked open quarry (there is no more underground mining) just south of Swanage – you go along the Panorama Road and pass the municipal caravan site to find it. This produces, besides good freestone, quite a lot of stuff which the old quarrymen would have discarded: stone that does not split in rectangles but can be used for crazy paving. A long section of dinosaur tracks was discovered here and is now in the Natural History Museum at South Kensington.

Langton Matravers is a straggling rather ugly quarrymen's village, and many quarrymen still live in it. Downshay Farm and Afflington Farm are on the Purbeck Marble outcrop and it has been worked at these places.

Worth Matravers is a superbly pretty village and its Square and Compass Inn is, quite rightly, a famous hostelry. You can buy there for a very few pennies a large-scale local map of the cliffs, with such splendid topographical names on it as Scratch Arse. Worth Matravers has a certain sort of medical fame owing to the fact that a man named Jesty who lived there vaccinated his wife and children with live cow pox virus twenty years before Jenner, the man who is generally credited with the discovery of vaccination. Jesty wisely refrained from vaccinating himself. His epitaph is in the churchyard. Worth has a lovely church.

St Aldhelm's Head, once wrongly called St Albans Head, has on it a most unusual and distinguished building. This is a Norman chapel, perfectly square in plan, and when you enter it you find a perfect stone vaulted ceiling supported by a massive central pillar. One enters it for the first time to receive a shock of surprise, and I would like to recommend it to any aspiring knight errant to watch his arms in. It was built between 1150 and 1200 to serve as a beacon to save the bodies of seamen and an oratory for a priest to pray for their souls if the beacon failed to do its work. It stands there 354 feet above sea level.

Chapman's Pool, which is part of the Encombe Estate and has a private motor road going down nearly to it, and a toll gate in the summer to collect money from motorists, is a strange little hole cut by the sea in a kind of rock that we meet here for the first time on the south coast: the Kimmeridge Clay, here a soft, black, crumbly shale. The Kimmeridge occurs underneath the Purbeck and Portland limestones but here the strike of the rocks brings the Kimmeridge above sea-level. It will be seen that Hound's Tout Cliff, just to the west of Chapman's Pool, is capped with the hard limestone. The erosion of the soft shaly clay by the sea here has caused such strange little hollows as Chapman's Pool and also the generally confused and jumbled nature of the adjoining shore, into which masses of limestone must in the past have collapsed. An Iron Age dwelling was excavated at Chapman's Pool in 1855, but there is no building here now except a few tarred shacks of local fishermen and these look rather like Iron Age dwellings themselves. Drawn up by them are a few small boats. There are foundations of more substantial dwellings, however, for in the last century the shale was mined and sent away for purposes which we shall discuss when we get to Kimmeridge. At Clavel's Hard are old mine levels into the shale from which oil shale was extracted.

Encombe House was built by John Pitt about 1735. William Moreton Pitt, a successor, was a prison reformer and tried to improve life on his estate by setting up a sail cloth and cordage mill at Encombe and other enterprises. Like many reformers he went bankrupt and had to sell his estate to the 1st Earl of Eldon.

The shore to the west, the Kimmeridge Ledges, is a chaos of tumbled rocks and should be given a good berth by boats. Of course, what has happened is that the sea has eaten into the soft Kimmeridge Clay of the cliffs and this has allowed great masses of Portland and Purbeck Stone to crash down into the breakers. These act as breakwaters to delay, at least, further erosion.

Kimmeridge Bay, whence the important geological formation of the Kimmeridge Clay takes its name (it is found far away in extensive outcrops in Lincolnshire and Yorkshire), looks deserted now (although not quite), but it has an interesting history. As this history is based (like all history) on geology we might as well consider the latter first.

The Kimmeridge Clay Series is enormously thick. Recent borings by the oil company here have shown a depth of it of 1,651 feet. This clay was laid down in a muddy sea which followed the clear warm water that formed the Corallian Beds of the later Jurassic period. It consists of alternative layers of soft shale and harder shaly stone. In the Upper Kimmeridge is found *Pliosaurus grandis*, a marine reptile with a seven feet long head and fore paddles of six feet nine inches, that must have swum about in that muddy sea. The upper part of the series consists of Paper Shales, which are bituminous: the top three feet only being known as 'Kimmeridge Coal'. This 'coal' has been the ruin of several men's fortunes.

Late in the seventeenth century Sir William Clavel built a massive stone quay, a hundred feet long, half way across Kimmeridge Bay to shelter ships come in to load bituminous shale. A gale of 1745 knocked it down and now it would be hard to find a trace of it. If you go there in a southerly gale now you will realise that no stone sea wall founded on crumbling shale would have a hope of survival. Early in the eighteen hundreds a London company contracted, of all fantastic things, to light the streets of Paris with gas extracted from this Kimmeridge shale. The gas stank, and blackened people's faces, and the enterprise foundered. Sir William Clavel also started an alum works at Kimmeridge and also a glass factory. The glass was made by firing the furnaces with the 'coal', a ton of glass requiring a ton of good coal to make it. This, like the other enterprises, came eventually to nought. Sir William also built Smedmore House, fine Jacobean, and sometimes open to the public, and the tower on the headland east of the bay. All these enterprises brought him to the Marshalsea, and it took three generations after him to pay off his debts. Another quay was built in the bay in the nineteenth century, with a big lime kiln in it. Limestone was probably burnt with the 'coal', too. In the nineteenth century there was some success, and the little bay was often crowded with shipping, small schooners and ketches, and there was a big fleet of beaching fishing boats. Shale was shipped round to Wareham to be sold for six shillings a ton there. As a fuel it was spoiled by its high sulphur content, though.

There is a rich vein of industrial archaeology to be worked at Kimmeridge, which might prove more profitable than the vein of bituminous shale.

But even the people of the Iron Age used Kimmeridge 'coal' – turning it on lathes to make armlets. The central pieces thus cut out were waste, and were thought by the Victorians to be primitive money, or by some people to be offerings to the god Hercules for some reason or other. The Romans used the stuff, which is hard and takes a shine, for trays and table tops. And now British Petroleum has an oil well here, and they have just struck oil again on the Arne Peninsula. The shale itself is oil bearing, and it exudes oil into the sea, sometimes giving the latter an oily appearance. If the Arab oil sheiks get too importunate no doubt a way will be found of extracting the oil cheaply and getting the sulphur out of it.

There are still a few part-time fishermen using Kimmeridge Bay, with boats and lobster pots and tarred huts, and one full-timer, a Mr Marshall.

And now we come to the most splendid and dramatic section of the Dorset coast, and one which we can seldom proceed along owing to the fact that it is all fenced off by the Army. This coast, and some twenty square miles of the hinterland, are used as a tank range by the Royal Armoured Corps. We can sail along it, though, sometimes, and when we do we pass Gad Cliff, where the Portland Limestone juts out to sea masking the Kimmeridge Clay below it, Worbarrow Tout, again made of Portland, at Worbarrow Bay the sea has cut into the Wealden Clay Sands and Marls that were laid down such a long time after in the estuary of the great river that flowed out to sea near here in Lower Cretaceous times. The western end of the Purbeck Hills here makes a great chalk cliff over five hundred feet high. Arish Mell is a weird little gap in the hills – and here the Atomic Energy Research Station at Winfrid's Heath pour their radioactive waste out into the sea. At Mupe Rocks the Portland Stone comes up again and then we come to the marvellous little sea-cut basin of Lulworth Cove.

At **Lulworth** the sea has eaten through the hard ridge of Portland Stone to fan out into the soft Wealden Beds behind and carve out this crater-like cavity until stopped by the harder chalk of the Purbeck Hills behind. It is delightful to sail along the apparently unbroken cliffs here and then suddenly to see this little hole in a wall and sail into it. Only have your anchor and cable clear, ready to let go the moment you are into it, or you, like the sea, might be brought up by the chalk of the Purbeck Hills.

Hard on the east shore of the little cove the tank range country ends and west of this it is lawful to go. Just inside the forbidden ground, on the headland that guards the eastern side of the cove, is the remains of a fossil forest. When the Portlandian Sea retreated shallow fresh water and deltaic conditions followed with occasional periods of dry land. It was during one of the latter that the forest grew, on the soil that is now known as the Portland Dirt Bed.

On this eastern headland, too, are the remains of Little Bindon Chapel, formerly a chapel of ease served by the monks of Bindon Abbey and later used as a barn. Bindon Abbey was revived by monks from France in the eighteenth century, but they were driven out from here during the Napoleonic Wars in case they might be spies. Thomas Hardy imagined Napoleon actually landing here, before they were driven out, to spy out the country he was set to conquer. The mortal remains of twenty-two of these monks had to be exhumed from the main monastery when tank shells began to desecrate their graves.

Lulworth Cove itself, still a popular anchorage for small boats, was once more important. Old prints of it show a sturdy pier on the west side where there is no pier now, and quite big ships at anchor. Edward Weld, the local squire, recorded in his diary for 22nd June, 1750: 'We went on board to visit Captain Hanbury in ye *Hazard* sloop, in West Lulworth Harbour: 150 tons, fifty men, seventy-five feet long.' Later he recorded that she remained ten days. But as anyone can see Lulworth is not tenable in a southerly gale: you either have to beach or get out of it.

Lulworth was once a great base for privateers and pirates. In Elizabethan times piracy was the great industry here and there are reliable records of many piratical goings-on. Even as late as William III's reign there were privateers based on Lulworth, and there is the case of Master Peter Joliffe, of Poole, master of the hoy *Sea Adventure*, who – spying a French privateer attacking an English fishing boat – attacked the Frenchman, freed the fishing boat, and forced the French ship to go aground at Lulworth, where she was taken. And this in spite of the fact that he was out-gunned and out-manned. Master Joliffe was awarded for this deed a massive gold watch and chain by 'Sailor Billy', or William III.

Like most such small inlets in the coast Lulworth was long a fishing port and still is now. A man named Miller fishes full time, working some two hundred and fifty lobster pots, and is the only man I know who admits that it is the English fishermen themselves who are responsible for overfishing the lobster grounds and not just marauding Frenchmen. Thirty years ago a man could make a good living with twenty lobster pots here. Now he has to have two hundred and fifty if he is to survive. The more pots men put out the fewer lobsters they ultimately catch. They all know this, and yet no individual fisherman can afford to act on the knowledge for if he did he would rapidly be starved out of business. The number of pots should be – and must be one day – restricted by law, and then men could earn a good living again with half the effort and far less capital outlay and there would be far more lobsters. Mr Miller has to take his boat to Weymouth in the winter time and fish from there: Lulworth is untenable. Miller shoots his pots mostly on rough ground about seven miles off-shore. He does another sort of fishery quite close in, with another sort of pot, a miniature one like a tiny wire-mesh rat-trap. In these he catches prawns. The traps are baited with fish.

West Lulworth, which must have been a village of sheer delight, is absolutely overwhelmed by tourists in the summer time. They come in an intolerable flood, and the only time to see the place for the people is in the off-season. Pleasure seekers, and discerning ones I should say, have been coming for a long time. In 1791 the actor and dramatist John O'Keefe came here for the sea bathing. When he asked an old fisherman why *he* didn't go swimming, too, the latter replied: 'Not I master – I keep out of the water as much as I can. And I'm sure I can't see why, for my part, you London folk come down here, at vast expense, to souse and sop yerselves in salt water.'

Stair Hole, just to the west of the cove, is a spectacular illustration of the way the ravening sea smashes a breach in the hard Portland limestone and gouges out the Wealden clays behind. The time to see it is in a southerly gale in the winter, when great seas founder against subterranean holes at the bottom of the limestone ridge, causing explosive pressures to build up within and then thunder out into the strange little bay, or gorge, within. The experience of watching this is awe-inspiring and beautiful, and awe-inspiring, too, are the fierce contortions of the Portland and Purbeck Rocks to the east of the bay.

Our way to the west now is barred by 'the grounds' of a large Edwardian-looking villa which come right to the crumbling edge of the cliffs and are fenced off, thus blocking the Dorset Coastal Path, a form of selfishness that fortunately one sees less and less of in this country.

Inland, past Lulworth Camp, huge and full of tanks and tankmen, is **East Lulworth**. Lulworth, by the way, is Old Friesic for The Place of Lulla. Lulworth Castle, which we can gaze at from the outside but can't safely enter because the roof has collapsed and the place is unsafe, was started in 1588 by Henry, Lord of Bindon. This Henry was a roaring swashbuckling fellow who beat his wife, chased his daughter, and spent a month in the Marshalsea Prison for outrageous behaviour. His daughter managed to marry against her father's wishes and Queen Elizabeth had to intervene to save both daughter and mother from the wrath of their husband and father. After the death of this importunate fellow the place went to his brother (a 'peevish fool' we are told), who sold it to the Earl of Suffolk, who completed it in 1609. In 1641 it was sold to Humphrey Weld, Governor of the Isle of Portland, a Roman Catholic, and Weld's descendants still hold it. James I stayed here in 1615. Parliamentary troops seized it in 1643 but did not dismantle it, although they did melt down the roof for bullets for the siege of Corfe Castle. Charles II stayed here and so did George III. The latter was so pleased with his entertainment that he gave the Weld of the day permission to build a Catholic chapel – the first allowed officially since Mary's reign. The only proviso was that it must not look like a chapel, and it doesn't, and stands now to the north-west of the castle. Unfortunately, the castle was allowed to burn down in 1929 and there it stands, a gaunt, gutted, and dangerous ruin. There is a fine picture gallery in the Stables, though, with some famous Brussels tapestries. For those who, like most of us, have little Latin and less Greek, the translation of the inscription on the two new (*and as yet unused*) graves in the south-east corner of the Anglican church can be translated:

I say that such marriages are a gain to men or else to wed is not worthwhile.

The graves are intended for the present incumbent of East and West Lulworth, the Reverend John Stone, and his wife, to whom he has been married for fifty years.

Durdle Door is famous and much photographed, with its wonderful arch of Portland Stone. Then comes Bat's Head standing boldly out to sea, the fine Celtic field system of the Warren, the great White Nothe showing a spectacular Jurassic–Cretaceous unconformity (the Portland and Purbeck Rocks were tilted strongly before the Upper Greensand was laid upon them), Ringstead Bay has a fault which brings the Kimmeridge Clay back to the surface again, which is why there's a bay here for the sea has eaten into it, and we even get here another outcrop of the Kimmeridge 'coal'. The Burning Cliff behind really was burning once. Spontaneous combustion ignited the bituminous shale.

Ringstead village was destroyed, either by the French or the Black Death or both, around 1420, but has risen from the ashes as holiday bungalows. The chancel of the ancient church is now part of a house. **Osmington Mills** is on a stream which cuts through Corallian Rock. The church of Osmington has a strange sixteenth-century monument with very un-Christian sentiments engraved on it. John Constable spent part of his belated honeymoon here in the vicarage and he painted the village. The horse and rider cut in the turf of the downs to the north is George III – put there in gratitude for his having deigned to visit the place, by local people. Poxwell and Warmwell have fine seventeenth-century manors. Overmoigne Court is fine, too, but earlier.

CHAPTER 20

Weymouth and the Isle of Portland

Weymouth is the result of the amalgamation of Old Weymouth and **Melcombe Regis**, shortly before the Armada came to grief. The two towns were forced to combine by Queen Elizabeth and in their combined strength were able to send six gallant ships against the Armada: the *Galleon*, *Catherine*, *Heath-Hen*, *Golden Royal*, *Expedition* and another. A Spanish ship was brought into Weymouth as a prize. George III and Queen Charlotte came here in 1789, accompanied, fortunately for us, by somebody with keener perception than either, and Fanny Burney has left a marvellous account of it all in her diaries. When the royal head was dunked under the water of the English Channel a band, hitherto concealed in an adjoining bathing machine, struck up 'God Save the King', and there were many other such charming touches. Afterwards the king made seven or eight more such visits, often being guarded while he was there by a strong detachment of the Royal Navy lest Bonaparte should swoop across the Channel and carry His Majesty away. The first bathing machines appeared at Weymouth in 1748, and a local law laid down that there was to be at least fifty yards between bathing machines used by the different sexes.

But Weymouth goes back further than its bathing machines. Radipole was a port in Roman times, and we know that the manors of Weymouth, Portland, Wyke Regis and Elwell were presented to St Swithin of Winchester by Edward the Confessor to atone for false allegations made against his mother. (She proved her innocence by walking blindfold and barefoot over nine red hot ploughshares.) Later these manors were part of the dowry of Eleanor of Castile, wife of Edward I. In 1347 Weymouth sent ships to Calais, in 1377 it was raided by the French, in 1471 Margaret of Anjou landed here to begin the campaign that ended at Tewkesbury.

Melcombe, just the other side of Radipole Lake or the harbour, was given a charter in 1280 by Edward I conferring on it exceptional privileges. It was a staple town under Edward III (meaning one of the few ports from which it was legal to export wool). It had the distinction of being the first place in England to know the Black Death, which was brought back to the port by pilgrims from the

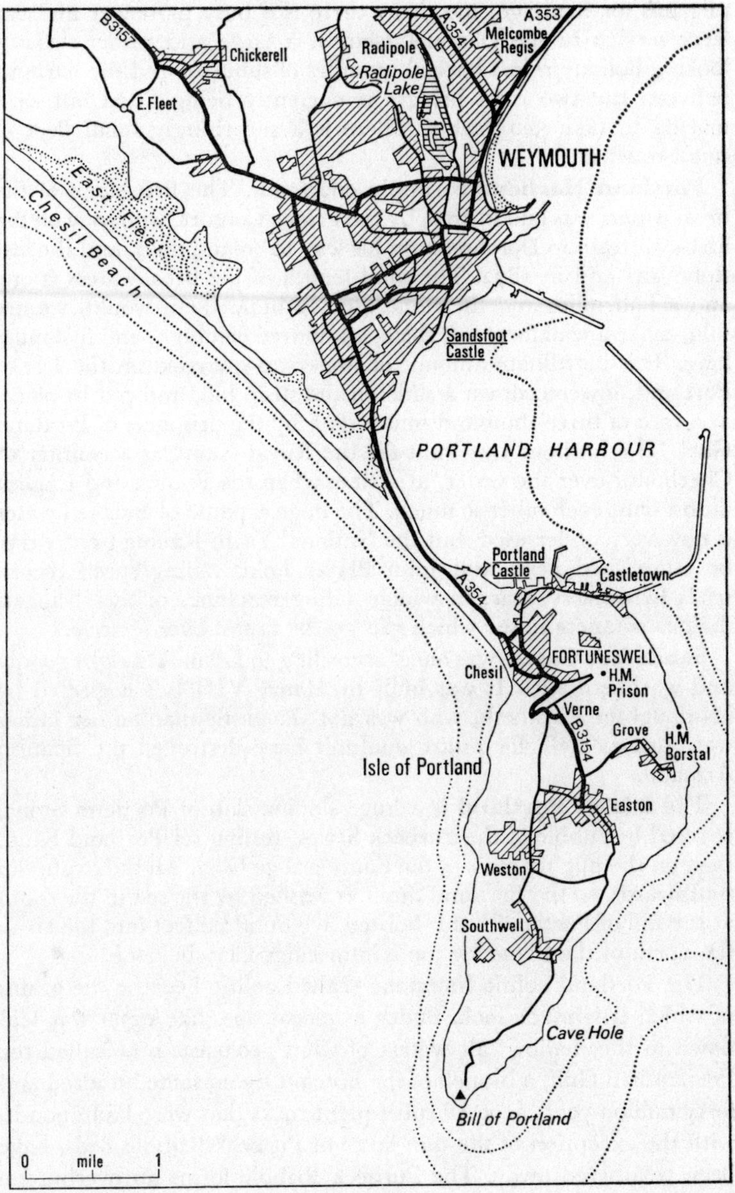
B3157
Chickerell
E. Fleet
Radipole
Radipole Lake
A354
A353
Melcombe Regis
WEYMOUTH
East Fleet
Chesil Beach
Sandsfoot Castle
PORTLAND HARBOUR
Portland Castle
Castletown
A354
FORTUNESWELL
Chesil
H.M. Prison
Verne
B3154
Grove
H.M. Borstal
Isle of Portland
Easton
Weston
Southwell
Cave Hole
Bill of Portland
0 mile 1

Holy Land in 1348. The port was a major embarkation port for pilgrims for Santiago, too. Now there is a busy passenger and car ferry service to the Channel Islands, a large and rather elegant-looking holiday resort backed by miles of suburbs, and the harbour between the two road bridges is currently being fitted out as a marina to take 360 yachts. There is a surprisingly small fleet of small trawlers.

Portland Harbour is simply enormous. The first stone of the breakwaters was laid in 1849 by the Prince Consort, who rode on the first-ever train to Dorchester on his way to go and do it, and the last stone was laid in 1872. The total length of the breakwaters is one and a half miles and the stone used to build them would, we are told, make a wall forty feet thick, a hundred feet high, and five miles long. This inordinate amount of stone was quarried on the Isle of Portland, lowered down a slide on the steep hill, and put in place, at a rate of three thousand tons a day, by the prisoners of Portland Gaol. The harbour was built for the Royal Navy, as a counter to Cherbourg over the water, at a time when the French and English didn't trust each other so much. The huge expanse of enclosed water is now very under-used, but the National Yacht Racing Centre is to be established here, and John Player holds sailing speed record trials here every year, in which sailing machines of the strangest designs compete to see which can go the fastest over a circle.

Sandsfoot Castle was once, according to Leland, 'a right goodly and warlike castle'. It was built by Henry VIII but neglected by his daughter Elizabeth, who was not the castle-maniac her father was. Just as well, for *castles* wouldn't have destroyed the Spanish Armada.

The **Isle of Portland** is a huge sloping slab of Portland Stone, covered by rubble of the Purbeck Series, resting on Portland Sand, then on the mighty mass of the Kimmeridge Clay. All the strata dip southwards, so the Portland Stone is washed by the sea in the south at the Bill of Portland but is hoisted five hundred feet into the air in the north of the island by the Kimmeridge Clay below it.

The Portland oolitic limestone (called oolitic because the grains of which it is made look, under a microscope, like eggs) was laid down in the shallow salt waters of what geologists now called the Portlandian Gulf, a branch of the Boreal Ocean, some hundred and forty million years ago. All subsequent rocks that were laid upon it, with the exception of the thin layer of Purbeck Rubble Beds, have been weathered away. The Purbeck Rubble forms an overburden which has to be removed before quarrying can commence of the valuable Portland Stone below. Much of it has simply been dumped into the sea over the steep cliffs.

Some people find the Isle of Portland an ugly place, all stone, no trees, scanty grass, and ugly houses. Personally I find it beautiful and of great interest. It is sad that a lot of hideous council houses have been allowed to go up – particularly at Weston and Fortuneswell. Surely this is one place in the world where *all* building should be of native stone!

To circumambulate the island first (you see little of it from the sea) we will start at **Fortuneswell**, which is where we enter the island from the mainland. (It is a near-island actually.) This has the attraction of a town built up a steep slope, for the buildings look down over each others' roofs, in a fine jumble, and except for the modern council estates a fine jumble of great blocks of Portland Stone. This building material lends a strange dignity to even the humblest buildings, perhaps because of the large size in which the blocks are generally dressed. The little place is richly endowed with good pubs, which is not surprising considering that not only was it (and still is) a place of quarrymen and fishermen, both thirsty professions, but also there is the Royal Navy hard by to lend a thirst. In Fortuneswell one has the impression of a fine, lively, prosperous working-class life and the people are very friendly. **Chesil**, down by the shore, where the noise of waves breaking on the enormous shingle bank is incessant, still houses fishermen who earn a living from the sea, launching their very small open boats from the steep shingle. It is sad that they have gone over, most of them, to small clinker-built transom-sterned boats and have deserted their traditional *lerrets*. The transom-sterned boat has the advantage that it is easy to hang an outboard motor from the stern of it, the lerret is primarily a pulling boat and there are not enough strong arms for pulling boats any more. Why the Chesil men have never evolved inboard-engined *punts* or luggers such as the Deal and Hastings men have is not clear. Unless it is just that the lerret, admirably suited for their conditions before the invention of motors, just was not adaptable to motors (it is not) and they have not yet had time to evolve an engined craft suitable for their conditions.

There are three derelict lerrets lying up on the beach at Chesil (fortunately we shall meet some non-derelict ones farther along the great Chesil Beach). They are double-ended, flat-floored, clinker-built craft of low freeboard, prettily shaped, from seventeen to twenty feet long, and they pull six oars double-banked. The oars are *copsea* oars – rather like the coble oars of the Northumberland coast.

That is they do not ship in rollocks but have shaped planks fastened on to their sides with holes in them and the holes go over thole pins, or upright iron pins sticking up from the gunwale of the boat. You cannot catch a crab with these oars (although in a sea they can very easily knock you over) and if you let go of them, to handle fishing gear, for example, they do not fall overboard but remain there ready to be used again. Although primarily rowing boats in days of sail, they set two sails, a lug foresail (or mainsail really) and a sprit mizzen. Like the Northumbrian coble they were launched bow first into the sea – the two bow oarsmen sitting ready to pull as soon as the boat hit the breakers – and they came to land stern-first. Unlike the coble, which was flat-floored in her after half but deep-keeled forward, lerrets were flat-bottomed all the way, and therefore would have made indifferent sailing vessels. They did not make the marathon sailing voyages far out to sea that the cobles had to make. They were very much surf boats, built for launching through often considerable surf, being rowed a short distance to do their fishing, and then landing again in the surf. It would be interesting to compare them with the Sheringham and Cromer Crabbers (much deeper-keeled but also double-ended) and, even more interestingly, some of the Portuguese beach boats, used for practically the same work. The lerrets are said to be named for one of their number which was named the *Lady of Loreto* by her owner, who had seen the church of that dedication in Ancona when he visited that place as a sailor. My suspicion, for which I have no sensible grounds, is that the name is much older than this.

Although a certain amount of potting was done from lerrets the primary fishery was seine-netting for mackerel, and occasionally other fish. A seine net is a long wall of net, leaded at the bottom and corked at the top, which is carried out to sea in a boat, one end being held ashore by men on the beach, the rest of the net being paid out of the boat, which describes a big half-circle, the other end of the net returned to the shore again, when both ends of the net are hauled in to the beach, and the net shortened until the *cod*, or *belly*, or *hose* as it is called by Chesil Beach men alone, and which is a widened and bellied length of heavier and stronger mesh net, is dragged up triumphantly, or not as the case may be, with whatever it has in it. Sometimes the net is not carried in the boat but paid out from the beach. The remaining lerrets at Fortuneswell cost *five pounds* when they were built (what would it cost to build one now?). They always had a first shot of the season on Good Friday, whether any mackerel had been sighted or not. The crew that caught the first mackerel bore it in triumph to Devenish's Brewery, whereupon they were awarded a voucher which entitled them to a gallon of free beer at any Devenish pub. The boats always used to shoot the seines westward before midday and eastwards after, which is a good indication of the mildness of the long-shore tide along the beach here, for it was hardly a factor. A lerret crew would have to be some dozen men, six to pull the oars, one on board to handle the net, and the rest waiting on shore to haul in the net. Everyone, including the boat owner, was paid on a share basis. Huge hauls of mackerel were sometimes obtained, but often the laborious business of shooting and recovering the enormous net (forty fathoms long, forty-five feet deep) was for nothing, or a few mullet.

Castletown, built on the Kimmeridge Clay at the base of the high end of the island and very cramped for space, has still the flavour of the old navy. **Portland Castle** is another of Henry VIII's efforts, open in the summer but in the winter closed off by the Navy. The Stone Quay is here, from which so much Portland Stone has been shipped about the world and, amazingly in this country of complete dominance by the motor lorry, some stone is still shipped off from time to time by sea. The little railway, incidentally, that came to the isle in 1863 has long since been destroyed: a seemingly maniacal act for a stone-exporting peninsula cut off from the mainland by roads as indescribably congested as the ones through Weymouth.

The Verne is a colossal fortress, with a citadel covering fifty acres which was once garrisoned by three thousand men, and it was built up on the highest point of the isle by prison labour. Assuredly the convicts of nineteenth-century Portland earned their bread and water. This vast fortress, in which the British Lion was supposed to skulk away from the Gallic Cockerel, is now occupied by the prisoners themselves. Their old prison, which we come to at **Grove**, is now a Borstal. Nobody can say that either institution adds to the air of cheeriness of the Isle of Portland. St Peter's-at-Grove church was built by convicts. There is much mosaic work in it done by female prisoners, working under the supervision of a lady named Constance Kent, who had been convicted for the murder of her stepbrother. The roof of this church is of Finnish redwood, held together entirely by wooden pins or trunnions: no metal was used. There is much of a rather poignant interest about this church, which was the garrison church of the Verne Citadel. King's Pier, down at the foot of the steep cliffs by the sea here, was in 1846 reported to be 'rendered ruinous by the sea'. It was the pier from which much of the king's own stone was shipped: the king, being Lord of the Manor of Portland himself (as the Queen is now), could exact a proportion of all the stone quarried. Folly Pier, Durdle Pier, and several others were all used in days gone by for shipping stone out.

Easton is a splendid little town, with enormously wide streets like a South African *dorp* (where the streets had to be wide for turning spans of twenty oxen pulling wagons), the houses are solidly built of that finest of all freestones, and everything on a sunny day is dazzling white or light grey. No place could be less English-looking. Down towards Pennsylvania Castle (a folly turned hotel) is a little thatched house which is a museum. It features in Hardy's *The Well-beloved* as 'Avice's Cottage'. It was bought by Dr Marie Stopes and presented to the Council for preservation. It has huge ammonites and other fossils of the Jurassic, and many strange objects. It is sad that there is not in it a really comprehensive collection exhibiting the geology of Portland, and also the Portland quarrying industry.

Just beyond 'Avice's Cottage' is the Rufus, or Bow and Arrow Castle, now ruinous, very old, once attacked successfully by Robert, Earl of Gloucester in the Barons' Wars. Pennsylvania Castle, hard by, was built about 1800 for John Penn, the grandson of the William Penn who founded the other Pennsylvania in America. John was the Governor of the Isle of Portland.

South of **Southwell** are Celtic field systems, and south of these a big area of raised beach rich in sea-shells, and now farmed, chiefly, by the boys from the Borstal, who grow a great many vegetables on this salty and wind-swept spot, for themselves and other guests of Her Majesty.

The **Bill of Portland**, called Portland Bill by landsmen, is a very dramatic place, although spoiled somewhat by surely too *many* naval wireless aerials – surely they can't need *quite* so many – who on earth are they wirelessing to? There is the modern lighthouse looking very sleek and fine, an older one once the home of Dr Marie Stopes and now a restaurant and several jolly wooden cafés. We gaze out off this flat barren slab of rock to the Shambles, a shoal four miles out to sea and a very dangerous place to be in a small boat when a strong wind is blowing against the tide. It looks, in rough weather, a horrible place and indeed it is, having claimed many a good ship, including the *Abergavenny*, captained by the brother of Wordsworth the poet. She went aground there in 1805 and Captain Wordsworth was lost with his new bride and three hundred men. The Shambles Light Vessel has now been replaced by a Lanby (which is described under Owers). There is a whim, or crane, down by the water east of the Bill, similar to hundreds that were once on the isle, still used for lowering the boats of part-time fishermen into the water and lifting them out again. Cave Hole near here goes far into the rock, and in 1780 a forty-ton ship was driven far into it by a gale. The Pulpit rock, to the west of the Bill, needs no description: it is just there.

Back north again, and just north of Weston is a building of great interest and great beauty: the church of St George, Reforne. Built about 1777 it is a grand and stately building, very metropolitan in style and feeling, and its interior is perhaps the country's best example of the eighteenth-century style of worship. There is a great mass of high-backed enclosed pews with two high fierce pulpits dominating them all. You could see the parson – and he could see you, but you could not see your neighbours, nor whether they were doing naughty things like crossing themselves, or bobbing to the east. No trace of 'altar worship' here – the rough plain table that stands where the altar might go would not look out of place in a very humble kitchen. Outside, the church is surrounded by a positive *sea* of gravestones, many of them elaborate. The church has, thank God and a band of local enthusiasts, recently been restored and is a building of the first interest.

For people who, like myself, love contrast, there is the Reforne Gospel Hall about two hundred yards east of St George's.

Now for a short word about the quarrying industry, and the history of the Isle and Royal Manor of Portland.

Roman remains, stone coffins, coins and sling stones have been found. Portland has been called the Isle of Slingers, for Portland men were once famous for this art, and of course they had plenty of ammunition on Chesil Beach below. If the art is not taught in Portland schools instead of rounders then it ought to be. The quarrying of stone is not an old industry on the Isle – amazingly the first parish church there (now no longer existing) was built of Caen stone!

The isle in olden days was very much a place apart from the rest of England. The Crown owned the manorial rights, there was much commonage on which grazed small hardy sheep of a breed peculiar to the isle and now no more, every islander had rights of commonage, but there were not many islanders: in 1696 there were seven hundred in a hundred and twenty houses. The islanders long clung to the pre-Norman custom of *Gavelkind*. That is their property was divided, at death, equally among their children, girls having the same rights as boys. Wives were free to leave their property to whom they would, independently of what their husbands wanted. The islanders met in a Court Leet and still do. It meets every November in the Pennsylvania Castle Hotel.

William Pitt reported to Elizabeth I that there were some stone quarries in the cliffs when he surveyed the isle, but what excited him most was the Kimmeridge 'coal', which occurs here at the top of the Kimmeridge Series as it does elsewhere, and, of course, outcropped right round the north of the isle under the Portland Sand. He recommended that the queen, as Lord of the Manor, should abrogate this to herself, leaving only enough on the Isle to keep the military garrison warm, and to hell with the rest of the inhabitants. Certainly there was no *wood* for them to burn! The Crown levied twelve pennies a ton on stone quarried on common land, Charles II gave half of this back to the islanders as a reward for their loyalty to his father during the Civil War and Queen Victoria gave back three-quarters.

It was Inigo Jones who started the great popularity of Portland Stone in London and elsewhere. When the Banqueting Hall at Whitehall was burned down in 1619 he was commissioned to build another, and he used a quantity of Portland Stone in its construction. After this orders from London came in thick and fast, more and more piers were built for loading it, more and more quarries opened up.

The quarrymen were a race apart, and said to have been as tough as the stone they hewed. Wesley wrote a hymn when he was on the isle (having wrestled in vain to save the souls of the islanders), with the lines:

'Strike with the hammer of thy word
And break these hearts of stone!'

The quarrymen were completely independent of any master. If they felt like it they would go to sea in their boats and catch fish instead of working in the quarry. If they saw what they took to be an ill-omen on their way to work – they would not go there. They would go to the pub and spend the day drinking it away. They were notable for the amount of beer that they consumed. They had strange customs – they would not marry a girl until they had already got her with child and when they did there were strange ceremonies, such as one where the happy couple walked right round the Isle with people behind them firing blunderbusses. When a young quarryman was married he would jump over a pinch-bar in the quarry to symbolise that he was leaving the carefree bachelors and joining the married men. People from off the Isle were called *Kimberlins* and not encouraged, unless they had something tangible to offer, but it is noteworthy that the Portlanders were never slow to go to the aid of shipwrecked mariners, *Kimberlins* or not.

Needless to say they took their idiosyncratic behaviour into the quarries with them. The unit of quarrymen was built up around a crane. A gang might be four men and a boy, and they would have their one crane, which they owned, and they served it and it served them. Huge blocks of stone would be broken out, as described in the last chapter for the Isle of Purbeck quarries, the blocks separated from the rest of the rock either by 'reaming up' – driving plugs and feathers along its bottom so as to break it out upwards, or 'reaming out' – driving vertical wedges along its back so as to break it out laterally. While this was done the four men would strike the wedges with their sledge-hammers to the rhythm of a song sung by the boy, who sat cross-legged on top of the stone to sing it. The song he sang was generally one known as 'The French Song', which has been collected by the English Folk Song and Dance Society. From time to time a man would 'start' his wedge (it would come loose and he would have to re-adjust his feathers) and when this happened he was in duty bound to shout 'Bout!' and he would then have to pay for half a gallon of beer. It was the boy's chief job, besides providing musical accompaniment, to keep his elders and betters supplied with this beverage.

The Purbeck Rubble overlying the Portland Stone varies from twenty to forty-four feet, and all this had, in days of old, to be removed by men with wheelbarrows if they were not indeed, as some of them were, quarrying underground. The rubble would either be thrown over the cliff or else dumped in country already quarried out. Nowadays this overburden is removed by machine, and furthermore there is a use for it now because it is crushed up for concrete aggregate, road metal, or other uses. This exposes the first layer of the Portland Series, locally called the *Roach.* This is rich in fossils called 'Portland Screws' (*Ceritheum portlandicum*) and cockles generally known as 'horse-heads'. The Roach is too fossiliferous to make the best building stone, but it was used in the new Waterloo Bridge and in the Eighth United States Army Memorial at Cambridge.

Then comes the *Top Tier,* formerly called the *Whitbed.* This is what the quarrymen are really after. Under this is the Middle (rather fossiliferous), then the *Bottom,* or *Base Bed Freestone.* This again is very good building stone.

When the steam crane took over from the hand-operated one the crane gang increased from four men and a boy to seven or eight men and a boy. Not long ago there were 1,200 men working down in the quarries on the isle. Now there are not more than about twenty-five (although many more work processing the stone on the surface). Except for that of Mr Sansom of Southwell all the quarries are owned by one big group of companies, all connected. Much of the stone now is crushed for making such stuff as *Portcrete*, a 'reconstituted stone', and much of the better stone is sawn by diamond-toothed circular saws into thin sheets of *cladding*, which can be stuck on to walls of cheaper material to give the false impression that the building is built of Portland.

In the seventeenth century large quantities of a plant called *cuckoo-pint* was shipped up to London, where it was sold as 'Portland Sago' and consumed in the belief that it was an aphrodisiac.

'In November 1457 was seen a cock coming out of the sea, having a great crest on its head, a great red beard, and legs half a yard long. He stood on the water, crowed three times and every time turned himself about and beckoned with his head North, South and West. He was in colour very like a pheasant, and when he crowed he – vanished' (Hutchins).

Thus the Isle of Portland.

CHAPTER 21

Chesil Beach to Lyme Regis

THE Saxon for shingle was *cisel*, and from this **Chesil Beach** derives its name. It is sixteen miles long, by some counts, gently curving, forty feet above sea level at the Portland end and half that at the Bridport end, about a hundred and seventy yards wide at Abbotsbury and two hundred at Portland. At the Portland end the pebbles are bigger, some up to a pound in weight and about as big as goose eggs. They diminish in size as you go west until at West Bay the pebbles are about a quarter of an inch across and are known as pea-shingle. A local fisherman, if he lands on the beach at night, can tell roughly where he is by looking at the size of the shingle. The pebbles are largely of flint and chert, but there are some pebbles of Jurassic rock which probably have come a long way from the west and some pebbles near the Portland end derive from the Portland Beds. At West Bay the pea-shingle is quarried, being scraped up from the beach with bulldozers and loaded into lorries with power shovels.

There are many theories as to the origin of this strange and impressive phenomenon. One is that during the last Ice Age when so much of the world's water was tied up in ice a great plain stretched out from here where the sea now is. Rivers running south across it from the higher land of England carried pebbles – some of them from as far away as Cornwall, from where it is obvious that some of the pebbles originated. When the ice melted and the sea rose, decade by decade, the advancing waves rolled these pebbles back, stroking them into the long regular ridge, and where the ridge is now is as far as it's got. Of course, any storm beach, and that is what this is, must be from time to time surmounted by the sea, for the simple reason that its topmost pebble was put there by a wave and by no other agency. Thus in 1825 the H.M.S. *Ebenezer*, a ninety-five-ton ordnance sloop, was dumped right on top of the beach, and a few years later, on a night in which ten ships were driven to their doom on Chesil Beach, a 500-ton ship was carried right over the beach and dumped in the lagoon behind! The *Ebenezer*, by the way, was successfully launched again.

Unless you are a strong swimmer, and know what you are doing,

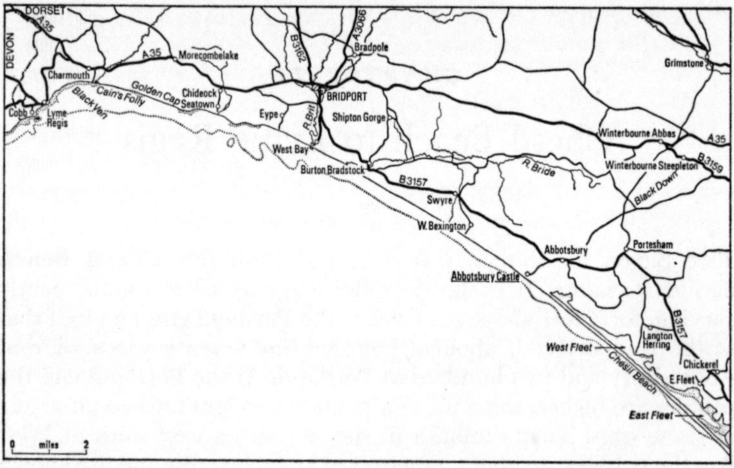

do not bathe from Chesil Beach. Even in calm weather it can be very difficult to get out of the water again – quite small waves can come and pull you back and the ever-shifting shingle makes foothold difficult. People *do* swim from the beach but they are people who know what they are doing. Of course, if you have a strong companion ashore with a rope to throw to you to help you get out you are much safer. When old men used to beachcomb (for Spanish pieces of eight we are led to understand) one used to walk along near the water's edge with a rope tied round him and the other would walk along, higher up, ready to haul his old mate up should he fall into the sea.

As for wrecks, there have been plenty of them. A sailing ship, finding herself embayed in West Bay in a severe on-shore gale, might find it very difficult to claw out to windward, her anchors would never hold, and she would inevitably be flung up on Chesil Beach. When in November, 1795, a fleet of troop transports was sailing down Channel, the *Piedmont*, *Venus* and *Catherine*, the wind freshened and headed them, fog came in, and all three – with a passing merchant ship for good measure – were driven on to the Chesil. Of the very few men who did manage to scramble ashore nearly all were badly bruised or had bones broken, and none would have been saved but for the gallant efforts of the local people to save them. True after rescuing as many people as they could the locals turned to rescuing such things of value as they could lay their hands on, but can you blame them? The prayer of poor people living near the coast in days of old was: 'Lord I ask not that a ship should be wrecked – but if one *is* wrecked let it be wrecked *here*!' There's nothing unreasonable about that. Allegations of the deliberate luring of ships to destruction are almost never founded on good evidence. The credibility of landlubbers on this matter is endless. For example, the fact that a local fisherman, Richard Bishop of Swyre, was sent to gaol in 1822 for 'unlawfully making a light on the sea coast' has been taken as evidence that he was trying to lure ships. It is obvious to any seafarer that in fact what he was trying to lure was a fellow smuggler. What ship's captain, in God's name, would steer towards Chesil Beach because he saw a light on it! The Lord did look kindly on the people who lived behind Chesil Beach sometimes, though. In 1748 the *Hope of Amsterdam* came ashore with £50,000 worth of gold in her. One hopes that the locals had some of it.

The Fleet, the lagoon that runs behind the beach for part of its length, is shallow and muddy, the water brackish, and in these days of heavy applications of soluble nitrates to the land, sometimes very insalubrious. Punts of a distinctive kind are kept on it, from which men fish for eels, either with stationary nets with trapped pockets locally called *fyke* nets, or with what we call in East Anglia the *pritch*, or Neptune's trident, which is jabbed into the mud. Mullet and bass that come in from the sea are also caught, and at the Portland end, where the fleet connects with the open sea in Portland Harbour through the narrow channel known as Small Mouth, large shrimps called 'Billy Winters' are trawled for.

Lerrets still fish from the beach: there is one based at Chickerel belonging to the Northover family, one at Langton Herring, three at Fleet (which the fishermen call Park Wall) and at Abbotsbury there are several seiners but they are not lerrets. Except at Abbotsbury, where the Fleet ends and people can walk to their boats, the lerret crews have to cross the Fleet in their punts, then launch their lerrets from the beach into the open sea. Conversely the fish, if they catch any, have to be dragged over the steep shingle of the beach on sleds, transferred to the punts, taken across the Fleet and there put into vans. It is a laborious process. The lerrets spend all their time on the beach, being hauled to the Fleet side of it in the winter when not in use. Most crews keep a tractor on the beach for hauling the lerret out of the water, and also, nowadays, for hauling in the heavy seine net. Nets, being of nylon now, will take the strain. At Park Wall there is a windlass instead of a tractor and the men must haul the net ashore themselves. The complete crew of a lerret nowadays is eight men and a boy, but skippers find it hard to get crews and often have to work short-handed. Two hundred stone of mackerel is considered a good haul, but in the summer of 1973 one crew landed a thousand stone in two days!

The fishermen are all part-timers and traditionally always have been, although in the past the time when they were not working their lerrets was spent fishing or wildfowling on the Fleet, or doing casual work for local farmers. A relic of this farming standby remains in the saying of the men that – when the mackerel are conspicuous by their absence in the summer when they should be there – 'the fish have gone hay-making'. A description of the lerret as a type can be found in the last chapter, under Fortuneswell.

The Fleet itself is an eerie place, guarded by the great unbroken and somehow rather daunting wall of shingle from the sea, with pleasant soft green country, with an indented shoreline, to landward. The Fleet supports thousands of wigeon from time to time on its growth of *Zostera marina*, or Wigeon Grass, although there is strong competition for this from far too many swans. Swans are nice, but a hundred swans are nicer than a thousand. There is limited shooting on the Fleet by members of the Wildfowlers' Association. Six punts, and no more, are allowed to be used for the stalking of wildfowl, and these are not allowed to have punt-guns mounted in them but the shooting is to be done with shoulder guns. Thus the stock of wildfowl is not depleted.

The Fleet was used by the R.A.F. for practising for their dam-busting exploits in the Second World War, and two of their dummy bombs are still, at the time of writing, in the mud. They are to be salvaged, though, and placed in museums.

East Fleet is a tiny village which was practically wiped out by the gale and flood that flung the *Ebenezer* on to the beach in 1825. The church was then swept away except for the chancel, and this still contains brasses of 1603 and 1611 to members of the Mohun families. One of the Mohuns had nine sons and just the eight daughters. The new church is of 1829, Gothic Revival, and very romantic. Fleet House, now called Moonfleet Manor, is now a hotel. Meade Faulkner wrote a romantic novel called *Moonfleet* about it, full of smuggling and underground tunnels and derring-do.

The great monument that dominates the country from the top of Black Down, inland, was built in 1844 in memory of Admiral Sir Thomas Masterman Hardy, who was born on this estate in 1769, was Nelson's Flag Captain aboard the *Victory* at Trafalgar, and was a fine sailor in his own right.

Abbotsbury is a most charming place, when not full of other trippers besides ourselves. The village is predominantly seventeenth century, preserved very carefully, and its thatched roofs kept in order, the great church is beautiful, but as there is a really excellent guide for sale in the Post Office (which describes fascinating local customs of the fishermen and others) I will forbear to describe it, except to say do not miss the barrel ceiling of the chancel, built in 1638, with its delightful and delicate plaster moulding, the Early Jacobean pulpit with bullet holes in it from Cromwell's trigger-happy men (they also managed to put holes through the *roof* – two white pegs in the roof of the north aisle mark where), the lovely 'St Catherine's Panel' in the glass of the south aisle, which is very moving.

The story of the bullet holes is well told by Sir Ashley-Cooper himself, in the report he sent to the Parliamentary Committee after the bullets were fired. Sir Ashley led his men against the men of Colonel Strangeways, who was holding the Manor House for the king. 'We came to Abbotsbury just at night,' wrote Sir Ashley, 'and sent them a summons to which they returned a slighting answer . . . and hung out their bloody flag. So a party of musketeers under Major Bainton was ordered to storm the Church, which was garrisoned by thirteen men because it flanked the house. This, after a hot bickering, we carried, and took all the men prisoners . . .' The full report, which describes the eventual blowing up of the Manor House together with many of the attackers when the powder magazine went up, is told in that most excellent local guide.

The abbey was old and important before it was pulled down. The tradition is that there was a church here in Roman times (so we can certainly suppose a pagan temple before that). In 1044 one Orc, or Orcus, a house-carl of Canute or Knut, with his wife Thola, founded a Benedictine Abbey here. Sadly little remains of it. The great abbey church was many times the size of the parish church of St Nicholas which remains. There are a few bits of masonry and enough foundations existing to show the outline of a great religious house. The fifteenth-century monastic barn is famous, and enormous, and still with us. Its full length was 272 feet long by 31 feet wide – very long and narrow for a barn. Part is thatched, part unroofed: it was once all tiled with stone. There was a water wheel on one side of it which was for working a threshing drum. The north porch has a turret and winding staircase. It is a fine and remarkable building.

The walk up to St Catherine's Chapel is well worth making, not only because it is a noble little building, vaulted like St Aldhelm's Chapel at Worth Matravers and built entirely of stone, but also because of the fine view you get from up there, of the Fleet, of Chesil Beach, and of the little village down below. The beautifully tended market garden to the south of the village, and the fruitful garden plots of the villagers, give an idea of what the whole country must have looked like when it was peopled and cultivated, as it once was as evidenced by the multitude of Celtic and Saxon field systems that cover the hillsides of this part of Dorset, many of which can be seen from this very point. The Celtic fields are distinguishable by being more or less rectangular and nearly as broad as they are long. The later Saxon field systems are the typical strip lynchets. The reason for the difference was that the Celts only had a scratch-plough: a simple plough that did not invert the soil such as is used in such places as Egypt and India to-day. With this they had to be able to cross-plough to break the soil properly and therefore their fields had to be wide enough to admit of cross ploughing. The plough they had, which was brought over from France in the Late Bronze Age, was called the *ard* (modern Welsh for plough is *aradr*, Spanish is *arado*). It was not until Belgian settlers arrived, shortly before the Roman invasion, and brought the heavy, iron, breasted plough which would invert the soil, that cross-ploughing became unnecessary and the typical strip-lynchet became possible. This lasted until men were displaced in favour of sheep and as we see from the top of St Catherine's Hill the once cultivated and productive hillsides are still nothing but sheep pasture.

As for the chapel it is fifteenth century and served, and still serves, as a sea-mark for mariners, and when it was built no doubt had a monk or two to tend a light on its roof and pray for the souls of such mariners as failed to be warned by it. There is a hollow pillar inside and if a girl drops a pin into this and wishes, St Catherine will vouchsafe her a husband. If she's pretty, that is.

The famous Abbotsbury Swannery is just a part of the Fleet on which there are an awful lot of swans. Personally I would like to see fewer swans and more wigeon. But thousands of people go to see the swans (which have been televised until they are quite blasé about it), and pay to do so, and there have been swans there for a long time for in Tudor times it was written that 'from all time whereof the memory of man is not to the contrary there was, and yet is . . . a game of wild swans', but in those days they had the sense to eat some of them. Henry VIII grabbed the swannery, of course, when the abbey was dissolved, and now it is cared for by the Ilchester estate.

A nice custom that has survived at Abbotsbury, possibly from pagan times, is Garland Day, which, like New Year's Day in certain parts of Wales, is held thirteen days after the day on which it should be held according to the Gregorian calendar. Garland Day is held on 13th May instead of 1st May, for the people refused to accept the alteration in the calendar. Garlands are made by the children and paraded around. A lively picture of the garlands being taken out to sea and cast on the waters was painted by P. R. Morris for the 1923 Royal Academy, and is reproduced in the Abbotsbury local guide book. And the boats depicted, being rowed by bearded fishermen and with pretty girls in them holding the garlands, are *lerrets*.

Abbotsbury Castle, to the right of the road two miles west out of the village, is a fine iron age fortress with a good view. North of the village are the Grey Mare and her Colts which are Bronze Age barrows perhaps four thousand years old, and there are stone circles here.

West Bexington is a little place of holiday bungalows where the Admiralty Underwater Weapons Establishment, which has its being in Portland Harbour, comes and does experiments. At **Swyre** in 1506 the Archduke Philip of Austria got shipwrecked.

Burton Bradstock was once important, is now pretty and unspoiled and has a fine church. It vied with Bridport in the matter of making ropes and nets, until stopped by Henry VIII, who made laws in favour of Bridport and thus knocked Burton Bradstock out of the industry. Bridport's triumph backfired, though, as restrictive trade practices often do. The Burton rope makers, no longer allowed to practise their craft in their home village, wandered far and wide, mostly to the north of England, and started up the industry wherever they went. Rope making thus established in the vigorous and populous north of England, with its water power and other advantages, soon knocked Bridport's monopoly out. Grove House Mill is still in the village, and there Richard Roberts wove good sail cloth in the early nineteenth century, and it was to another Roberts of Grove House, Captain Francis Roberts, of H.M. Brig *Helena*, that Thomas Masterman Hardy was allotted, at the age of twelve, as 'Captain's servant'.

Shipton Gorge is named for the Gorge family, a member of which, Sir Ferdinando, founded New Plymouth in North America (although he never went there), and his son, Robert, was Governor of New England in 1623. Sir Ferdinando was a great sailor and soldier, too.

And so we come to **West Bay**, which was thus misnamed when the railway came to it and tried to make it a big seaside resort, for **Bridport Harbour** was what it was up to then and should be again. West Bay is the name for the eastern end of Lyme Bay and it is confusing that Bridport Harbour should have been thus named. The East Cliff, east of Bridport Harbour, is a fantastic-looking formation when seen from the cliff below. It is a softish sandstone with horizontal bands of a harder concretionary stone which give it its strange ridged appearance. It is a little liable to drop bits of itself on the heads of the unwary so do not sit too near it. East of the harbour here it is crowned with Inferior Oolite. These sandstones of the Upper Lias run inland as far as the Cotswolds. There is a small outcrop of it at the base of the cliff west of the harbour, then a fault which has brought down the Lower Fuller's Earth Beds and above them, after another fault, the Forest Marble. The Fuller's Earth Beds are endearing if for nothing else than that they contain a layer called the Zig-zag Zone, so called because it contains the ammonite *Zigzagicerous zigzag*.

If you arrive by sea, the proper way to arrive at Bridport, approach with caution, and not at all with a fresh on-shore wind blowing unless you know what you are doing. The entrance nearly dries out and there can be nasty breaking seas in it. Except that it is not obstructed by a broken piece of wall it is very similar to Southwold Harbour in Suffolk.

The coast of this part of England is receding – it has been calculated by some people (surely pessimists?) at a rate of as much as three feet a year. But if such a recession has been going on, or anything like it, for many centuries, it is certain that in pre-Roman days the shoreline was very much farther out than it is to-day, and it has to be supposed that the River Brit (on which stands the modern Bridport Harbour) joined the River Bride, and that they both ran into the sea through one mouth. It is thought that their combined waters would have cleared a channel out through the ancient Chesil Beach (which would not have been as large as the present one) and that thus there would have been a natural harbour for ships, and that there was probably a lagoon formed by the two rivers behind the advancing shingle which would have made a good natural anchorage. If this was so then it would have been the only harbour for a long stretch of coast: the whole of Lyme Bay from Exmouth to Weymouth. This, and the fact that the soil in the alluvial valleys of the hinterland derives from outcrops of the Upper Liassic and Inferior Oolite, is responsible for the fact that fishing nets of polypropylene are manufactured in Bridport to-day. The rationale of this extraordinarily long chain of cause and effect is this: a natural harbour (in the days before there were any artificial ones) made it possible for such people as Phoenician traders if indeed there were any such people – perhaps it would be much safer to say traders from the Mediterranean – to come here with their ships. The importance of the alluvial soil derived from the two kinds of rocks mentioned is that this soil is very suitable for the growing of hemp

(*Cannabis sativa*). Hemp was brought in very early times from the Far East, and cultivated in the Mediterranean countries because of the fact that the tissue surrounding the soft pithy interior of the stems is *bast*, that is, it is made of strong interlocking cellulose cells. The stem of the plant is therefore very good for rope making. Hemp seeds brought by the early traders (could they have been *pot* smokers?) got planted, whether by design or accident, throve in these deep-soiled alluvial valleys of south Dorset, and a rope and twine industry grew up, and thus a net-making one. And when man-made fibres ousted natural ones for the making of fishing nets the old-established net industry went over to such substances as polypropylene.

But to get back to where we were: Bridport Harbour, now so ridiculously called West Bay. It is clear that as the sea encroached, and drove the Chesil Beach back and back, the time came when the Brit and the Bride found separate exits into the sea. Then their separate efforts would not have been enough to force an open channel naturally: the Brit would have tended to percolate through the shingle just as the Bride does, a mile and a quarter to the east, to-day. So men would have had to interfere to keep their harbour open: the harbour that was no doubt their lifeline because they would have had to have exported their one product, rope, by sea. No doubt they got to work with shovels to clear the ever-encroaching shingle and no doubt they also got the idea of building training walls. The long fight against the shingle started and goes on to this day, and odd reports of the campaign have come down to us. For example, in 1388 John Huddersfeld improved the harbour and was allowed to charge a halfpenny a horse load of goods going to it or coming from it. By 1395 a Customs Officer had been appointed. By 1444 an indulgence was granted by the Bishop of Sarum to reward people who helped repair the harbour. In 1619 the bailiffs and burgesses launched an appeal for £3,000 to repair their harbour: they only got £67.

But the problem was attacked effectively in 1722 by the passing of an Act of Parliament for the restoration of the harbour, and in 1740 John Reynolds, a Cheshire man, undertook for £3,500 to build piers through the beach and create a harbour inside. This was very successful and Bridport became a harbour in which it was said that forty ships might lie in safety. At first a gate used to be put across the entrance in southerly gales to stop the big seas from crashing in and doing damage. (There is such a barrier at Mousehole in Cornwall.) The storm gate was done away with, though, in 1823 when the extension to the basin to the east was made, allowing craft to creep round out of the direct scend of the sea, and it was probably at this time that the excellent system of sluice gates was constructed. This allows the fresh water coming down the river, combined with the impounded top of the tide, to rush out violently at low tide to scour the harbour out. This system is thought to be unique by the men of Bridport but it is not. It is to be found at Bridgewater among other places. But it worked in 1823 and it works now. By 1830 over five hundred ships a year were using the harbour and there was a considerable shipbuilding industry building up to a thousand tons. The area to the west of the harbour is still known as the Old Shipyard, although now all built up.

Bridport Harbour is still occasionally used by a German coaster bringing timber in from the Baltic, or sometimes fertiliser, and then going on to Cornwall to load china clay for Europe, and occasionally a load of shingle or sand, scraped up from the beach, goes out. There are four good little trawlers working full time and a number of part-timers of one sort and another. There have been ominous rumblings of marinas to come. Let us hope they will never be more than rumblings.

Bridport Harbour or West Bay is completely spoiled as a village by Pier Terrace, which is a *monstrous* building, not so much built as *plonked* there in 1882 and quite out of scale with and out of place with everything else in the village. It would look fine in some vulgar Mediterranean casino resort. It is said by architects to be a work of architectural merit but how any architect could be so *rude* as to plonk it there right in front of the charming and entirely fitting Bridport Arms Hotel is beyond understanding. It has nearly been burnt down twice. Perhaps *jamais deux sans trois*. Maybe next time the fire will have its way and the inhabitants (well insured, we hope) removed to a more suitable place.

While on the subject of fires, on the Green just east of the river above the sluice gates is a noble fire engine. Built by Merryweather of London it came to Bridport in 1902 and it won the First Grand Prize for a Patent Steam Fire Engine. It deserved to. It was pulled at first by horses but later, we are told, by a Daimler shooting brake which once belonged to His Majesty Edward VII.

And so up to **Bridport** itself, which is a noble little town with great wide streets with long narrow alleyways running off them, and predominantly Georgian houses. The pavements of the wide streets were once wider than the streets, for these were used for drying and sorting out nets and ropes. The long narrow alleyways, and also the long narrow gardens behind the houses, were once used as rope walks and spinning walks. Bridport is an industrial town, but an industrial town built in the age of good taste. Everything is fine, solid and spacious. The arcaded Town Hall was designed by William Taylor in 1785 (near it is a chemist's shop which was a hotel once in which Charles II slept when he was trying to escape from England). There is a civilised air about the whole place.

The beginning of the town's great industry, as we have seen, was the cultivation of hemp in the surrounding countryside. Hemp requires a deep, rich, loamy soil and here it was. The hemp would be harvested (the male plants in July and the female in September), the seed threshed out of the female plants, and the stems either 'dew-ripened' or laid in water, to *ret.* (This retting of fibrous plants is a process necessary with most vegetable fibre production: one finds somewhat noisome pits full of brown water and coconut coir on the Malabar coast, or jute soaking in pits in much the same way in Bangla Desh.) After retting the stems of the hemp were combed in a scutching mill, which removed the unwanted and now slightly rotted pith from the fibre. Then, after drying, the long strong fibres were spun into *yarn*, then twisted back on themselves to make *twine.* Hemp spinning yielded very slowly to mechanisation: the long fibres were less easy to spin by machine than the short fibres of cotton or wool. Rope would then be made in a rope walk. Three or four strands of twine would be fastened to hooks (called *cogs*) fitted round a frame called a *jack*, the cogs were made to revolve by boy-power, each cog twisting individually in the same direction, and, finally, the twisted strands were transferred to a central hook and allowed to twist back into each other to form a rope.

I have seen a m'Kamba tribesman in East Africa make a very good light rope ten foot long by beating some of the long spiked leaves of the aloe or sisal cactus with a stone, then twisting the tough fibres into yarn and twine and then laying the rope by walking backwards away from a tree. This is the fundamental process of rope making and it hasn't changed.

Flax (*Linum usitatissimum*) was also grown at Bridport. This is a much shorter plant with softer fibres. The seed is threshed out and pressed for linseed oil and the residue used for cattle cake. In the old days at Bridport the seed was imported annually from Riga, broadcast in mid-April, and at the end of July the immature plants drawn by hand by women and children and laid in swathes to dry. The seed (though not ripe enough for planting) was beaten out and the stalks 'barked and swingled' (in other words well-beaten), and then sent to the flax-dresser. Spun, it made a softer, whiter yarn than hemp and was woven, at Bridport, into sail cloth for which, in sailing ship days, there must have been a colossal demand. Every severe gale meant complete new suits of sails for hundreds of ships.

Flax is still used for sail cloth by the discerning. The remaining East Coast sailing barges (now all converted to yachts) still have their sails of No. 2 Flax, well 'tanned' with esoteric mixtures of linseed oil, kutch, fish oil and the rest, and some still good after many decades of hard use and constant exposure to weather.

The age of rope-making at Bridport is conjectural beyond 1211. But in Domesday Bridport was a 'vill of 120 houses', which was a large place in those days and there can be no doubt but that at that time the place owed its prosperity to rope, for in King John's day mention was made of the fact that the place had produced rope from time out of mind of man. An entry in the Pipe Role of 1211, still to be seen at the Public Record Office, has this:

> . . . and for 1,000 ells of cloth for making ships' sails and for 3,000 weights of thread of hemp according to the measure of Bridport for making ships' cordage £48 9s 7d by the same writ. And for the expences of Robert the Fisherman who stayed at Bridport making his nets 39s by the same writ.

And in 1213 King John ordered that the men of Bridport were to work: 'night and day as many ropes for ships both large and small, and as many cables as you can, and twisted yarns for cordage for ballistae.'

In the fifteenth century 'Italian Hemp' (still imported) began to come in to England from Genoa and Normandy and this caused a slump at Bridport. In the time of Henry VII there was an important ropewalk in Burton Bradstock, but Henry VIII made an order giving Bridport the sole right to all hemp grown within five miles of the town, which effectually knocked out Burton Bradstock. It was after this that the displaced rope makers of Burton Bradstock wandered away to the north of England and spread the virus of rope-making there. Camden, in Elizabeth I's time, mentions a special law which reserved all Bridport rope for the use of the Navy. In the late sixteenth century the industry declined badly owing to the importation of large quantities of hemp from Holland and Russia. For reasons of climate this was better than the Dorset hemp, and as it was easier to ship it into London and the south-eastern harbours than to take it as far west as Bridport, it caused rope industries to be set up there. Another cause of Bridport's depression was the silting of the harbour. But the revival of the harbour in 1740, the Newfoundland cod trade with its great call from west country ships for rope and lines, and convenient rope-using wars on the Continent, brought prosperity back: hence the good prosperous-looking houses of the last half of the eighteenth century. In 1793 1,800 people were employed in Bridport and 7,000 in Dorset in the rope industry.

By 1800 net making had become more important than rope. Rope making, being fairly unskilled, could be done at Portsmouth and Chatham and other places farther east, while many of the skilled Bridport people turned to the more demanding trade of net making. But the demand for rope in sailing days must have been pretty well insatiable. You have only to look at the anchor cables on board H.M.S. *Victory* to realise the vast tonnage of hemp that went into a big man of war, or a big merchant ship for that matter. After 1810 iron wire rope began to come in, but even so most running rigging was hemp nearly to the present day. And rope was needed ashore, too, for a hundred purposes, one of the more macabre being for hanging people. Leland wrote, in the sixteenth century, that 'Bridport makes fine daggers'. Bridport made no daggers, but either Leland was trying to pull our legs or having his leg pulled. The fact was the cant expression for being hanged in those days was 'stabbed with a Bridport dagger'.

Bridport can probably now claim to be the world centre of the net-making industry, and this now all centres on the firm of Bridport-Gundry, which was formed by an amalgamation of some of the surviving independent firms.

Samuel Gundry set up as a factor in the net-making industry in 1665. That is he did not manufacture himself, but bought the hemp crop and put it out to outworkers who turned it into netting, and then he found a market for it. In 1670 William Hounsell built the first spinning mill. Hitherto spinning had all been done in people's back yards. The Jumper netting loom came to Bridport from Scotland in 1840 and this caused wholesale going over from cottage industry to factory-work. At this time the demand for nets was rocketing. The great fleets of sailing trawlers demanded endless netting for their trawls, the herring drifters of the North Sea, with their forays west for the Mackerel Voyage, too, needed many miles of drift net each. No longer could a fisherman buy twine and braid his own nets in the winter time in his cottage. Fishing was becoming a big industry. By 1900 there were fifteen net-making firms operating in Bridport. As machinery became more complicated and expensive, amalgamations were inevitable, and the final one came in 1963 when the Joseph Gundry group joined Bridport Industries to form Bridport-Gundry. This firm is known to every sea-fisherman in Europe at any rate, and in many a far-flung corner of the world, too. The *range* of fishing engines that they produce is extraordinary. The firm employs about five hundred people inside the factories and another five hundred out-workers who work at home in the traditional way.

West along the coast, **Eype** is pronounced eep. At Seatown men earn great sums (one is told) picking the right pebbles up on the beach here, to be sent away for grinding up for pottery shellac, and other substances, and the Anchor Inn here has a bar for 'children only'.

Chideock, pronounced Chiddock, had a castle. The Arundells got it in the fifteenth century and harboured Catholic priests. In the Civil War it changed hands several times between the two sides and was finally totally destroyed by Parliament, the bill for its destruction being £1 19s 0d, which seems modest. On the mound in the centre of its earthen remains there is a wooden cross with the words: 'Castle built by Sir John de Chideock 1380, destroyed by Parliament 1645, from its gates five Christian martyrs were taken'. These were Catholic priests taken and butchered between 1597 and 1642. The story is told in the excellent guide on sale within the church. In the church is a magnificent effigy of Sir John de Chideock.

Golden Cap is a dominating coastal hill 617 feet high, capped with Upper Greensand resting on Middle Lias Beds. Below are the Green Ammonite Beds, with the 'Three Tiers' – bands of sandstone at the base of the Middle Lias between them. The Green Ammonite Beds are rich in ammonites, the empty chambers of which are filled with green calcite. By the fine farmstead at the foot of Golden Cap on the west are the ruins of St Gabriel's Chapel, built thirteenth century as a chapel of ease to Whitechurch Canonicorum but disused since 1841. At **Morecombelake** is the Dorset Knob Biscuit Factory.

The cliff called **Cain's Folly** contains many ammonites and belemnites. We have now arrived, and are well into the great Jurassic exposure, famous among geologists, of the highly fossiliferous beds that run from this part of the coast right through England to emerge at the sea again in the cliffs of North Yorkshire. This exposure is described in greater detail in *Companion Guide to the Coast of South-West England,* which continues our present excursion, but the really interested should buy No. 23 of the *Geologists' Association Guides,* published by Benham and Company Limited, and obtainable very easily in Lyme Regis.

Charmouth is now a quiet Regency seaside resort where (as far as the outsider can see at least) not much happens. It was much praised by Jane Austen. But after the Battle of Worcester Charles II fled to Lyme Regis disguised as a groom, accompanied by Miss Juliana Coningsby riding pillion behind him, and with his friend Lord Wilmot riding another horse and posing as the young lady's eloping lover. The captain of a ship, a Charmouth man named Stephen Limbry, was to pick the party up and take them to France but, when he went home to sleep and told his wife about the strange party who had offered him so much money, that astute lady guessed that the party contained the fleeing prince and *locked her husband's trousers up* so that he could not go.

The party were by then at the Queen's Arms in Charmouth, and the ostler there also suspected the true identity of Charles and he went to tell the parson about it (a Puritan named Bartholomew Wesley, John Wesley's grandfather) but that divine was in prayer and could not be disturbed (some versions say he was preaching), which gave the royal party time to get away. Wilmot's horse cast a shoe, and when he went to the farrier that man, who knew shoes made in different counties, recognised that one was made in Worcestershire, and confirmed the ostler in his belief that this was the royal party. The ostler at last managed to get through to the pious parson, who went to the Queen's Hotel and told the landlady that she had acted as a 'maid of honour'. Catherine of Aragon is also supposed to have slept at the Queen's Arms in 1501. Her badge in plaster is in the hotel.

Black Ven is made up, in its lower parts, of the Black Ven Marls, with Belemnite Marls above. In 1908 a fall of cliff here started the bituminous shale to burn, causing people to speak of the 'Lyme Volcano'. In the Blue Lias underneath are ammonites, fish and in 1811 a twelve-year-old schoolgirl, Mary Anning, unearthed a complete Ichthyosaurus, which she sold to the Lord of the Manor for £25 (her brother had found the head first in case there should be too much jubilation in Women's Lib circles). Mary was the daughter of a carpenter who sold fossils to visitors as a side-line. In 1824 she found a Plesiosaurus, and four years later the first Pterodactyl to be discovered in Britain. There is a window in Mary's memory in the parish church of Lyme Regis.

Lyme Regis has been settled at least since 774 – for in that year Cynewulf, King of the West Saxons, granted land here for salt pans. Edward I gave the town a charter in 1279 (since then it has been *Regis*), Lyme was a big port in its day and sent four ships to the Siege of Calais in 1347, in the fifteenth century it was much harried by the French. The Cobb is famous, being one of the oldest artificial harbours in the country. In Edward I's reign it was first built, perhaps of wood or perhaps of stone. In Charles II's day we know that the interstices between the stones were not cemented. It was badly smashed by a great storm of 1824. It was somewhat spoiled by the building of a car park a few years ago which has stopped the sea from running through the harbour from the west and thus scouring the sand out. It is really an unsatisfactory little harbour and one feels that more should be done to make it more commodious and more secure. It dries out at low water and only affords partial shelter from easterly and south-easterly gales. Sometimes fleets of yachts sail over from France and find scant mooring space. There is a small fleet of trawlers: the flag-ship perhaps being the *Barbara Allen*, skipper John Wayson or 'Hurricane Joe'.

There were stirring times in Lyme in the Civil War. Prince Maurice besieged it for two desperate months in 1644 and the townsfolk held out in an heroic manner. After the Earl of Essex had raised the siege Parliament voted £2,000 to the town, and £150 to the Governor to supply boots and shoes to the inhabitants.

The Duke of Monmouth, pretender or not, landed at the Cobb in 1685, after having spent nineteen days at sea getting there from Holland. He had been encouraged to go and dispute the British crown by William of Orange. Monmouth was the son of Charles II and Lucy Walter, the beautiful girl from Pembrokeshire with whom he had been living and who went and joined him in exile. Charles II repudiated their marriage when he obtained the throne, but Monmouth claimed that the marriage had been a legitimate one and that he was the heir to the throne. He also accused James II of having murdered Charles II. Monmouth soon raised an army of Dorset Protestants, marched to Castle Field near Taunton and there unfurled his flag, and was thereafter completely routed by the king's forces at Sedgemoor. Judge Jeffreys was sent to punish the defeated and he hanged half the males who could be proved to have been implicated and deported the rest to the colonies. Twelve Lyme men were hanged on the shore at the spot where Monmouth had landed.

The River Lim drove several mills, and some must have been flax mills. In 1825 we know that 25,000 tons of flax was imported into Lyme from Riga. The little town is charming, the Lim running in a deep chasm out to sea impressive, the small museum just over it extremely idiosyncratic and interesting, with its good section on fossils and geology and its paintings and other relics of the great landslip on the cliffs farther west (see *Companion Guide to the Coast of South-West England*) and the interior of the church is lovely.

A few hundred yards along the beach past the Cobb we come to the Dorset–Devon border and the end of this book. Here a vast hangar has been converted into an Adventure Centre by the Dorset County Council.

Index

INDEX

INDEX

Numbers refer to chapters which describe the coastline indicated